SCHOLARSHIP IN WOMEN'S HISTORY: REDISCOVERED AND NEW

Editor

GERDA LERNER

A CARLSON PUBLISHING SERIES

For a complete listing of the titles in this series,
please see the back of this book.

Private Woman, Public Person

AN ACCOUNT OF THE LIFE OF JULIA WARD HOWE FROM 1819 TO 1868

Mary H. Grant

CARLSON
Publishing Inc

BROOKLYN, NEW YORK, 1994

Please see the end of this volume for a listing of all the titles in the Carlson Publishing Series *Scholarship in Women's History: Rediscovered and New*, edited by Gerda Lerner, of which this is Volume 5.

Library of Congress Cataloging-in-Publication Data

Grant, Mary Hetherington
    Private woman, public person : an account of the life of Julia
Ward Howe from 1819-1868 / by Mary H. Grant.
        p.   cm. — (Scholarship in women's history ; 5)
    Revision of thesis (Ph.D.)—George Washington University, 1982.
    Includes bibliographical references and index.
    ISBN 0-926019-66-X
    1. Howe, Julia Ward, 1819-1910—Biography. 2. Women authors,
American—19th century—Biography. 3. Feminists—United States—
Biography. I. Title. II. Series.
PS2018.G73   1994
818'.409—dc20   94-20240
[B]

Typographic design: Julian Waters

Typeface: Bitstream ITC Galliard

Jacket and Case design: Alison Lew

Index prepared by Scholars Editorial Services, Inc., Madison, Wisconsin.

Printed on acid-free, 250-year-life paper.

Manufactured in the United States of America.

Contents

Editor's Introduction to the Series xi

Acknowledgments xxi

	Introduction 1
I.	Nature: Parents and Grandparents 5
II.	Nurture: Nursery Days, 1819-1830 15
III.	"Young Ladyhood," 1831-1842 29
IV.	Marriage, 1843-1846 55
V.	Children, 1846-1850 75
VI.	Passion Flowers, 1850-1854 95
VII.	Student and Writer, 1854-1857 115
VIII.	Civil War, 1857-1862 129
IX.	Sammy, 1863-1864 147
X.	Philosophy, 1864-1867 159
XI.	Conviction, 1867-1868 181
XII.	Conversion, 1868 193

Notes 205
Bibliography 241
Index 253

For my parents

Editor's Introduction
to the Series

An important aspect of the development of modern scholarship in Women's History has been the recovery of lost, forgotten or neglected sources. In the 1960s, when the practitioners of Women's History were so few as to be virtually invisible to the general profession, one of the commonly heard answers to the question, why is there nothing about women in your text? was that, unfortunately, women until the most recent past, had to be counted among the illiterate and had therefore not left many sources. It was common then to refer to women as among the "anonymous"—a group that included members of minority racial and ethnic groups of both sexes, most working-class people, colonials, Native Americans and women. In short, most of the populations of the past. These ignorant and erroneous answers satisfied only those who wished to stifle discussion, but they did make the issue of "sources" an urgent concern to practitioners of Women's History.

To historians who had done work in primary sources regarding women, it was obvious that the alleged dearth of sources did not exist, but it was true that the sources were not readily available. In archives and finding guides, women disappeared under the names of male family members. The voluminous records of their organizational work were disorganized, uncatalogued, and not infrequently rotting in file boxes in basement storage rooms. Since few if any researchers were interested in them, there seemed to be little purpose in making them accessible or even maintaining them. There were no archival projects to preserve the primary sources of American women comparable to the well-supported archival projects concerning Presidents and male political leaders. There were only a few and quite partial bibliographies of American women, while the encyclopedic reference works, such as the *DAB* (*Dictionary of American Biography*) or similar sources traditionally neglected to include all but a small number of women notables.

When the three-volume *Notable American Women: 1607—1950: A Biographical Dictionary* appeared in 1971, (to be followed by a fourth volume in 1980), it marked an important contribution to sources on women.[1] This comprehensive scholarly work consisted of 1,801 entries, with a biographical essay and a bibliography of works by and about each woman under discussion. It readily became obvious to even the casual user of these volumes how few modern biographies of these notable women existed, despite the availability of sources.

The real breakthrough regarding "sources" was made by a "grand manuscript search," begun in 1971, which aimed to survey historical archives in every state and identify their holdings pertaining to women. This project was started by a small committee—Clarke Chambers, Carl Degler, Janet James, Anne Firor Scott and myself. After a mail questionnaire survey of 11,000 repositories in every state, to which more than 7,000 repositories responded, it was clear that the sources on women were far wider and deeper than anyone had suspected. Ultimately, the survey resulted in a two-volume reference tool, Andrea Hinding, ed., *Women's History Sources: A Guide to Archives and Manuscript Collections in the United States.*[2]

The project proved that there were unused and neglected sources of Women's History to be found literally in every archive in the country. Participation in the survey convinced many archivists to reorganize and reclassify their holdings, so that materials about women could be more readily identified.

The arguments about "illiterate women" and absence of sources are no longer heard, but the problem of having accessible sources for Women's History continued. Even after archives and libraries reorganized and reclassified their source holding on the subject, most of the pertinent materials were not available in print. Many of the early developers of Women's History worked on source collections, reprint edition projects and, of course, bibliographies. The rapid and quite spectacular expansion of the field brought with it such great demand for sources that publishers at last responded. The past twenty years have seen a virtual flood of publications in Women's History, so that the previous dearth of material seems almost inconceivable to today's students.

For myself, having put a good many years of my professional life into the development of "source books" and bibliographies, it did not seem particularly urgent to continue the effort under the present conditions. But I was awakened to the fact that there might still be a problem of neglected and forgotten sources in Women's History as a result of a conference, which Kathryn Sklar and I organized in 1988. The Wingspread Conference "Graduate Training in U.S. Women's History" brought together 63 representatives of 57 institutions of higher education who each represented a graduate program in Women's History. As part of our preparation for the conference, we asked each person invited to list all the dissertations in Women's History she had directed or was then directing. The result was staggering: it appeared that there were 99 completed dissertations and 236 then underway. This was by no means the entire national output, since we surveyed only the 63 participants at the conference and did not survey the many faculty persons not represented, who had directed such dissertations. The questions arose—What happened to all these dissertations? Why did so many of them not get published?

When Ralph Carlson approached me at about that time with the idea of publishing "lost sources" in Women's History, I was more ready than I would have been without benefit of the Wingspread survey to believe that, indeed, there still were some such neglected sources out there, and to undertake such a project.

We used the dissertation list from the Wingspread Conference as a starting point. A researcher then went through all the reference works listing dissertations in history and other fields in the English language from 1870 to the present. Among these she identified 1,235 titles in what we now call Women's History. We then cross-checked these titles against the electronic catalog of the Library of Congress, which represents every book owned by the LC (or to define it differently, every book copyrighted and published in the U.S.). This cross-check revealed that of the 1,235 dissertations, 314 had been published, which is more than 25 percent. That represents an unusually high publication ratio, which may be a reflection of the growth and quality of the field.

A further selection based on abstracts of the 921 unpublished dissertations narrowed the field to 101. Of these we could not locate 33 authors or the authors were not interested in publication. Out of the 68 remaining dissertations we selected the eleven we considered best in both scholarship and writing. These are first-rate books that should have been published earlier and that for one reason or another fell between the cracks.

Why did they not get published earlier? In the case of the Boatwright manuscript, an unusually brilliant Master's thesis done in 1939, undoubtedly the neglect of Women's History at that time made the topic seem unsuitable for publication. Similar considerations may have worked against publication of several other earlier dissertations. In other cases, lack of mentorship and inexperience discouraged the writers from pursuing publication in the face of one or two rejections of their manuscripts. Several of the most valuable books in the series required considerable rewriting under editorial supervision, which, apparently, had not earlier been available to the authors. There are also several authors who became members of what we call "the lost generation," historians getting their degrees in the 1980s when there were few jobs available. This group of historians, which disproportionately consisted of women, retooled and went into different fields. Three of the books in this series are the work of these historians, who needed considerable persuasion to do the necessary revisions and editing. We are pleased to have found their works and to have persisted in the effort of making them available to a wider readership, since they have a distinct contribution to make.

The books in this series cover a wide range of topics. Two of them are detailed studies in the status of women, one in Georgia, 1783-1860, the other in Russia in the early 1900s. Two are valuable additions to the literature on the anti-woman's suffrage campaigns in the U.S. Of the four books dealing with the history of women's organizations, three are detailed regional studies and one is a comparative history of the British and American Women's Trade Union League. Finally, the three biographical studies of eighteenth- and nineteenth-century women offer either new information or new interpretations of their subjects.

Eleanor Miot Boatwright, *Status of Women in Georgia, 1783—1860*, was discovered by Professor Anne Firor Scott in the Duke University archives and represents, in her words "a buried treasure." An M.A. thesis written by a high school teacher in Augusta, Georgia, its level of scholarship and the depth of its research are of the quality expected of a dissertation. The author has drawn on a vast range of primary sources, including legal sources that were then commonly used for social history, to document and analyze the social customs, class differences, work and religion of white women in Georgia. While her treatment of race relations reflects the limitations of scholarship on that subject in the 1930s, she gives careful attention to the impact of race relations on white women. Her analysis of the linkage made by Southern male apologists for slavery between the subordination ("protection") of women and the subordination of slaves (also rationalized as their "protection") is particularly insightful. The work has much information to offer the contemporary scholar and can be compared in its scholarship and its general approach to the work of Julia Spruill and Elizabeth Massey. When it is evaluated in comparison with other social histories of its period, its research methodology and interpretative focus on women are truly remarkable.

Anne Bobroff-Hajal's, *Working Women in Russia Under the Hunger Tsar: Political Activism and Daily Life*, is a fascinating, excellently researched study of a topic on which there is virtually no material available in the English language. Focusing on women industrial workers in Russia's Central Industrial Region, most of them employed in textile production, Bobroff studied their daily lives and family patterns, their gender socialization, their working and living conditions and their political activism during the Revolution: in political organizations, in food riots and in street fighting. The fact that these women and their families lived mostly in factory barracks will be of added interest to labor historians, who may wish to compare their lives and activities with other similarly situated groups in the U.S. and England. Drawing on a rich mixture of folkloric sources, local newspapers, oral histories, workers' memoirs and ethnographic material, Bobroff presents a convincing and intimate picture of working-class life before the Russian Revolution. Bobroff finds that the particularly strong mother-child bonding of Russian women workers, to which they were indoctrinated from childhood on, undermined their ability to form coherent political groups capable of maintaining their identity over a long period of time. Her thesis, excellently supported and well argued, may undermine some commonly held beliefs on this subject. It should prove of interest to all scholars working on gender socialization and to others working on labor culture, working-class activism, and class consciousness.

Rosemary Keller, *Patriotism and the Female Sex: Abigail Adams and the American Revolution*, is a sophisticated, well-documented interpretation of Abigail Adams's intellectual and political development, set firmly within the historical context. Compared with other Abigail Adams biographies, this work is outstanding in treating her seriously as an agent in history and as an independent intellectual. Abigail Adams emerges from this study as a woman going as far as it was possible to go within the limits of the gender conventions of her time and struggling valiantly, through influencing her husband, to extend these gender conventions. This is an accomplishment quite sufficient for one woman's life time. Professor Keller's sensitive biography makes a real contribution to colonial and women's history.

Elizabeth Ann Bartlett, *Liberty, Equality, Sorority: The Origins and Integrity of Feminist Thought: Frances Wright, Sarah Grimké and Margaret Fuller*, is another work of intellectual history. It attempts to define a common "feminism" emerging from the thought of these important nineteenth-century thinkers and concludes that feminism, in order to sustain itself, must balance the tensions between the concepts of liberty, equality, and sorority. The lucid, well-researched discussions of each woman's life and work should appeal to the general reader and make this book a valuable addition to courses in intellectual history and women's history and literature.

Mary Grant, *Private Woman, Public Person: An Account of the Life of Julia Ward Howe from 1819 to 1868*, is a sensitive, feminist study of Howe's life and thought up to the turning point in 1868, when she decided to dedicate her life to public activism in behalf of women. By carefully analyzing Howe's private letters and journals, the author uncovers a freer, more powerful and creative writer beneath the formal *persona* of the author of "The Battle Hymn of the Republic" than we have hitherto known. She also discusses in detail Howe's fascinating, never published, unfinished novel, "Eva and Raphael," which features a number of then taboo subjects, such as rape, madness and an androgynous character. This well-written biography reveals new aspects and dimensions of Julia Ward Howe's life and work.

Jane Jerome Camhi, *Women Against Women: American Anti-Suffragism, 1880-1920*, and Thomas J. Jablonsky, *The Home, Heaven, and Mother Party: Female Anti-Suffragists in America, 1868-1920*, are complementary studies that should be indispensable for any serious student or scholar of woman suffrage. They are, in fact, the only extant book-length studies of anti-suffragism. This important movement has until now been accessible to modern readers only through the somewhat biased lens of contemporary suffragists' observations. They consistently underestimated its scope and significance and did not engage with its basic paradox, that it was a movement by women against women.

Jane Camhi's comprehensive study of nationwide anti-woman's suffrage movements makes this paradox a central theme. Camhi analyses the "antis' " ideas and ideology and offers some thought-provoking theories about the competing and contradictory positions women took in regard to formal political power. Her insightful profile of a noted anti-suffragist, Ida Tarbell, is an additional contribution this fine book makes to the historical literature.

Thomas Jablonsky's study is focused more narrowly on the organizational history of the rise and fall of the movement. The book is based on extensive research in the organizational records of the anti-suffragists on a state and national level, the records of Congressional hearings, biographical works and the manuscripts of leaders. Jablonsky takes the "antis" seriously and disproves the suffragists' argument that they were merely pawns of male interest groups. He offers a sympathetic, but critical evaluation of their ideas. His detailed attention to organizational efforts in states other than the major battle-grounds—Massachusetts, New York and Illinois—make this book a valuable resource for scholars in history, political science and Women's History.

The four remaining books in the series all focus on aspects of women's organizational activities. Taken together, they reveal the amazing energy, creativity, and persistence of women's institution building on the community and local level. They sustain and highlight the thesis that women built the infrastructures of community life, while men held the positions of visible power. Based on research in four distinctly different regions, these studies should prove useful not only for the intrinsic worth of each, but for comparative purposes.

Darlene Roth, *Matronage: Patterns in Women's Organizations, Atlanta, Georgia, 1890-1940*, is a thoroughly researched, gracefully written study of the networks of women's organizations in that city. The author's focus on conservative women's organizations, such as the Daughters of the American Revolution, the Colonial Dames, and the African-American Chatauqua Circle, adds to the significance of the book. The author defines "matronage" as the functions and institutionalization of the networks of social association among women. By focusing on a Southern city in the Progressive era, Roth provides rich comparative material for the study of women's voluntarism. She challenges notions of the lack of organizational involvement by Southern women. She traces the development of women's activities from communal service orientation—the building of war memorials—to advocacy of the claims of women and children and, finally, to advocacy of women's rights. Her comparative approach, based on the study of the records of white and African-American women's organizations and leadership—she studied 508 white and 150 black women—is illuminating and offers new insights. The book should be of interest to readers in Urban and Community History, Southern History, and Women's History.

Robin Miller Jacoby, *The British and American Women's Trade Union Leagues, 1890-1925: A Case Study of Feminism and Class*, is a comparative study of working-class women in Britain and America in the Progressive period. Although parts of this work have appeared as articles in scholarly journals, the work has never before been accessible in its entirety. Jacoby traces the development of Women's Trade Union Leagues in Britain and America, exploring their different trajectories and settings. By focusing on the interaction of women's and labor movements, the author provides rich empirical material. Her analysis of the tensions and overlapping interests of feminism and class consciousness is important to feminist theory. Her discussion of protective labor legislation, as it was debated and acted upon in two different contexts, makes an important contribution to the existing literature. It also addressees issues still topical and hotly debated in the present day. The book will be of interest to labor historians, Women's History specialists, and the general public.

Janice Steinschneider, *An Improved Woman: The Wisconsin Federation of Women's Clubs, 1895-1920*, is a richly documented study based on a multitude of primary sources, which reveals the amazing range of women's activities as community builders and agents of change. Wisconsin clubwomen founded libraries, fostered changes in school curricula and worked to start kindergartens and playgrounds. They helped preserve historic and natural landmarks and organized to improve public health services. They built a sound political base—long before they had the right of suffrage—from which they trained women leaders for whom they then helped to secure public appointments. They worked to gain access for women to university education and employment and, in addition to many other good causes, they worked for world peace. Steinschneider's description and analysis of "women's public sphere" is highly sophisticated. Hers is one of the best studies on the subject and should prove indispensable to all concerned with understanding women's political activities, their construction of a public sphere for women, and their efforts and successes as builders of large coalitions.

Margit Misangyi Watts, *High Tea at Halekulani: Feminist Theory and American Clubwomen*, is a more narrowly focused study of clubwomen's work than are the other three, yet its significance ranges far above that of its subject matter. Watts tells the story of the Outdoor Circle, an upper-class white women's club in Hawaii, from its founding in 1911 on. Its main activities were to make Hawaii beautiful: to plant trees, clean up eyesores, preserve nature and rid the islands of billboards. To achieve these modest goals, the women had to become consummate politicians and lobbyists and learn how to run grassroots boycotts and publicity and educational campaigns, and how to form long-lasting coalitions. Above all, as Watts's fine theoretical analysis shows, they insisted that their female vision, their woman-centered view, become an accepted part of the public discourse. This case study is rich in theoretical implications. Together with the other three studies of women's club activities it offers not only a wealth of practical examples of women's work for social change, but it also shows that such work both resists patriarchal views and practices and redefines them in the interests of women.

Gerda Lerner
Madison, Wisconsin

Acknowledgments

In writing this book I have piled up as many debts of gratitude as I have bits of biographical data. I thank the staffs of the Houghton Library at Harvard University, the Schlesinger Library at Radcliffe College, the Manuscript Room of the Library of Congress, the Sophia Smith Collection at Smith College, and the Rare Books and Manuscripts Division of the New York Public Library. All were unfailingly helpful.

My adviser, Linda Grant DePauw, shared freely her skill as a scholar, her talent as a writer, and her insights as a mentor. For this introduction to the historian's craft, I will always be grateful.

Members of the George Washington University faculty have been generous with time and advice. I am particularly indebted to Leo P. Ribuffo, Lois W. Banner, and Phyllis M. Palmer for their suggestions at various stages of this manuscript. Other scholars, too, have offered their professional judgment. Deborah P. Clifford, collateral descendant and biographer of Julia Ward Howe, has been exceptionally helpful at every stage of this project. I am indebted as well to Elisabeth Griffith, Noralee Frankel, Karen J. Blair, and Katharine C. Black for many improvements in style and analysis. Whatever faults remain are the results of my decisions, not their suggestions.

I have collected debts of other kinds. To Jean G. Andrews, who proofread the final copy, to the staff at the Church of St. Martin-in-the-Fields in Philadelphia, to the faculty of National Cathedral School in Washington, D.C., and to various neighbors, friends, and relatives, I am indebted for countless acts of helpfulness and encouragement. My sitter, Mrs. Katie Taylor, deserves special mention for her willingness to provide superior child care at a moment's notice. Above all, to my husband, Richard W. Grant, I am grateful beyond expression.

Private Woman,
Public Person

Introduction

The February snow had stopped falling, and in the early morning light a small woman, dressed entirely in black except at her throat and wrists, watched as the dark mountains and evergreen forests of Vermont flew past her train window. She had taken the midnight run from Boston to Montpelier. When the train pulled into the station, the small, plump figure clambered down from her Pullman, lugging a heavy pocketbook. She had stuffed this bag with books and folders of papers. A fresh collar and cuffs were tucked in, too, for later that day she would need them.

The station, still dark and chilly, was unfamiliar to Julia Ward Howe. Stiff, sleepy, and a little nervous, she peered around to see if someone had been sent to meet her. Suddenly she spotted Mary Livermore stepping down from another car. "Oh, you dear big Livermore!" she cried.[1] At once all was well. The veteran traveler and lecturer took the novice under her wing. After resting at a hotel, they donned their fresh white collars and cuffs and made their way to Montpelier's Village Hall. On the speaker's platform with them sat Lucy Stone and Henry Blackwell. They all made lengthy addresses, and when they finished, both Mary Livermore and Julia Ward Howe looked around with satisfaction. The year was 1870, and Vermont was about to review its Constitution. An amendment had been proposed that would secure the ballot for all women of the state. Both women had spoken in its favor; they believed they would carry the day.[2]

They were wrong. All but one of the delegates elected to the Vermont Constitutional Convention voted against the proposal.[3] Howe was undaunted, however. She continued to press for women's rights, in state after state, until her death in 1910.

Julia Ward Howe had not always been dedicated to improving the status of women. She began her career at the age of forty-nine, after a sheltered adolescence and twenty-five years of domestic life. Julia was born in 1819 to a wealthy New York family. After an erratic education, much of which she conducted on her own, Julia Ward married Samuel Gridley Howe. Four children were born in the six years after her marriage; in the ensuing nine years, Julia added two more to her flock. During this time, she wrote poetry, plays, and fiction, some of which was published. "The Battle Hymn of the Republic" remains her best-known work.

Despite these publications and a bit of work on behalf of some philanthropic agencies, Julia Ward Howe remained a private person during these years. She occupied herself with her studies and her large, difficult family. From 1844 to 1863, the care of six small children consumed her time. Of all her suffrage colleagues, only Elizabeth Cady Stanton had hands this full, but Julia Ward Howe had no Susan B. Anthony to help her. Julia enjoyed entertaining at musical parties or dinner. When she could, she invited literary and political people for grander affairs. She cared intensely about social success. But while her social life did take Julia out of her strictly domestic circle, it was hardly public activity. It served her personal needs, not those of her community.

Of her abundant writing, Julia published only a part. Most of it she wrote for herself, a mirror of her inner life. Intermittently during the 1850s and 1860s, Julia wrote pieces for publication in newspapers and journals. With rare exceptions, these were reviews, poems, fiction, or reports on society "doings." They brightened the journals, perhaps, but they shed no light on social movements and pursued no reform objectives.

Her husband, Samuel Gridley Howe, known to friends as Chev, was a widely recognized leader among midcentury reformers. Julia, however much she admired his "moral courage," did not throw herself into his causes. There was good reason for this. Chev was an irascible and unsupportive spouse. He could not abide, in any form, any sign of independence in his wife. He picked away not only at her estate, demolishing her once substantial income, but also at her self-esteem. He criticized her for doing the things she most loved. He took charge of the household, sharpening her sense of inadequacy in that department. He moved the family around constantly, ever eager for the change that kept Julia off balance. He even challenged her competence as a mother. With argument, silence, infidelity, and indifference he fretted Julia for most of their married life.

To many, then, it seemed peculiar that Julia was selected, in November 1868, as the first president of the newly formed New England Woman Suffrage Association. As her experience in Vermont in 1870 shows, Julia had no background in lecturing and traveling on behalf of reform. Indeed, her support for woman suffrage was all of one day old when Julia took the president's chair at the association's convention.

Yet private and domestic life had prepared Julia Ward Howe to serve the interests of women in ways her critics could not see. In rearing a family, Julia acquired a rhetoric that other middle-class women could relate to and believe. Stout and lace-capped, she looked like the respectable matron she was. It was a look she cultivated and used to her advantage. She brought thousands of women to the cause because she knew how to talk to them out of her—and their—experience. Loneliness, isolation, depression, and a lack of outlet for talents were frequently women's lot. Julia knew this well, and she devoted the last forty years of her life to its remedy.

Family life did more for Julia Ward Howe. By 1868 it had toughened her. The deaths of her parents, her favorite brother, and her youngest child taught Julia how to manage emotional pain and her own tendency to depression. A marriage ravaged by quarrels with a domineering husband led Julia to a theory of individual moral responsibility on which to base both her eventual independence and much of her feminist theory.

Study and writing provided Julia with an emotional sanctuary. They gave her a workshop in which to hammer out her own values. They offered a taste of what a self-sustaining life could be like. If the pursuit of philosophy and religion reinforced the private dimensions of Julia's existence, they also nourished her self-esteem and her ability to think, judge, and operate independently. Moreover, the fruit of all this study would become the core of Julia's feminist theory. She came to believe in the primacy of individual conscience, the absolute necessity for free action of individual moral will, and the role of both sexes in advancing human progress. This was not the stuff of successful stump speeches, but it was the architecture for the moderate woman's movement she eventually led.

Julia's major task, then, in the years of her young adulthood and midlife, was to transform her inner, private experiences into the stuff of public leadership. She would have to find her own convictions, her own voice, and her own platform. Ironically, those institutions traditionally used to keep women "in their place"—religion and marriage—provided the crucible for this transformation. The process, slow and often fiery, turned the lead weights of her life—boredom, isolation, frustration, and depression—into the gold of clarity, hope, courage, and articulate conviction. This book is the story of that alchemy.

ONE

Nature:
Parents and Grandparents

These are my people, quaint and ancient
Gentlefolks with their prim old ways
This, their leader, came from England,
Governed a state in early days.

I must vanish with my ancients
But a golden web of love
Is around us and beneath us
Binds us to our home above.

One evening when she was in her eighties, Julia Ward Howe ignored the pleas of her family to stay at home and slipped out to a meeting at Boston's Old South Church. In a brief address, she alluded to her escape, comparing it to those of her great-great-uncle, General Francis Marion. "General Marion was known in his generation as the 'Swamp Fox'; and when I succeed in eluding the care of my guardians, children and grandchildren, and coming to a meeting like this, I think I may be said to have inherited some of his characteristics."[1]

This comparison was typical, for Julia Ward Howe delighted in her ancestors. She attributed various different personality traits in herself and her children to one or another of her relatives. From Cutler relations Julia believed she had inherited red hair, warmth of temper, and effervescent humor. From the Wards came "force and integrity of purpose, a strength of character, and a certain business instinct."[2]

Both of her parents, Julia Rush Cutler Ward and Samuel Ward, likewise prided themselves on their distinguished ancestry. The great events of colonial and Revolutionary history intertwined through the lives of their relatives. To

Wards and Cutlers, American courage, canniness, and triumph were part of their blood.

Julia's grandmother, Sarah Mitchell Hyrne Cutler, was the niece of Francis Marion, the famous "Swamp Fox" of the Carolinas. She was reared in comfort and elegance on a wealthy Carolina rice plantation. Nevertheless, she joined "a company of ladies who banded together for some new departure of a patriotic intent. . . . They called themselves 'Daughters of Liberty.' "[3] Sarah Mitchell was considered socially prominent enough to dance with General Washington at a ball given in his honor.[4]

Like many young women of the southern elite, Sarah married early. She was fourteen when she became engaged, and family legend has it that she wept upon being told that she must now give up her dolls.[5] Her husband, Thomas Hyrne, was indulgent. He established her in an elegant house in Georgetown, South Carolina, well suited to the lavish entertainments she loved.[6] Her aristocratic life-style of luxury and leisure crashed to a halt two years later, however, when her husband died. Like many women of her era, widowhood left her with nothing but an inadequate pension, debts, and the need to remarry quickly. After four years of widowhood, she married Benjamin Clarke Cutler of Long Island, "a genial handsome man much given to hospitality."[7]

At the time of her second marriage, Sarah Mitchell Hyrne was charming, attractive, and somewhat given to eccentricity. She pinched snuff, ate with her knife or her fingers, and delighted in launching "audacious but good-natured sallies."[8] Confident of her opinions and sure of her style, Sarah Mitchell Hyrne Cutler embarked on her second marriage, at the age of twenty, as an experienced woman of independent views.

Julia Rush Cutler was the daughter of Sarah and Benjamin Cutler. She was one of five children who occupied the family house on Long Island. When she was six, her parents sent her to board at Mrs. Isabella Graham's school.[9] Isabella Graham was a Scottish woman, widowed in 1773. In 1789 she arrived in New York City, hoping both to practice her Calvinist faith in "the country where the Church of Christ would eventually flourish" and to open a school successful enough to sustain her family.[10] She combined social distinction with vigorous Presbyterianism in her classes, instilling her pupils with religious feeling, concern for the poor, and the rudiments of learning.[11]

In 1810 Benjamin Cutler died, leaving his wife with barely enough money to pay for immediate needs. Julia's education ended, and she went home briefly to join her family. Her mother, faced with little income, a large family, and no means of self-support, decided to use what talents she had—social wisdom and experience—to ensure the prompt marriage of her older daughters. In the winter of 1811-1812 she took Eliza and Julia to spend the winter in a polite boardinghouse on Manhattan, under the watchful eye of Mrs. Graham.[12] After a short stay to get them settled, Sarah left her daughters and returned to Long Island to supervise the care of the younger children.

Eliza Cutler was the oldest daughter. Her education was limited and her accomplishments few. Although her family loved her for her lively sense of humor, her upright character, and her firm sense of purpose, these qualities were not much in demand among eligible bachelors. Eliza, moreover, was unusually tall, with hairy moles on her face and large, uneven teeth.[13] Potential husbands did not materialize from her boardinghouse companions.

Unlike her sister, Julia was a very pretty girl. Her passions were literature and parties, and she thrived on the cordial atmosphere of the boardinghouse. Her temperament was a bit uneven: moody and impulsive one moment, irritated and depressed the next, cheerful, even frivolous, the next.[14] Since she was only fifteen, she hardly took seriously her mother's idea that she might end the winter with a solemn proposal of marriage in her hands.

Yet a proposal did arrive, much to Julia's consternation, in January 1812. Her suitor was Samuel Ward, a bachelor she had assumed was engaged. Her senior by more than ten years, Samuel had seemed more a substitute father than a potential husband.[15]

Samuel Ward was twenty-five in the winter of 1811-1812. He was tall, energetic, and fond of horses. Furthermore, he was handsome, with short, curly hair, clean-shaven cheeks, a long, finely chiseled nose, and a firm chin.[16]

His background was Yankee. Samuel's great-grandfather and grandfather were governors of Rhode Island. When the first Continental Congress was convened, the second Governor Ward chaired the Committee of the Whole. Although he knew that independence from Great Britain would be declared, he never lived to see it. He died of smallpox before the Declaration of Independence was completed.[17]

Governor Ward was a friend of George Washington, and his descendants cherished the correspondence between the two. One of these letters praised the performance of the governor's son, "a sensible, well-informed young man." This was another Samuel, who rose to the rank of lieutenant colonel during the course of the Revolution.[18] When the war was over, young Colonel Ward moved his family from Newport to New York, rightly sensing that economic opportunities were rising in the great port city. With him went his wife, Phoebe Greene Ward, and his family of young children.

Phoebe Greene was a member of another distinguished Rhode Island family. Her paternal ancestors had also been governors of the state and officers in the Revolution. Phoebe's mother, Catherine Ray, had been a noted beauty in her day and a correspondent of Benjamin Franklin's. Phoebe's life was not so glamorous, however; her days were filled with the rearing of ten children, seven of whom attained adulthood.[19] Her fifth child was another Samuel Ward.

Since his father could not afford a college education for him, young Sam was apprenticed at the age of fourteen to the banking house of Nathaniel Prime, who later formed a partnership with Rufus King, noted Federalist politician and diplomat.[20] The offices were on Wall Street, cheek-by-jowl with those of the stockbrokers. It was an excellent situation for the young apprentice. He quickly mastered the arts of banking as well as those of investing. His flair for commercial transactions, his sobriety, and his integrity soon brought him appropriate reward. At the age of twenty-two he was named partner, and the firm's masthead was changed to Prime, Ward and King.[21]

Samuel's distinguished ancestry, combined with his financial success, would have given him a degree of social prominence had he desired it. The Knickerbocker aristocracy was losing its grip on New York high society, and Yankee merchants of Samuel Ward's caliber were making their way up the social ladder. Samuel did not choose this path. By nature he was grave and disinclined to parties and crowds of people. More important, he was dedicated to his work.[22] When still an apprentice, he was asked what he intended to do with his training. "I mean to be one of the first bankers of the United States!" he replied.[23] To his interest in banking, Samuel added active participation in reform causes, such as temperance, and an interest in education. He was rich, optimistic, and upwardly mobile. And he very badly wanted to marry Julia Cutler.

While Samuel waited for a response to his proposal, Julia returned to her family in Jamaica Plain. He wrote her tender, affectionate letters, revealing that strong emotions lay beneath his sober businessman's exterior. "Dearest best of friends the pen almost intuitively flies to my fingers to convey to you the feelings of my heart, to tell you that it unceasingly throbs for you and you alone."[24] He counseled her about her health, her reading, and her religion.[25] He sympathized with her over the difficulties of leaving home.[26] He impressed upon her his vision of married life. "The time that we can steal from the pleasures and duties of society shall if agreeable to you be devoted to a course of reading. . . . Seated by our comfortable fireside in winter, the business of the day or the pleasures of the evening being over, the cold winds of winter shall whistle around our little mansion and find peace and happiness within."[27]

The romantic notion of two people united in intellectual interest and common purpose had molded Samuel's ideal of marriage. He subscribed, too, to the emerging perception of women as entirely domestic creatures whose hands and minds should be devoted expressly to the comfort and companionship of family members.

> The duty of the husband is to provide every comfort for, and to love, cherish, & support, the friend of his bosom. To this end all his efforts are directed—he labors and toils incessantly—his reward is, the smiles of his dear partner—surely, then, the wife should endeavor to make Home, dear Home, chearful and comfortable—should cheer with her smiles and sooth with her caresses the object whose energies are occupied in their mutual welfare.[28]

> [In women] that character is most estimable where great firmness is combined with great gentleness & that retiring timidity which captivates the soul of men.[29]

These ideas were not original with Samuel; they had been circulating among members of the wealthy urban classes since before the Revolution. But this scene certainly departed from the past experience of other Ward women, who had worked on family farms. Julia would be the first Ward wife who would be expected to live a life filled entirely by entertaining and household concerns, an ornamental and domestic role divorced from the business activity that was Samuel's world. In domestic matters as well as in business ones, banker Ward was in the forefront, accommodating to the changes of a modernizing society.

Evidently young Julia found such sharp role prescriptions less appealing than did her fiancé. After all, a domestic life had not brought her twice-widowed mother security and comfort. Besides, Sarah Cutler was clearly of an independent cast of mind, and her daughter had some of that same spirit. Fond of literature, poetry-writing, and religious meditation, Julia hoped to have some life of her own. Nevertheless, she acquiesced to Samuel's plans, with wit if not wholehearted agreement with his theories. "Am I not rational for once in my life—yes I am & I hope in time to be cured entirely of all my *wayward* fanaticals, & to be settled down into a good, natural, honest, plodding soul without an idea beyond making a pudding or cleaning an andiron."[30]

Thirty years later, the same romantic ideal, then sentimentalized and elevated to the status of a cult, would confront another Julia.[31] Like her mother, Julia Ward would first hesitate and then concur, but she never adapted to marriage as easily as her mother, Julia Cutler Ward.

On October 12, 1812, Julia Cutler married Samuel Ward. They moved to a small house on Marketfield Street, but Julia spent the hot summer of 1813 in the country with her family. She was already showing signs of the tuberculosis that would progressively weaken her until her premature death in 1824. The country air was expected to provide a cure.

The Wards' marriage was an affectionate one. During the early years, before pregnancy and disease had worn her out, Julia's letters bubbled with physical references and teasing asides. "Sometimes indeed a sweet thought *will* steal into my heart, reminding me of those delightful moments when I sat on your knee & pressed my lips to yours."[32] In a later letter she teased Samuel about his aversion to being "kissed up on hot nights" and inquired whether he would sleep with her during the winter.[33] Their physical and emotional intimacy endured throughout their marriage, as Samuel indicated. "Love letters between us old married folks might to many appear very ridiculous—but I feel almost as much in the vein for one as when 'first I wooed you to these arms'—and I love you dearest with more ardency than when you were my young & blooming bride."[34]

Illness formed a counterpoint to these loving messages. Julia remained high-strung and nervous. Her letters to Samuel repeated references to her fragile state: "The noise and bustle of city life . . . makes me ill all day." "My nerves are shattered when I see anyone kiss anyone else." "This morning, I burst into tears at the noise Francis made in running across the room." And after a long vacation in the country, designed to restore her health, she wrote, "You must not expect to find me . . . as able to endure as I was last winter, for I am still very nervous if put out of my usual course."[35]

She suffered from severe headaches that made the slightest noise unbearable. Colic and congestion in her lungs were additional woes. Although these sufferings were very real, they were also convenient. Julia learned to turn them to her advantage. They provided a reason to escape the heat of a New York City summer and a justification for returning to her mother. (These country vacations may have been a futile attempt at birth control as well.) Once established in Jamaica, illness gave Julia a good excuse to avoid housework.

More important, ill health gave her an acceptable way of dealing with her strong-minded husband. The issue of houses is a case in point. Their first house on Marketfield Street—her husband's choice—was cold and cramped, surely unsuitable for an invalid. Another possible house was "cold and disagreeable in winter, on account of the entry," she reported.[36] Eventually Julia got a house on Bowling Green that suited her tastes. Julia's invalidism gave her a certain amount of power in the marriage, which her husband had not counted on.[37]

Friends and relatives admired Julia Cutler Ward's tact and charm. Her daughter remembered later in life that, "She died . . . so beloved and mourned by all who knew her that my early years were full of the testimony borne by surviving friends to the beauty and charm of her character."[38] Julia used this tact to survive her husband's patriarchal ideas. When she was away from him, her letters contained hints of dissatisfaction. As soon as he pursued these, she suggested the remedy that suited her. She always phrased her suggestions in a self-effacing manner: "But I know you will do everything for the best & rest assured I shall be *more* than satisfied with all your arrangements."[39] She preserved a facade of submissiveness while engineering a life-style that pleased her.

Julia took care to preserve a part of her life independent of her husband. Fond of reading religious poetry, she also wrote and published religious verse, even when ill health and an expanding family took up her time. Her work appeared in Rufus Griswold's *The Female Poets of America*.[40] Samuel Ward had no objection to this. Writing poetry was, after all, a genteel occupation. It simply did not interest him, so he had nothing to do with it. By cultivating this private recourse, Julia avoided turning over all her energies and thoughts to the demands of her family.

Julia also succeeded in overcoming her husband's objections to religious activity. Julia Cutler Ward's own interest in religion began shortly after Sammy's birth, when her tuberculosis flared up once more. Faced with death and the tragedy of leaving her new family behind, she wept inconsolably. Laudanum was used to quiet her, but Julia insisted that only a talk with Mrs. Graham, her old teacher, could reassure her.[41]

Mrs. Graham had the popular sentiment of the time in her favor as she reasoned with her old pupil. The fires of the Second Great Awakening of religious fervor were building up to the "grand climax" of 1825-1837.[42] Isabella Graham had been well warmed by these fires. Together she and her fearful pupil prayed and read passages of the Bible. Her message had Puritan foundations. Graham instructed Julia in the depravity of ordinary men and women, the terrible justice of an almighty God, the eternal fires of hell, the

11

saving grace vouchsafed to the sanctified, and the battle between good and evil as reflected in the personal struggle for salvation. Isabella Graham abandoned the old Calvinist tenet of predestination, however. Like the preachers of the Second Great Awakening, she argued that a person's "ability to be saved was a matter of his own will, yet actual conversion was supposed to be exclusively the work of the Holy Spirit. Complete submission to the will of God would somehow put one in the way to be saved. Righteous behavior was both a token of the person's correct state of mind and a symbol of Heavenly favor."[43]

Along with other evangelicals of the early nineteenth century, Isabella Graham aimed at a merger of piety and morality, of theology and action.[44] She believed that everyone had a responsibility not only for the salvation of his or her own soul, but also for the salvation of all. She was convinced that reformed souls should turn their attention to the reform of society. Graham herself had founded several societies for this purpose in New York City. Most prominent of these was the Society for the Relief of Poor Widows with Small Children, organized in 1797. Some of Graham's former pupils taught there. Other alumnae contributed their time to additional projects of Graham's, including the Orphan Asylum and the Magdalen Society.

So it was that in addition to explaining the Bible to the anguished Mrs. Ward, Isabella Graham turned the attention of her old pupil to various benevolent enterprises. In particular, the Society for Promotion of Industry among the Poor interested Julia. From 1814 on she gave this enterprise both her time and her money.[45]

The doctrine of reform to which Julia Cutler Ward subscribed embraced institutions and individuals. Consequently, in tandem with her own religious studies, Julia initiated an effort to convert her husband. Initially her attempts met with resistance, but by the early 1820s Samuel had adopted many of his wife's views. In a letter to his absent wife in 1822, he thanked her for her counsel and admitted that, "Pride, ambition & hardness of heart I have mistaken for nobler emotions."[46] Samuel Ward was, by the time of his wife's death, entirely willing to let her study and pray according to her own lights. Further, he had so far concurred in her ideas that he turned to her minister brother for spiritual guidance when Julia was gone.

In the course of time, Julia had succeeded in combining elements of her mother's aristocratic background with the modern, and often more restrictive, views of her husband. By manipulating the domestic role that her husband had decreed for her, Julia carved out for herself a position of dignity and influence in the family. She had won the independence to travel without her husband

and the opportunity to study and write as she saw fit. She claimed a voice in family decisions. She gained the respect of her husband, who no longer treated her as a little girl, and of his father and brothers. No one doubted her right to grow intellectually and spiritually. The aristocratic heritage had been a strengthening influence for Julia, countering the pressures of a modernizing society. Her daughter, however, would grow up without such a buffer to ease her emergence into womanhood.

Although she had transformed her family role into one of strength, she had not been able to preserve her health. Julia Ward Cutler died on November 11, 1824, three days after the birth of her seventh child. She was twenty-seven. Puerperal fever was the direct cause of death, as it was for thousands of women in her era, but tuberculosis, constant pregnancy, and nursing had all taken their toll. Julia had borne her children in rapid succession. The first, Samuel, was born in January 1814, just fifteen months after her marriage. After a miscarriage in 1815, she gave birth to "the first little Julia" in 1816. Henry was born one year later. Baby Julia died shortly after her third birthday, so when another little girl was born—on May 27, 1819—she was named Julia, too. Francis Marion was born about nineteen months later, in 1821. Louisa followed in February 1823, and Anne Eliza was delivered less than two years later. Julia Cutler Ward had been pregnant or nursing for nearly twelve of her twenty-seven years.

Identification with ancestors had a long tradition in the Ward household. Her parents impressed on little Julia and her sisters and brothers that they had "a great deal to live up to and that there would be no excuse for them if they were lazy or incompetent."[47] The Wards, Greenes, Marions, and Cutlers, with their records of public service, provided a model of behavior for young Julia. She felt duty bound to continue the family tradition of community leadership and service. The honors and distinction that attended these ancestral careers were not lost upon her, either; Julia would always yearn for some sort of power and recognition. Furthermore, Julia's ancestors gave her an automatic claim to social distinction and community respect. It was not a large step from identifying with an ancestor's heroism to identifying with his claim to glory. As she saw it, their blood was hers. She was tinged with the same greatness that had attended them.

As was the case with many of the accomplished women of her generation, Julia had no trouble identifying with the male achievements in her family. She managed to dilute the connection between maleness and leadership, political

13

service, force of character, and business sense. She saw these personal qualities as available to her. Perhaps she did so out of sheer need; her family was, after all, "patriarchal in its dimensions," and she had no other choice.[48] Yet there were women—Sarah Mitchell, Catherine Ray—whose presence, although not physical, was felt. Julia cherished their memory long into adulthood. Family legend has it that Julia preserved not only the Ward correspondence, but also Catherine Ray's orange silk wedding stockings.[49] Perhaps these startling hose were more than a keepsake. Perhaps they were a reminder of women of character and distinction, blood relatives who were independent, beautiful, and renowned. Wards, Cutlers, and all their connections kindled ambition and bolstered Julia's sense of worth.

TWO

Nurture: Nursery Days, 1819-1830

Another kiss, and yet another
"Love me very much, my mother?
Teach me good words, high and grand
Show me stars with your dear white hand.
Give me ribands and pretty flowers
Take your gold plaything and tell me the hours.
Give me sweet cuddling place, close to your breast
Little bird's mother sits warm in her nest."
At night, the creatures all turn to stone
And I lie in my cradle, silent and lone.

Little Julia Ward was five years old when her mother died. She was old enough to remember her parent and to remember learning of her death. In her *Reminiscences* she recalled their last days together. "I remember this summer as a particularly happy period. My younger brother and I had our lessons in a lovely green bower. . . . My mother often took me with her for a walk in the beautiful garden, from which she picked flowers that she arranged with great taste. . . . And then, one bitter morning, I awoke to hear the words, 'Julia, your mother is dead.' "[1] The juxtaposition of the idyllic last days with the tragedy of her mother's death re-creates in the reader a sudden pang, a hint of the child's shock and grief. It is a subtle sign of the seriousness of Julia's loss.

For Julia's father, the news was a crushing blow. For several weeks after his wife's death, he lay in his room, suffering from "fever and ague." The physical pain, he later reported to his oldest daughter, was a welcome relief from the mental anguish he was suffering.[2] He refused to see his baby daughter until his own father, alarmed at the state of affairs in his son's household, himself placed Anne Eliza in her father's arms.[3] This happy introduction initiated Samuel's recovery, but he could not bear to stay long in the house he had shared with his dear wife. He sent back the new furnishings she had ordered (but never seen), and he bought a new house on the outskirts of the city.[4]

Julia does not mention the reaction of the other Ward children in her *Reminiscences*. There must have been grief, anxiety, and bewilderment, however. Hushed voices, footsteps at odd hours, a grief-stricken father locked up in his room, sudden appearances and disappearances of relatives, and an odd new baby sister disrupted the familiar routine of family life. Furthermore, pious relatives made sure that Julia and her brothers and sisters recognized their loss. For Aunt Anne Ward, the death of her sister-in-law provided a perfect opportunity for Christian instruction. She guided the prayers of her nieces and nephews appropriately, noting with satisfaction that all of them "cried and it seemed as if their little hearts would break."[5]

Perhaps five-year-old Julia felt as though her heart really would break, for she had lost the loving attention of a kindred spirit. Julia was as high-strung as her mother. In a letter to her husband, Julia Cutler Ward wrote:

> I was obliged to whip Julia yesterday afternoon and have been sick ever since in consequence of the agitation it threw me into. . . . I felt *obliged* to try Solomon's prescription, which had a worse effect on me than on her. . . . I think it is the last time, however, blow high or low, for she is as nervous as her mama was at her age, at the sight of a rod, and screamed herself almost to death; indeed, her nerves were so affected that she cannot get over it and has cried all today, trembling as violently as if she had the ague all the time I whipped her and could not eat.[6]

Because of this shared temperament, Mrs. Ward took particular interest in her daughter, lavishing great care and attention on Julia's education. She picked Julia to accompany her on a trip through upper New York State during the summer of 1823. The fond mother reported Julia's antics in letters to Samuel Ward, delighting in the praise her daughter elicited. "Your daughter is universally courted and admired," she wrote, "and is as good & sweet as ever—she is really an uncommon child."[7]

Without her mother, Julia was at a serious disadvantage. As her daughter later summarized it, "The great misfortune of losing her mother shadowed her young life."[8] One problem was that Julia had no one to open the world of women to her. Early-nineteenth-century sex roles were restrictive, and Julia's father could not introduce her to their nuances. The conventional social thought of the first half of the nineteenth century defined a special sphere for women, one that gave them responsibility for religion, the instruction of children, and the running of households. This private domestic sphere was distinct from the more public spheres of men. Male responsibilities included those of the marketplace, the political forum, and the professions. As the heads of families, husbands retained control of their children, their property, and the property of their wives. At home they expected to find solicitude for their comfort; they did not expect to contribute anything to the running of the household except money. This strict division between spheres of responsibility and places of work led to definite distance between men and women, and a certain distance between fathers and daughters.[9]

The distance between men and women had another implication for Julia. As women were thrown increasingly back on themselves for intellectual stimulation, emotional support, and daily assistance, a private "world of women" developed. In religious study groups, in sewing circles, in sickrooms, and in confinement, they turned to one another. Women became one another's closest friends and intimate companions.[10]

After her mother's death, however, there was no one to help Julia find her way in this world. Her Aunt Eliza, who had come to live with them, had neither the interest in nor the time for instructing her nieces in the subtleties of feminine behavior and association. As a consequence, Julia had no access to "the milieu in which women could develop a sense of inner security and self-esteem."[11] Later she would create some of this lost experience with her sisters and a Boston friend. But for a long time, Julia was isolated and rather lonely.

Furthermore, Julia had lost an important role model. Her parents had managed to reconcile their very different temperaments, styles, and backgrounds. They never allowed financial or domestic worries to smother their affection, and each learned to tolerate the other's tastes and preferences. Julia never got the opportunity to see this marriage at work. She never saw her mother in action, dealing with her strong-willed father, and getting her way in the end. She never witnessed the process of sorting out differences, the use of acceptable techniques of persuasion, or the arrangement of compromises. As a consequence, she went into her own marriage ill prepared, with vague notions about married bliss. When marital difficulties cropped up, Julia had no model for successful dealings between man and wife.

At the time of their mother's death, the Ward children led a sheltered life. When the family lived near the Battery, the children were taken for walks by their nurse, but even then they could not romp freely. The girls' clothes made vigorous play difficult, since their shoes were thin kid and their dresses fine cambric. Warm coats were unheard of, even in winter; a thin wool pelisse was all they had.[12] The girls caught cold easily, and this was held up as evidence that long outings in the fresh air were unwise.[13] In summer, a cumbersome woolen veil was tied over Julia's face lest she acquire new freckles.[14] This clothing was designed in part to reflect the girls' social position. The fine fabrics and impractical outerwear signaled wealth and a life of leisure. Yet they were also emblematic of the restrictions on the Ward children's lives. Flimsy shoes and coats restrained them out-of-doors; Banker Ward restrained them indoors.

Especially after his wife's death, Ward determined that his children should rely on one another for amusement. Outings were "confined to the family circle."[15]

> My father had become deeply imbued with the religious ideas of the time. He dreaded for his children the dissipations of fashionable society, and even the risks of general intercourse with the unsanctified many. . . . The early years of my life were passed in the seclusion not only of home life, but of a home most carefully and jealously guarded from all that might be represented in the orthodox trinity of evil, the world, the flesh, and the devil.[16]

Mr. Ward regarded frivolous companions as the devil's accomplices. Consequently, worldly amusements declined in the Ward household, even as wealth and material comfort increased. The children were given dancing lessons, but no place to dance. They were not allowed to play cards or give parties. Although his brothers were connoisseurs, Samuel Ward admitted no wine to the table; neither did he permit tobacco.[17] Julia regretted the isolation that cut her off from the ordinary experiences and lessons of childhood. "No one dreamed of turning the enamelled pages of the garden for us. We grew up consequently with the city measure of the universe—your own house, somebody else's, the trees in the park, the strip of blue sky overhead, and a great deal of talk about nature read from the best authors."[18]

Thrown on their own devices, the children invented their pleasures. Julia, showing early literary and dramatic flair, devised short plays for her brothers and sisters to perform. One drama, *The Iroquois Bride*, provided Julia with a choice part. As the ill-fated bride, she clambered up a stool that served as the precipice where she was to meet her lover, brother Henry. Their mock mutual suicide by stabbing came to a hasty conclusion when horrified elders realized what was going on.[19]

Henry, two years her senior, was Julia's favorite. The two children had their first lessons together, and Julia sobbed when Henry was taken off by himself to visit relatives or to go to school.[20] But her other brothers were good playmates, too. The whole nursery ran and screeched with excitement when Sam, the eldest, played ghost or when Marion, the youngest boy, played the outlaw.[21]

In 1825, when Henry was sent off to join Sam at Round Hill School, Julia turned to the company of her sisters. The girls had large families of dolls, which enjoyed a far more frivolous life than their small mistresses. Julia, Louisa, and Annie devised for them the lavish parties they could not have, and they permitted far more acquaintance with spiced punch and mud puddles than their own sheltered lives allowed.[22] These vicarious pleasures gave the girls an outlet for unfulfilled wishes and for their pent-up social energy.

Julia's position as the eldest daughter gave her a special role in the trio. She was "Miss Ward"; she must set an example; she must fill a mother's place in attending to the development of character in her younger sisters. Apparently Julia, dreamy and fond of reading, escaped this unnatural burden by devoting herself to literature. From time to time, however, she decided to plunge into the business of supervising her sisters, sometimes with comic results. One day she insisted that her charges compose some religious verse. Louisa stoutly refused, but cheerful little Annie produced two lines: "He feeds the ravens when they call/And stands them in a pleasant hall."[23]

Religion remained a topic of major importance in the Ward household. Julia read *A Pilgrim's Progress* at the age of nine; Francis improved his siblings with morning sermons. A letter from eight-year-old Julia to her ten-year-old cousin reflects her familiarity with the language and ideas of the Calvinist pulpit. "Dear Cousin, I hope that you will say the Prayer which my Brother has written for you. I hear with regret that you are sick, and it is as necessary as ever that you should trust in God; love Him, dear Henry, and you will see Death approaching with joy. Oh, what are earthly things, which we must all lose when we die—to our immortal souls which never die!"[24]

Julia combined her love of literature with this religious training in her first efforts at poetry. Her identification with her mother was forthright, as she explained to her father. "Expect not to find in these juvenile productions [a collection of her poems] the delicacy and grace which pervaded the writings of that dear parent now in glory. . . . I entreat you to remember that they were written in the eleventh, twelfth, and thirteenth years of my life."[25] The titles reflect a child's effort to invest stock religious phrases with personal meaning. They also reveal the degree to which Julia had internalized the religious principles of her parents. At the age of fifteen, she wrote a poem entitled, "Vain Regrets written on looking over a diary kept while I was under serious impressions."[26] She had already adopted the practices recommended by the ministers of the period as the best means of capturing the adolescent heart—journal keeping, self-analysis, recognition of sinfulness, and regret.

Samuel Ward must have rejoiced in his daughter's gravity. Following his wife's death, his religious beliefs had grown stronger and more stringent. He was, according to his daughter, an "ardent evangelical."[27] His wife, his brother-in-law, and his local parish church had nurtured the slow conversion of a man initially hostile to "Mad Devotees" to one entirely in sympathy with them.[28] The loss of his wife and of his father confirmed in his mind the importance of a grave, sober, and religious life. He embraced the concept of spiritual benevolence, with its concern for the souls of others. As a result, he was grief-stricken when his father died without adopting evangelical views.[29] He accepted, too, the burden of stewardship, the view that everyone had a responsibility to rectify public and private wrongs. As his children could attest, he was ready to correct and reprove them lest he fall into the error of indifference.

There is no doubt that Mr. Ward's beliefs were deep and heartfelt, but for men of his age and position, evangelical religion had certain advantages. His reputation as a man of character was enhanced by his religious views, which in turn enhanced his business. Prime, Ward and King enjoyed not only high regard but also great prosperity during his career there. A colleague wrote of him:

> There exist undoubtedly, in regard to the trade in money, and respecting those engaged in it, many and absurd prejudices. . . . It is no small triumph to have lived down, as Mr. Ward did, this prejudice, and to have forced upon the community in the midst of which he resided, and upon all brought into connection with him, the conviction that commerce in money, like commerce in general, is to a lofty spirit, lofty and ennobling, and is valued more for the power it confers, of promoting liberal and beneficent enterprises, and of conducing to the welfare and prosperity of society, than for the means of individual and selfish gratification or indulgence.[30]

Money was, according to this view, a noble end in itself, and a "lofty spirit" was the monarch that ennobled it.

Because money, and the spending of it, could be seen as a virtue, Samuel Ward did not hesitate to buy things for his own comfort and for that of his family. He invested in furnishings, horses, and carriages that were both handsome and expensive. Banker Ward regarded this not as frivolity, but as evidence of substance. He recognized, as well, the power of money to extend his views about piety and morality. In particular, money could be dispensed, through the agency of the benevolent societies, to secure secular order. The ideal society, after all, would certainly include obedience to authority, orderly and sober behavior, and the prompt payment of debts. To members of the wealthier classes, whose property and businesses depended on the quiet cooperation of the working class, religion meant not only the salvation of souls, but also the stability and integrity of society as a whole.[31]

The benevolent societies, financed in great measure by men like Samuel Ward, were the means of enforcement. On the one hand, they reached out through colporteurs and missionaries to spread the gospel to individuals throughout the country. On the other hand, they took an early interest in politics, trying to preserve economic virtue by keeping the Federalists in office.[32] The leaders of the community were to be those who embodied both religious and financial success, the latter being some evidence of the former. Through the benevolent organizations, they would become the enforcers of moral norms, a "cultivated, responsible, stable aristocracy."[33]

In keeping with the benevolent thrust of the evangelical Episcopalianism to which he subscribed, Ward gave generously to several benevolent enterprises, including those his wife had championed. His special concern, however, was education. He was a founder of New York University. He befriended Joseph Green Cogswell, principal of Round Hill School, and he helped finance this innovator's educational experiment.[34] The school reflected exactly the concerns of the evangelicals. Cogswell insisted that his pupils board there so that he could supervise their character development. His contention that no education was complete unless it stressed moral training as well as intellectual development placed Cogswell right in the middle of the swift currents of evangelical Christianity. Not surprisingly, Samuel Ward sent all his boys to Round Hill.

Ward's concept of education was as broad as it was religious. He built a wing onto his house to serve as an art gallery. He filled it with pictures, including originals by Thomas Cole. He built a study filled with books for his sons' perusal.[35] His expenses did not stop there; he provided the children with a large garden and a ring for riding horses.

Although he entrusted his sons to Cogswell, Ward did not for a moment abandon his role in their spiritual and moral development. To Sam he wrote, "Your twelfth birthday fills your father's heart with memories of your angel

21

mother, blest in heaven. For her, for your poor father, for yourself and your friends, strive to be all that is virtuous, good, and wise. Relax not, dearest boy."[36]

His daughters, too, concerned him. Ward governed Julia's reading as much as possible and personally hired and fired her tutors. Julia's niece later recalled that her grandfather "distrusted feminine methods and procured for his daughters a learned tutor who taught them just what he would have taught boys."[37] Ward watched the character development of his daughters as closely as he did his sons, reprimanding any thoughtless or unkind behavior or expression.[38] "My little acts of rebellion were met with some severity," Julia recalled in her old age.[39] His granddaughter observed that "this sterner role impressed itself so deeply on the minds of his children that the anecdotes familiar to our own generation echo it." She also perceived the motivation behind such strictness: "It was in fact this very anguish of solicitude, this passionate wish that they should not only have, but *be* everything desirable and lovely, that made him outwardly so stern."[40]

In providing so thoroughly for his children's education and training, Samuel Ward may have wished to offer those advantages that had been lacking in his own upbringing. But he also sought to create a world, pure and self-sufficient, that would shield his children from the "fashionable world." He hoped to protect them from examples of frivolousness, irreligion, and waste.[41] This "anguish of solicitude" also determined that the family would have to find its entertainment and stimulation by turning inward on itself. The children, with their cousins, aunts, and uncles, would have to form a microcosm of the ideal society where God—not the devil—prevailed. Here the forces of youthful growth and social change could be curtailed. The energy they generated could be directed to religious and benevolent ends.

Samuel Ward was not alone in this desire. Lyman Beecher, for example, had urged the restoration of family discipline as a means of reinforcing social and religious institutions and authority.[42] Indeed, the notion of the family as a replication of the bonds and obligations of the larger society was as old as the Puritans. Samuel Ward succeeded, at least for a time, in creating this ideal. He was able to do this in part because he bought a new house at 16 Bond Street.

In 1825 Bond Street was at the northern end of New York City. "The city was then so remote, one could hardly see the houses to the south across woods and fields."[43] Since there was only one other resident there at the time, a Jonas Minturn, it was indeed an unspoiled land. Ward's friends protested, "You are going out of town!"[44]

22

Neighbors and relatives in town attributed the move to Samuel Ward's grief. They thought it entirely understandable that the unhappy widower would find the associations of his old house too painful to bear.[45] But in selecting a new home, Samuel Ward had more on his mind than a mere change of scene. Had he wished, he could have invested in one of the fashionable new brownstones going up downtown. Instead, he selected an unknown neighborhood. The investment was hardly a sure one. The fashionable districts being built all over the city might never connect with Bond Street, and the value of the real estate might appreciate too slowly. City services might not extend sufficiently far to guarantee new building north of Bond Street, further devaluing the investment. Ward ensured the safety of his investment, however, in a simple and effective way: he convinced his father and brothers to join him as neighbors. The street immediately became a wealthy neighborhood, populated by men whose prestige would assure adequate city services and sufficient social respectability. Soon the empty lots filled.[46]

Thus, by the early 1830s, Bond Street was an elegant neighborhood, lined with distinguished mansions. In 1835 Ward built a new house on the corner of Bond and Broadway. Appropriately named The Corner, this house confirmed the wisdom of his initial investment. Now he could afford spacious rooms, marble trimmings, silk draperies, an art gallery, and a huge library.[47] The security of his investment was sure.

The development of the Bond Street neighborhood revealed that family life and financial gain supported and extended each other. Most important to Samuel Ward, however, was that the family and financial decisions he had made had helped create the secure, protected society that he desired for his children. In a street filled with Wards, Samuel could indeed become the "enforcer of moral norms." What the children saw around them were the activities and habits of evangelical men and women; their strictness and piety were the standards of the Ward children's world. The street came close to the ideal society that had bloomed in Samuel Ward's imagination. Removed from the gaiety and frivolity of the city, populated by other religious families, and guarded by family discipline, it was a world unto itself. Here the Ward children could be guided toward that perfection of character that would renew society. Stewardship, then, fit nicely with good business sense. Ward had managed to integrate theology, family, neighborhood, and capital into a "little commonwealth" characterized by stability, wealth, and Christian virtue.

Aunts and uncles gave almost as much character to Julia's young life as did her father and siblings. Among the dozen or so relatives clustered around the

23

new house was Eliza Cutler, Julia Cutler Ward's older sister. Perhaps there had been some debate about who should take charge of the household after Mrs. Ward died. There is evidence that she had mentioned her sister, Louisa Cutler McAllister. This sister lived in South Carolina, however, and she had a family of her own to manage.[48] Inevitably the task fell to Eliza, who had helped her mother raise one generation by providing all sorts of domestic help after her father died.[49]

She now undertook to rear a second family. Her education had been slim, and perhaps she was ill prepared for the challenges of running a household in urban New York. She had no flair for entertaining, and her language was "inelegant," even "coarse," to the ears of her well-bred nephew.[50] The art of navigating the seas of upper-class life escaped her. Instead, she was capable, earthy, and blunt. She was also possessed of a lively wit. For example, one day the housekeeper of a certain millionaire dwelt at length in conversation on her master's fine style. "Mr. So-and-so keeps this; Mr. So-and-so keeps that," she boasted. "Yes," replied Eliza Cutler. "It is well known that Mr. So-and-so keeps everything except the Ten Commandments."[51]

As she worked to feed, clothe, and instruct the six young Wards, Aunt Eliza turned to the language and discipline she knew best, the somber tenets of her evangelical faith. She, almost as much as the children's father, filled Julia's youth with clear and fearful images of heaven and hell. Her letters to young Sam, away at school in Northampton, Massachusetts, resounded with dark notes of evangelical warning: "Every pleasure has its pain—and God intended it should be so." "Remember that 'to be good is to be happy—Angels are happier than men because they are better.' "[52] She used the children's grief and the natural guilt that children feel from time to time about a parent's death to ensure their good behavior.

> Remember my beloved nephews all your sainted Mother taught you—which now she is no more—& you are doubly bound to perform first out of love to her—& then out of respect to her memory—she is now in heaven. If you wish ever to behold her, you must be good.[53]

> Set a good example . . . for the sake of your Angelic Mother's memory—think that she looks down from heaven upon her dear children & realize that sin will divide you from her forever.[54]

Such messages of sin, death, and separation may have worried Julia. When she was a little older, she would write a great many poems about death, grief, and dead mothers.[55]

To make matters more difficult for Julia, Aunt Eliza did not care particularly for her eldest niece. Perhaps she had had enough of caring for difficult temperaments. At any rate, she rarely mentioned Julia in her letters to her nephews, except to describe an occasional book that Julia liked. She talked much more enthusiastically about Louisa and Annie and their brothers.[56] The lack of sympathy between the two deepened Julia's isolation.

Benjamin Clarke Cutler also spent a good deal of time with the family when Julia was young, but he was no refuge for a little girl. He had been swept up in New York's religious enthusiasm as an adolescent when his father, Benjamin Clarke Cutler, Senior, had died. Religion provided a solace and a direction for his grief. He drew up a document ("An Instrument of Solemn Surrender of Myself, Soul and Body, to God!") in which he articulated his determination to serve God and challenge the devil ("Prince of Hell! I am thy enemy, thy implacable enemy, from this time forth and forevermore."). He pursued this course steadily, with some worldly success. He eventually became rector of St. Anne's Church in Brooklyn. Family anecdotes concerning him reflect not only his seriousness of purpose, but also a trace of latter-day amusement. "Once during his early ministry, he was riding in a crowded stagecoach. One of the passengers swore profusely and continuously, to the manifest annoyance of the others. Presently, Dr. Cutler, leaning forward, addressed the swearer. 'Sir,' he said, 'You are fond of blasphemy; I am fond of prayer. This is a public conveyance, and for the remainder of our journey, as often as you swear aloud, I shall pray aloud, and we shall see who comes off best.' "[57]

Julia is said to have stamped her foot and complained, "I don't care for old Ben Cutler!"[58] She had her reasons; he too felt compelled to impress on his nephews and nieces the grave danger that imperiled their souls. He wrote to Sam warning the boy that his good behavior was no insurance against hell. "Men may appear to be good . . . yea they may be like sepulchres which contain the bones of the dead: Outwardly they may be fair . . . but inwardly these sepulchres are full of dead men's bones and of all uncleanness. . . . Now a man who is only outwardly good is like a 'whited sepulchre' Math 23-27. To men he seems fair, but to God he seems foul."[59]

Uncle Ben's letter, however doleful its message, meant well. Although he and the other adult relatives emphasized the dark side of human nature and the threatening aspects of orthodox religion, they did so to protect the Ward children, not to harm them. Their father's careful provisions for their comfort and instruction and their aunt and uncle's concern for their welfare filtered down to the Ward siblings a message of love and concern. They knew they were cherished.[60]

Because of this emphasis on piety, religion would always be a tender subject for Julia, a way to strike sparks in her emotional life. Her childhood training forever impressed her with a belief in an all-knowing God, to whom she was directly responsible. It made her comfortable with prayer. As Julia tangled with questions of good and evil, doubt and belief, and purpose and role in her later life, she approached these questions from a religious standpoint.

To this collection of Cutlers were added an abundance of Ward relatives. Julia's two aunts spent most of their time on their father's farm on Long Island, so of all of her Ward connections, Julia knew these unmarried sisters least well. Aunt Anne was a woman of vigor, proud of her industry and frugality. She herself sold all the cheese the farm produced. She managed the farm and cared for Phoebe, the "invalid saint." Anne was religious, but not as intensely so as Phoebe, who, in an effort to live a godly life, stayed in darkened rooms and avoided, because her eyes could not endure it, anything white.[61]

The five Ward brothers—Richard, John, Samuel, William, and Henry—all lived in the city. Uncle Richard was the quietest and the least successful (he may have been an alcoholic). He lived with his brother, John, who left to him the bulk of the family estate when he died.[62] Uncle William married Maria Hall, and their four sons provided Julia with her only Ward cousins. William owned a substantial amount of New York real estate, including a valuable house called The Grange. Like Samuel, he was wealthy.[63] Uncle Henry was fond of music and of his nieces and nephews. Described as stately and handsome, he was never too dignified to consent to a request for music, and he would pound out polkas and waltzes on his piano for the benefit of the Ward children.[64] Uncle John was the best loved of all the uncles. After his brother Samuel's death in 1840, he lived with the Ward children until 1847 and was a "second father to them" until his own death in 1866. He liked cigars, dogs, and children. He was well known on Wall Street as a conservative banker and well known in town as a friendly, hospitable bachelor.[65]

The Ward brothers were rich. They were all involved in the commercial boom of New York City, generally in banking and real estate. They were widely known as a result of their successful business ventures, and they were respected for their conservative, sound financial judgment. All of these men were tall. Colonel Ward was at least six feet tall, and the extant descriptions of his sons all mention their unusual height.[66] This was in sharp contrast to the Ward women; Julia herself never exceeded five feet in height. Like a stand of friendly, giant trees around the Ward children, these men sunk their roots on Bond Street. Samuel Ward lived at 16 and then at 1; Uncle John lived at 8; Grandfather Ward lived at 7; and Uncle Henry lived first at 14, and then at 23.[67] Julia's life was indeed "patriarchal in its dimensions," and those dimensions were huge. These dimensions had special importance because of Samuel Ward's insistence that the children socialize with the family. Julia was always surrounded by big, powerful men. Sometimes she felt overwhelmed by them, and she hid when the family assembled.[68] They were kindly in feeling, but their size was distancing. They were not particularly approachable.

Despite all these well-intentioned relatives, Julia never believed that anyone in her family understood her need for young companions and ordinary childhood adventures. As she entered adolescence, Julia felt alone as she tried to comprehend the complicated world of manners, money, and men. She had few female friends and few activities that took her outside the family circle. In times of crisis, she had only her siblings, her studies, and her religion to fall back on.

THREE

"Young Ladyhood," 1832-1842

> Oh my Father, thou hast heard
> All my bitter cry.
> And hast bid thy gracious word
> Still my agony.
>
> . . . .
>
> Joyful humbled in the dust
> Now I bless thy name,
> At the thought of thy mistrust
> Glows my soul with shame.
>
> Now thy truth shall comfort me,
> Now that thou hast smiled,
> Father, glory be to thee
> Peace unto thy child.

The years from 1832 to 1840 encompass Julia Ward's adolescence. Actually, the term "adolescence" is potentially misleading, loaded as it is with modern connotations of high school athletics, rock-star mania, and acne medicine. Today's norms of extended education and protracted residence with one's family of origin were not characteristic of youth in the early republic. Joseph Kett has suggested "semi-independence" as a substitute.[1] Since his data derive from male sources, his term has dubious value for interpreting the experiences of young women. They rarely achieved the kinds of physical, social, and financial independence that Kett describes.

Julia Ward Howe's own term, "young ladyhood," has something to recommend it, at least for young women of her class.[2] It implies a kind of intermediate status—more than that of the dependent child and less than that of the married woman. This life stage was characterized by more domestic responsibilities than the child could perform, but fewer than those of a wife and mother. Although the freedom to schedule and attend social events was still limited by parents, social life was more extensive than it had been earlier. Most women remained in this intermediate and indeterminate stage until they married or left home to be teachers or missionaries. Since Julia did not marry until she was twenty-four, this meant a long and trying intermediate stage in her life cycle.[3]

For some young women, this stage was a relatively easy one. For others, it was difficult, attended by periods of brooding introspection and friction with authority. In a sensitive young person, these reactions could be pronounced and difficult to resolve.

Julia was a sensitive girl. Always quick to dive from peaks of gaiety to fits of anger or black depression and to soar back up again, she continued this pattern of behavior well into her twenties. As an old woman, Julia described her youthful self as "impressionable and sensitive." "My attachments were strong," she recalled, "my griefs violent. Religious questions interested me at an early age."[4] She described how her participation in musical trios and quartets, which always delighted her, was occasionally followed by an intense unhappy reaction. This feeling was as painful as the music had been pleasant, and it "induced at times a visitation of morbid melancholy which threatened to affect my health."[5]

The religious questions that interested her were the difficult ones of her father's orthodoxy, which combined the ideas of conservative Congregationalism with the practices of low-church Episcopalianism. Concern about damnation and salvation sharpened the edges of Julia's sensitivity. Combined with long years of uneasy intermediate status, and with her natural emotional intensity, these questions helped precipitate a serious crisis in Julia's life when she was in her early twenties. This crisis, its mode of expression, and the means Julia found for dealing with all reflected the intensely private, sheltered, inward-turning quality of Julia's young life.

The key to this sheltered environment was Samuel Ward. So important was Julia's father to her young ladyhood that she gave the title "My Father" to the chapter in her *Reminiscences* that deals with her early life.

Ward did the best he could to fill the shoes of his wife. At times, he offered his daughters excellent advice. To shy Louisa on the occasion of her first visit to Boston, he made the sort of sensible suggestion that Julia Cutler Ward would no doubt have tendered: "Listen to opinions on various topics and take an interest in whatever you are capable of understanding. And ask as many questions as are likely to be well-answered."[6]

Despite this obvious affection, Ward seemed to grow increasingly distant and severe as time went on. All Julia's memories of him mention his strictness. She described him as reproving the "smallest breach of good taste or decorum."[7] In another place she recalls that he was "a man of excellent tastes and a very strict disciplinarian" who allowed "no frivolous companionship or frivolous tastes." He was "very careful to reprove any thoughtless or unkind expression which fell from the lips of his children."[8] She referred more than once to his strict ideas of propriety and his "austerity of character."[9] Even the slightest deviation from good manners mattered to Ward. For example, he disliked Julia's kicking off her shoes at the dinner table. He cured Julia of this habit by sending her from the room, shoeless and terribly embarrassed, to fetch some seals he had left in another room.[10]

As time went on, Ward abandoned a number of pleasures that he deemed too worldly. He gave up smoking, urging his sons to do likewise.[11] He stopped attending the theater and refused to allow his children to go.[12] As an early member of the Society for the Promotion of Temperance, he gave away his fine wines, allowing neither his children nor himself to sample any of them.[13]

Impatient with these limitations and with his father's dislike of the fashionable world, young Sam clashed with his parent.

"Sir, you do not keep in view the importance of the social tie," urged Sam.
"The social what?"
"The social tie, sir."
"I make no account of that," rejoined the father.
"And I will die in defense of it!" rejoined the youth.[14]

His sternness meant that Julia was a little afraid of her father. Fear of displeasing him "acted as a constant check on her spirits," her brother Francis Marion observed. He likewise found his father cold and forbidding. In a letter to Sam, he reported that Ward, upon entering the house one evening, found his children "in high glee, singing, laughing, and talking. He chided them: 'Children, stand before the fire. I don't see why you can't sit down quietly instead of standing all together in the way.' "[15] None of the children understood why their overworked, gout-ridden father wanted peace and quiet when he got home. They all saw unwonted severity.

31

Julia did not understand either why her father permitted her to attend so few evening parties. "I did aspire to much greater freedom of association than was allowed me. . . . I seemed to myself like a damsel of olden times, shut up within an enchanted castle. And I must say that my dear father, with all his noble generosity and overweening affection, sometimes appeared to me as my jailer."[16] Whether or not his restrictions were fair, they chafed Julia, and sometimes she rebelled. Julia's most notable act of independence was an evening party that she arranged with the help of her brothers. First Julia secured the permission of her father to entertain a "few friends." Then her brothers Sam and Henry drew up the guest list while Julia hired a caterer, musicians, and even a crystal chandelier. When Ward came downstairs, he was surprised to find "as brilliant a gathering as could have been found in any other of the great houses of New York." While her father circulated through the company, Julia "became as possessed with terror as she had been with desire. She could think of nothing but her father's displeasure, of the words he might speak, of the glances he might cast upon her." Her father let fear and guilt be Julia's punishment. The next day, his reaction was mild, and the matter was dropped.[17]

As Julia grew older, she took on responsibilities that kept her out of society to an even greater degree. When the rest of the family went to Newport in the summer, Julia stayed behind with her father on Bond Street. These summers were difficult for Julia, who was shut in and lonely. "One day is just like another, tomorrow will be as yesterday and the day before were. The same long solitary morning, the same afternoon drive, on the same road, the same dull evening and sleepless night. But dear father seems to enjoy it, and therefore I am reconciled to it."[18]

Sam thought Julia was kept too much inside the house. In a long, impassioned letter to his father, he revealed how parental strictures had affected his sister.

> . . . poor Jule [is] the victim of a thousand false inequities and sensibilities. Smiling before you but weeping tears of blood at being forced to stay from Newport and the girls. You always exact too much of her in desiring not only that she obey you but be happier in so doing than in following up certain wishes of her own. . . .
>
> There are a thousand duties a mother would naturally perform. Of these you have not the slightest suspicion. The girls then at this season should be the chief study and care and hope of your life. Julia writes all day and half the night. One morning she wrote in 5 hours 16 pages. She is murdering herself. Yet she is

forced to this. In the tedium and heat of a large solitude her restless mind must need work. I have told you of these excesses before and you have given them a moment's thought & heeded them not afterwards. . . . Dr. Francis says she is destroying herself by eating [only] vegetables and you heed him not.[19]

Ward had no easy task in guiding his eldest daughter. On the one hand, Sam criticized him for being too strict. On the other hand, he dared not leave Julia to her own devices, for she did not show steady judgment. Her extravagance at the evening party was the sort of thing that worried him. Furthermore, Julia handled day-to-day responsibilities erratically. After requesting and receiving permission to run the household, Julia then decided she would not pour tea. Her refusal meant that she neglected one fundamental duty of any mistress of the house.[20]

Julia balked, too, at learning domestic skills. To please her father, she once attempted to bake a pie. This only convinced her that the whole process was tiresome and not worth the bother. She wrote her aunt about "the miseries of pie-making, of kneading up and rolling out the paste, of stewing, sweetening, and worse still tasting the gooseberries, of daubing one's self with butter, lard and flour—hands, face, and clothes; of tearing the paste to pieces in trying to transfer it from board to dish! In two hours I made three pies and hope that I may never again have the same painful duty to perform."[21] When her uncle presented her with some silk to make up a dress, Julia turned the gift over to the family seamstress.[22] All this suggested to Ward that Julia was not responsible enough to take entire charge of her own life.

Suitors were another problem. Julia loved to be admired and she was, along with her sisters, undeniably pretty. "Her red-gold hair was no longer regarded as a misfortune; her gray eyes were large and well opened; her complexion of dazzling purity. Her finely-chiseled features, and the beauty of her hands and arms, made an ensemble which could not fail to impress all who saw her." Swains called her "Diva Julia," and together with handsome Louisa and winsome Annie, she deserved her reputation as one of the "Three Graces of Bond Street."[23]

To her beauty and wealth, Julia could add a lively sense of humor. Puns and double entendres were a specialty. Julia's description of her state after a ball is typical: "It was Sad-sack, Me-rake, and Abed-no-go."[24]

Julia's family worried about the effect she had on men and the effect they had on her.[25] Evidence suggests that they were right to be concerned. A small manuscript poem reads

> There is one alone
> Whose blue eyes I sigh for
> There is one, only one
> Whose sweet smile I die for
> One! One alone!

This poem was folded up carefully into a tiny note, one inch square. On the outside, Julia sketched an angel playing a harp and wrote, "Cara, tu sola" and "Night after the choir."[26] The possibility that Julia was sending love notes to a harpist echoes in a fragment of a story that Julia wrote twenty years later. Julia describes a sensitive heroine, age fourteen (Julia's age when she wrote the poem), who falls in love with a harpist named Henri. The heroine's passion becomes so consuming that the girl neglects her studies and her health. Although Julia left the story unfinished, the manuscript implies that Henri was fickle and that the heroine was so stung by the force of her love and the pain of rejection that it took months for her to regain her health.[27] If the story is semiautobiographical, it is no wonder that Julia's father chose to guard Julia.

Other scraps of evidence from Julia's young ladyhood suggest her powers of attraction and her talent for flirtation. Her daughters recall a sea captain who, too shy to ask Julia for her hand in marriage, thrust his card into her hand. "*Russell E. Glover*'s heart is yours!"[28] Samuel Ward may have had to handle this case, just as he had broken up two earlier romances. One, when Julia was fifteen, was an attachment to a mysterious "T," whom her father forbade Julia to see.[29] Another involved a clergyman, whom Ward rebuked for having abused his hospitality by proposing to Julia.[30] Henry later convinced Julia to reject another minister whose heart, Henry feared, was as set on the Ward money as it was on Julia herself.[31] Her aunts banished another suitor, Christy Evangelides, a Greek student whom Ward had invited to live at Bond Street while he finished his studies at Columbia University.[32] Her last suitor, Joseph Greene Cogswell, fell in love with Julia, as did a nameless professor.[33] To a businessman with little leisure, acute gout, and substantial religious anxiety, Julia posed a rare tribulation. Ward had neither time nor energy constantly to chaperone her. Curtailing Julia's movements and limiting her acquaintances were the best safeguards he could devise.

He intended, though, to relax his restrictions in time. He once told his complaining daughter that he had "early recognized in me a temper and imagination over-sensitive to impressions from without and that his wish had been to guard me from exciting influences until I should appear to him fully able to guard and guide myself."[34] Unfortunately, Julia's flammable spirits were not cooled down by being bottled up.

Ward tempered his strictness with kindness. Julia admitted his generosity in allowing her to use the company parlor, the Yellow Room, named for its yellow silk draperies.[35] This room generally remained closed, but every morning Julia slipped inside to work at the desk her father had set up for her there. Furthermore, though his rebukes were frequent, they were usually gentle. When Julia lingered too long in bed, delaying breakfast, her father sent up a note: "It is half past 8 & the sun refuses his company today, do thou descend and illuminate us poor mortals in the lower regions. God bless thee, dearest daughter."[36]

At the age of sixteen, Julia ended her formal schooling. Her father did pay for extra tutors, however, and set no limits on what she might learn. When Cogswell left Round Hill School, for example, Ward employed him in his own household to instruct his daughters. Julia chose to study German, and Ward did not interfere with this even when he discovered, to his horror, a copy of *Faust* among her books. The German language opened new worlds of thought to his daughter, as she recalled: "I derived from the studies a sense of intellectual freedom so new to me that it was half delightful, half alarming."[37] If he saw any evidence of this stimulation, her father ignored it, and allowed Julia to proceed with her studies.

Nor did her father object when Julia requested lessons in mathematics and in declamation. He provided as well instruction in French, Latin, Italian, piano, singing, and dancing.[38] Her musical training far exceeded the standards of the day. A Mr. Boocock taught her piano "so carefully that after eighty years [her fingers] still retained their flexibility." Signor Cardini trained her voice so well that even as an old lady, she could be heard in the largest halls when she spoke. To these advantages, Ward added the use of a large library and the private art gallery.

Ward's liberal attitude toward Julia's education was particularly remarkable because no firm theory about intellectual training for young women had yet taken root. The broad and useful education that the New York Dutch had once extended to their daughters was out of fashion; mercantile families no longer trained girls to understand and handle various aspects of business.[39] Some wealthy families sought to prepare their daughters for ornamental roles by giving them a smattering of music, religion, drawing, French, and fine needlework. Other families trained girls in history and geography, as well as a bit of classical literature, hoping to fit them for roles as good wives and mothers.[40] No one view held sway, however. Julia was indeed fortunate in her father's willingness to let her study widely and intensively.

At sixteen, Julia determined to begin her studies on her own "in good earnest." These studies gave her a way to occupy her time since she was so rarely allowed out of the family circle. They also gave her the opportunity to cultivate her considerable intellectual gifts. No longer did she indulge in the daydreams with which she had once relieved the tedium of schoolroom recitations.[41] She buckled down to a daily routine of morning study and the practice of music in the afternoons. Since she was by nature unsystematic, and since she wished to be efficient and orderly in her studies, Julia asked her sisters to tie her in her chair when she began her daily stint. Only they could unloose her when the hours appointed for study were over.[42]

Julia cherished the dream of becoming a great writer. In her memoirs, she recalled that "a vision of some important literary work which I should accomplish was present with me in my early life, and had much to do with habits of study acquired by me in youth and never wholly relinquished. At this late date I find it difficult to account for a sense of literary responsibility which never left me, and which I must consider to have formed a part of my spiritual make-up."[43]

Her sense of "literary responsibility" may have been stimulated at about this time by a packet of letters that her father gave her to read. These were letters her mother had written, and in them Julia saw the intertwined strands of her mother's life. The importance of family to Julia Cutler Ward was apparent, as pregnancy after pregnancy appeared in these pages. Julia could not miss the unhappy suggestion that marriage meant childbirth and that childbirth meant death as she pondered her mother's missives. "I cannot be resigned to her loss," she wrote her sisters. "I will not dwell on this topic any longer, but it has of late occupied my mind to the exclusion of everything else."[44] Nor could she ignore the religious tone of Julia Cutler Ward's writings, for, at the end of her life, Mrs. Ward had been in a perfect agony concerning the worthiness of her soul.[45] Just as important, Julia saw clearly her mother's love of poetry and her fondness for writing it. This literary side of her mother's personality was not one the well-meaning aunts and uncles had stressed. It was new to Julia, and it gave her the opportunity to develop her own private image of her mother. The Julia Cutler Ward whom she now envisioned was certainly religious and virtuous, but she was also a poet who accepted publication. To discover this, just at the time she had decided to study seriously, was a boon.

She was inspired to sustain her mother's legacy, and she determined to write "some great work or works which I myself should leave to the world."[46]

Other influences were at work, too, spurring Julia to write essays and verse. Her father, fearsome, distant, and increasingly wrapped up in his work, had earlier encouraged her efforts at poetry. Perhaps a literary career would secure his continued admiration and a little more attention.[47] Her brother Sam, recently home from European studies, may have been a factor as well. Although she probably had no conscious intention of imitating him, his desire to make a reputation as a literary critic helped direct Julia's attention to that field.

With the exception of Sam, who encouraged her, and of her father, who remained for the most part in a state of benevolent disinterest in her studies, Julia's family thought her emphasis on reading and writing was peculiar.[48] It seemed odd to them that a wealthy young woman would devote so much time to study. Yet Julia's inclination had a certain logic. The study of mathematics, Latin, and philosophy was generally reserved for males. As such, it was a badge of male rationality and intellectual fitness. Furthermore, for Sam and for her Uncle John, study had been the avenue toward success and public stature. If study had worked for the men in her family, then, Julia hoped, it might serve as an "open sesame" for her. With this training and background, she would be able not only to produce the great work so dear to her heart, but also to have it accepted and recognized by other great minds as an achievement of substantial merit.

The hunger for real study belonged to Julia alone of all the Ward women. Only her brother Sam had similar intellectual powers. His education had been broad and unstinting: preparation at Round Hill School, mathematics at Columbia, travel in Europe, literary criticism with Jules Janin in Paris, and a degree from the university at Tübingen.[49] The Ward boys, whether they were talented or not, got a much better education than did their sisters. Julia could not have helped but notice the discrepancy. There is no record of any bitterness on Julia's part, but an undated autobiographical fragment suggests that this system of education according to sex, rather than talent, may have bothered her. "I made rhymes, and even dreamed of speeches and orations, often wishing that I had been a boy in view of the then limitations on a girl's aspirations. Was studious by fits and starts, learning easily, & fond of acquiring languages, passionately fond also of music. Very romantic in disposition."[50]

When she finally wrote her autobiography in 1898, Julia rejected this assessment of her youth in favor of a fuller, more complex description. She dropped the passage about wishing she were a boy. Yet "romantic" Julia could be practical in recognizing how greatly sex influenced her chances, and she may well have translated her resentment into fantasies about being a boy.

Since she could not be a boy or enjoy a boy's education, Julia did the next best thing. Although she could not assure herself of a rigorous, well-structured curriculum, she could talk to every learned man or woman she could find. She borrowed books; she quizzed visitors; she welcomed new tutors. From one of her father's protégées she learned Greek; Cogswell taught her German; another friend of her father's helped her with French literature. Sam encouraged her, of course, with this talk of literature, mathematics, and, of great interest to Julia, astronomy. Her brother's friend, Henry Wadsworth Longfellow, introduced Julia to the study of early British literature through *Beowulf*.[51]

Julia was not the first young woman to piece together an education in this way. An informal network of contacts with ministers, fathers, brothers, lovers, and husbands provided a means for determined women of the middle and upper middle classes to acquire a broad education. Women reinforced and fleshed out this system by exchanging books. They wrote essays for their friends to comment on. Parlor lectures and public readings extended this sort of informal educational system. For all of these women and for Julia Ward, their education was a triumph over the discriminatory approach to women's education then in vogue.

If they could not claim systematic exposure to all the disciplines, neither could the graduates of the best men's schools.[52] What women like Julia did acquire was a degree of liberation from religious dogma, the ability to exercise their critical faculties, and an openness to new ideas. Their experience whetted their appetites, making them strong and determined advocates of higher education for women. Furthermore, a sense of their own mental powers, along with confidence in their own opinions, emerged from this intellectual exposure, with broad impact on the activist movements of midcentury.

Whatever limitations she sensed, Julia's studies were rewarding to her. Mastering German, Latin, mathematics, and philosophy strengthened her sense of competence; it was one of the few areas of her life over which she exerted substantial control. Her sense of purpose and accomplishment grew as she began to see her articles in print.

Julia's first published work consisted on two articles, one of which was a critique of Larmartine's *Jocelyn*. Cogswell helped edit the essays, and Leonard Woods, editor of the *Theological Review*, published them.[53] These occasioned considerable comment among Julia's family and friends, "more . . . than their merit would have warranted," she observed later.[54] Uncle John commented that, "This is my little girl who knows about books, and writes an article, and has it printed, but I wish that she knew more about housekeeping."[55]

Charles King, editor of *The New York American*, also printed Julia's pieces. Julia intended that these were preliminary to her real contribution—"the novel or play of the age." "I indeed made some progress in a drama founded on Scott's novel of 'Kenilworth,' but presently relinquished this to begin a play suggested by Gibbon's account of the fall of Constantinople." These never saw the light of day, but poetry, always her favorite mode, proved successful. In the manner of the time, Julia wrote some sentimental stanzas describing the death of her music master.[56] This was eminently a woman's domain, as Lydia Sigourney, for example, had already demonstrated. No one reproved Julia for these efforts. Later successes, including publication of her poetry in O'Sullivan's *Democratic Review*, confirmed Julia's decision to devote herself to writing.

Perhaps as a consequence of this, Julia's education in the tasks of homemaking was sparse. None of her schoolmistresses taught any needlework except embroidery. Although she eventually learned to knit and sew for her babies, Julia never enjoyed these tasks, and she never did them well. She learned almost nothing about cooking or about managing a staff of servants. This sporadic engagement with household tasks was poor preparation for any young woman, even if she were to spend the rest of her life with a wealthy husband—and Julia was not to be so lucky.

Although Julia later regretted her inadequacy in these matters, at the time, this state of affairs could not have bothered her less. Her mind continued to burn with plans for a literary career. Her publications encouraged her to think she was on the right track. The acclaim they stirred up reinforced Julia's tendency to turn to the pen when her mind seethed with ideas. Poetry in particular took up more and more of her time. It allowed her to define her feelings, to vent powerful emotions in an acceptable way, and to give her experiences some order. Letters, too, enabled her to lay out the relationships between the activities of her daily life and the passionate responses she felt. The pen had become her ally and she would use it to combat inner difficulties and to assert her claim to a literary career for the rest of her life.

Studying and writing gave Julia confidence and ambition. These things far outweighed the disadvantages of a sheltered life in the long run. Another factor favorable to Julia's happiness was her collection of brothers and sisters.

Although her brothers were frequently away at school or college, or even abroad, they played a significant role in her "young ladyhood." They all were delightful company. They shared the Cutler wit, all were gifted musically, and they loved to eat, dance, and entertain. Sam, Harry, and Marion, as they were called, were the primary source of gaiety in Julia's otherwise very solemn youth.

When Sam returned from Europe in 1835, "His wit, social talent, and literary taste opened a new world to me and enabled me to share some of the best results of his long residence in Europe," Julia recalled.[57] Specifically, Sam urged Julia to use the wonderful library he had bought in Paris. Included in this collection were scientific works in French and in German as well as literary and philosophical classics. Here Julia could find the German Transcendentalists and the writings of John Locke. Sam owned daring works, too, including those of George Sand and Honoré de Balzac. Moreover, Sam supported Julia's literary endeavors, encouraging her to read widely and suggesting that she translate some of his literary essays.[58] "He brought into the Puritanic limits of our family circle a flavor of European life and culture which greatly delighted me," wrote Julia many years later.[59] Sam's interest in her intellectual life provided a variation on the father-daughter relationship that characterized the early lives of many notable women of the nineteenth century.[60] At a time when her father's early enthusiasm for her poetry had dwindled to lack of involvement, Sam stepped in to encourage Julia's efforts.

Furthermore, Sam was popular with hostesses. His popularity did not decrease, either, when in 1838 he married Emily Astor, granddaughter of John Jacob Astor. Under the chaperonage of Sam and Emily, Julia began to enjoy a social life. Sam urged his father to relax the rules, and Julia embarked on a round of parties.[61] Elegant soirées at the Astor mansion, presided over by the formidable Margaret Armstrong Astor, opened to Julia the world of balls, elaborate dinner parties, jewels, and fashion. Although Ward family evening parties remained the staple of Julia's social diet, her days of seclusion were over. Now she danced in brilliant ballrooms, her feet flying over the floral patterns "traced in colored chalks."[62] On a visit to Boston, Julia wrote happily, "I have three parties for next week, but shall be ready to go home on Saturday, or whenever convenient to you. . . . I am glad Boze [Annie] had a nice time at Mrs. Otis'—why do you not sent my mits, my apron, and the sleeves of my lilac dress? Pray send them on Monday, also my butternut, carefully put up. I want it for Mary who isn't well. I have seen a good deal of

Longo [Longfellow], and with much pleasure. Sumner also has been very kind and attentive."[63]

Under Emily's guidance, Julia's interest in clothes expanded. She wrote Sam, urging him to send on to Boston the following: "A silk dress for the evening, of latest fashion, white and pale blue; a skirt of tulle or muslin, whichever Emmie advises, lightly embroidered, *en tunique*; two complete trimmings for a ball dress, in geranium leaves and flowers; and two ornaments for the back of the head, *en bronze doré*."[64] Dressed in the height of fashion, with Sam and Emily as chaperone, Julia savored the whole of New York's extensive social season. Even her father was affected, opening his house to fashionable guests for the first time since his wife had died.[65]

Even after Emily's death in childbirth in 1842, Sam remained Julia's loyal friend. He took her for drives and guided her during her own engagement. He was the only one of Julia's siblings to take a lively interest in her literary career. He arranged for little extras—peaches, grapes, or wine—to arrive on Julia's doorstep throughout her life. Predictably, during Sam's long and checkered career, Julia was a devoted, supportive sister.

Francis Marion, the youngest brother, also took a genuine interest in Julia. He deplored her constant studying, but he devoted himself to her welfare as soon as he was on his own.[66] He was largely responsible for reorganizing the household in 1838 to allow Julia more influence in domestic matters. After their father's death, Marion and Sam arranged to buy property in Newport and New York City for the three sisters. He had excellent business judgment, and Sam welcomed his willingness to assume responsibility for the family.[67]

As much as Sam's encouragement and Marion's concern meant to Julia, it was Henry whom Julia loved best. When Henry went to Europe, Julia was bereft, as lost as she had been when they were in the nursery and he went off to visit cousins.[68] In the summer of 1840, he took Julia along with Francis Marion to the Catskills, where "we went down to the falls, where we passed the morning, climbing, and scrambling and singing like so many wildcats, in the afternoon walked up South Mountain, and did not keep still more than ten minutes in the whole day."[69] For a secluded city girl, this excursion was bliss, and it was Henry who arranged such treats.

In the spring of 1840, Henry proposed to Julia's friend, Mary Ward. Perhaps prompted by Henry's example, Julia decided to accept a proposal of marriage offered by a minister named Kirke.[70] Julia had refused offers in the past, but the knowledge that her brother would soon be striking out on his own may have spurred her to accept this proposal. Leaving the nest together

41

would be far less lonely than being left behind. At any rate, Henry urged Julia, in the bluntest terms, to reconsider. "I have stated to you what occurs to me for consideration—the want of sufficient acquaintance, the disparity of years, the arduous duties of the wife of any clergyman & the want of a permanent settlement. . . . However freely a gentleman in his situation may consider himself entitled to float in society, receiving the hospitality of friends, it cannot be desirable for a woman to lead such a life of dependence, for in no other light can it be viewed."[71] Henry was close enough to Julia to risk being a little harsh. He told her his opinion honestly, without hedging. Julia respected him so much that she broke off the engagement.

The brothers, when they banded together, were a force to be reckoned with. In the summer of 1838 they decided that they needed a change in household routine. Aunt Eliza, who had been in charge of the household since 1824, had married Dr. John Francis. Now she had her hands full with a troop of noisy sons. This gave the brothers an excellent opportunity to encourage her to leave the running of the household to them. Despite her initial reluctance to do so, Aunt Eliza left in the fall to devote her time to her own household.[72] Julia and Louisa shared control of daily household routine, although Julia's lack of skill and interest in that department meant that Louisa eventually handled all the responsibility.[73] This change, thoroughly to the taste of Julia and her sisters, could never have come about without the insistence of their brothers.

The brothers were windows to a larger world. They were sources of financial security, they were delightful companions, and they were trusted advisers. As much as they shielded and supported Julia, so much did she love them. Despite her attachment to her brothers, Julia's primary sources of emotional support were her sisters. Louisa and Annie remained throughout their lives Julia's closest confidantes. They supplied the emotional warmth and affection essential to Julia's well-being. With them, Julia began to build the "world of women" she had lacked as a little girl. Affectionate letters filled the mail when the girls were apart.

Julia to Louisa and Annie:

> I feel like a poor little exile, separated, for the first time from all of you, and to hear from you is my only consolation.[74]

Annie to Louisa:

> I know not how I could exist for one month without you. . . . Indeed, I agree with the old bird [Julia] that sisters are great blessings. . . . The happiest [hour] that I have passed for many months will be that in which the carriage drives up to the door, and I hear once more the dear voices of my blessed sisters.[75]

Julia to Annie:

> I love thee very tenderly my dear little Annie. Wevie [Louisa] is not so cheerful as I could wish.[76]

Julia to Louisa and Annie:

> My dear girls . . . God bless and protect you my darling sisters; the time passes here very pleasantly, and dear Mary is to me almost like another sister, yet I long to be with you again.[77]

As Julia began to realize how much her father and brothers expected her to teach and guide her younger sisters, she offered them serious advice. "I am happy in the hope that my sisters this time are behaving beautifully and are verifying my prediction that they will soon be the biggest kind of good girls. . . . Now farewell my darlings, and our father in heaven bless and keep you. Seek to be pure in mind, meek and lowly in heart, modest and maidenly in deportment—seek above all to be true to yourselves, to all men, and to Him who loved us and gave Himself for us."[78] Annie and Louisa took this solemnity in stride, teasing Julia for her sudden maturity by calling her "Old Bird."

The sisters helped one another out of difficult spots, giving advice about suitors, sending off clothes and books when one of them was traveling, and even, in Julia's case, purchasing a wedding gown.[79] Because none of the girls had the sort of schooling that would have enabled them to develop side networks of friends, they relied on one another.

This exclusive reliance on her sisters began to change when Julia met Mary Ward (no relation to the New York Wards). Mary's father, Thomas Ward of Boston, was Baring's representative in that city. The two Ward families had much in common, including a son named Sam, a source of confusion for generations afterward. Julia and Mary met in Newport in 1837 and remained close friends for the next several years. Julia's father had purchased a farm there earlier in the decade in order to escape the epidemics of cholera then plaguing New York.[80] Mary Ward's family found in Newport a quiet refuge from Boston's summer heat. At that time, Newport was a "forsaken, mildewed place, a sort of intensified Salem, with houses of rich design no longer richly inhabited."[81] Nevertheless, both girls were very happy there.

Both Mary and Julia were accustomed to solitude. Both loved literature, and both felt different from other young women by virtue of their intellectual leanings. Each rejoiced to discover a soul mate. Over the next six years, they exchanged visits and steady correspondence. Mary's letters to Julia brim with delight—even relief—at finding a confidante.

> I love you. I wish I were with you. I am both sad and happy. Sad for your sad moments, dearest, and happy, inexpressibly happy in your love. Before I knew you, Jules, I had no friend. . . . I said to myself, "My life so far has been completely isolated and alone—I have lived in a world of my own. . . . And each year I shall be more widely seperated from it, more utterly alone." Do you wonder that I love you as I do. No I think not, for you too know what it is to live *alone*. You too now have a new existence opened before you. . . . Others may tell you of themselves and the world—I will tell you but of my love and yours.[82]

Both savored the pleasures of sharpening their wits together, of practicing clarity of thought, and of discussing literary topics.

Two years later, their affection was as warm as ever. "My own sweet Jules, I shall never in this world have any friend who can fill your place, Jules, nor anyone whom I can love as I love you, so while our love is yet pure, and while you are yet spared to me, I will make the most of you—"[83]

This intensity of feeling was common among women of the early and middle nineteenth century. The female sphere in which they traveled, combined with their forced isolation from men and "masculine" pursuits, led women to seek not only each other's company, but also each other's affection.[84]

It is clear from their letters that neither wanted the demands of marriage to dilute their affection for each other. They fully expected to be able to carry on their old relationship regardless of whose roof they lived under. Perhaps this desire reflected their ignorance about marriage. Mary's letters outlined a picture of marriage that stressed self-sacrifice and submission to the wishes of the husband.[85] Equality of interest, open interchange of ideas, emotional support at difficult times, and frank advice tenderly given were not the sweets of marriage, but of female friendship. They were the antidote to the constant self-abnegation of marriage as she saw it.

Indeed, Mary came closer than anyone in her ability to understand Julia's feelings. They shared a tendency to depression and were able to discuss it freely; Julia would never enjoy this comfort with her husband. As an illustration of the anguish they both suffered, Mary's letter is interesting.

> I have been obliged, too, to struggle with and overcome the most desperate blue devils you can conceive of. I have suffered somewhat at various periods in my life, but I do not think I have ever been visited by such black and ugly devils as have since you left me been paying their court to me. I am very well always as long as I "keep down," that is, keep quiet and subdued, living in the present moment as if it were all, investing it with as much of the golden light as it is capable of receiving . . . but if I step out of this ever so little, if the slumbering spirit is roused, the heart sickens, the mind's strength is wasted, the whole creature is miserable.[86]

This ability to write at length to each other helped both young women exorcise their "devils." Friendship was a superb resource in their battles to overcome grief, fear, and disappointment.

Because of their shared sensibilities, Mary was able to give Julia advice on the terms she could best understand. When Julia's heart went out to Kirke, Mary counseled caution. "Think of this more seriously than you have done. . . . I would on my knees beseech you to pause and in no way bind yourself further than you already have done until another year shall have passed over you."[87] Later she cautioned Julia that her poems might not find a publisher's favor.[88] And as Julia struggled with grief and depression in 1840-41, Mary's consolation proved to be the most understanding and the most helpful.[89]

Friendship, siblings, and books all gave Julia comfort. They allowed her to toy with new ideas and to develop her own views of what she might become. The successful men in her family also suggested to Julia ways people could develop confidence and acquire the power to achieve their goals. Julia internalized a great deal of her brother Sam's experience, for example. Travel had freed him from family pressures and values so that he had been able to assess his potential and determine his future. Julia, in turn, always saw travel, especially in Europe, as a way to explore her feelings and ideas. Sam had returned with a huge collection of books; books and study became Julia's means of developing her ideas. Sam tucked his literary life in and around the demands of his business life; Julia learned to snatch time when she could, too. In short, Julia's dedication to studying and writing reflected many lessons gleaned from Sam's example.

Her father's life, too, suggested that individuals could exert some control over the shape of their lives. The religion he espoused stressed the responsibility of each individual for his or her own fate. This was a tool Julia would employ later as she defended her unconventional choices. Her father also taught—as did the other males in his circle—that people could acquire status by combining financial, religious, and community leadership, especially through involvement in benevolent enterprises. Julia was a careful student. She learned to link this trio of wealth, religion, and public power. In later years, she saw herself naturally cast in a leadership role, just as her father had been. Although she never enjoyed a vast fortune, she never lost her identification with wealth, and she retained an active role in religious life. Her leadership she saw as an obligation, just as her father had, a form of noblesse oblige. If others doubted her fitness, Julia had acquired a sense of moral aristocracy at her father's knee, and she never forgot her lesson.

Despite his new link with Astor wealth and social position, Ward never wavered from his firm conviction that true aristocracy was that of virtue, not wealth. Although he now had the opportunity to entertain lavishly the rest of New York City's elite, he resisted. As always, he protected his social status with a combination of business sense and Christian benevolence. He believed that benevolence marked him as a natural leader of society, as it served to reform and stabilize the city he lived in. Spending money as the Astors did could not appeal to him. To be sure, theirs was another route to social leadership in the fluid class structure of New York. Because it seemed fraught with moral danger, Ward shunned it. A few parties in The Corner could not shake a decade of habit, and the Wards continued to consolidate their status, their money, and their reputation as they had in the past.

The alliance, then, between Ward and Astor, while logical on the surface of things, was uneasy beneath. Astor kept Emily's money in trust, and Ward kept his eye on Sam's income. This had several implications for Julia's future. For one thing, after Emily died, Julia's connection with the Astors disintegrated. Second, her father's example of putting social action before money as a means to social prominence gave Julia an alternative when she faced married life with grand ambitions and few funds.

Her father's social preferences did not affect Julia's. She delighted in her new circle of friends and began to look for a husband.[90] Marriage held out several attractions for Julia in 1838. She was nineteen years old, old enough to marry and start a family. Also, marriage meant conformity to society's ideal. Wifehood was the only career contemplated for young women in Julia's class. Without a husband, Julia's status and livelihood were in doubt. As she entered her third decade without a suitable fiancé, Julia must have felt uneasy about her future. As long as she stayed in her father's house, she could never be free, nor could she claim the status of her married friends. A lifetime in the intermediate stage of young ladyhood meant a lifetime of restriction and dependence. As a consequence, Julia also saw marriage as an escape. Of course, the freedom from male authority that she longed for was rarely found in nineteenth-century marriage. To her young eyes, however, marriage meant a home away from her father's regulation.

To Julia marriage also meant the opportunity to extend her contacts with the literary and philosophical giants whom she had met through Sam and Emily and Mary Ward. As mistress of her own house, she could entertain and encourage young artists the way her father did young ministers. Although Julia thought she did not wish to be a "bluestocking" because bluestockings were not in good repute, she did envision a role that combined marriage and entertaining with intellectual endeavor.[91] In part Aunt Eliza, despite her limitations, provided a model for Julia. After marrying Dr. John Francis, Aunt Eliza had perked up considerably, and in 1841 Annie wrote of her as "never more happy than when surrounded by a cheerful laughing group."[92] This zest for jovial company became one of Julia's trademarks. Margaret Armstrong Astor provided an excellent example of the polished hostess. From her Julia got an inkling of the kind of social power a woman could wield by means of balls, dinners, marriages, and the like. Although Julia would never try to build family dynasties the way Mrs. Astor did, she glimpsed in the Astor mansion the ties among politics, money, family, and hospitality.

Visits to Mary Ward in Boston presented other possibilities. In Mary's company, Julia mingled with Boston's literati, including such intellectual women as Elizabeth Palmer Peabody, Fanny Appleton, Margaret Fuller, and Annie Fields. Julia found the literary salons of the Hub a welcome relief from the parlors of New York. She described them as "a circle of society composed of warm-hearted, intelligent people, not cold, carping critics, people who are disposed to make the best of you, who have sense enough to perceive your good qualities and charity enough to overlook . . . your faults."[93] Perhaps Julia had in mind the "conversations" conducted by Margaret Fuller, some of which she attended. Fuller was dedicated to helping women polish their strengths and overcome their limitations by developing their powers of analysis and criticism. All who recalled her remembered the kindness she displayed toward other women on these occasions.[94]

These interesting, interested women added a new dimension to the powerful hostess image Julia had brought from New York. If she were going to meld the two styles into a position of social and literary eminence, Julia needed one thing—her own house. Marriage was the key that would open the door to it all. But Julia's hopes crashed to a halt midway through her twenty-first year.

Samuel Ward died on November 27, 1839, forcing Julia into the two years of retirement customary at that time. He had worked feverishly to prevent the default of New York City's banks and to stabilize the currency in the face of Jackson's pet banking schemes. His family was convinced that he died of overwork. To Julia, who had held his hand until his last breath was released, the blow was severe. "I cannot, even now, bear to dwell upon the desolate hush which fell upon our house when its stately head lay, silent and cold, in the midst of weeping friends and children," she recalled in her old age.[95]

Like all fond children, Julia grieved not only for her loss, but also for the small acts of disobedience, the kindnesses left undone, past harsh words, and disloyal thoughts. "With my father's death came to me a sense of my want of appreciation for his great kindness, and of my ingratitude for the many comforts and advantages which his affection had secured to me."[96]

To guilt and loss was added another blow, the death of her brother Henry. He died of typhoid fever in October 1840. Julia nursed him day and night, cradling his head in her arms when he died. "When he closed his eyes, I would have gladly, oh, so gladly have died with him. The anguish of this loss told heavily upon me, and I remember the time as one without light or comfort." Julia suffered a "season of depression and melancholy during which I remained in a measure cut off from the wholesome influences which reconcile us to life."[97] She wrote poems reflecting her misery; a number of them she wrote in Henry's honor and collected in a little book.

These two deaths following quickly upon one another shattered not only Julia's dreams, but also her spirits. In the winter of 1840-41, she described herself as "weak," "erring," "unable to determine what ought to be done in simple situations."[98] To her sisters she wrote, "I view your sins and mine as enemies who often prove too mighty for us, and who must overcome us, if for a moment we imagine that we are able to meet them in our own strength."[99] This depression lasted for nearly a year.

Like most depressed people, Julia could see nothing encouraging in her future; past achievements seemed useless. No longer did she find comfort in her literary successes or in the warm welcome extended her by Boston's literary circles. The future looked dim and pointless.

At the same time, New York City was in the midst of a religious revival. To a young woman greatly in need of comfort, spiritual solace was attractive. Furthermore, the revival was a perfect outlet for her grief. Revivals were among the few means sanctioned in the early nineteenth century for anyone to express emotion. For Julia, the revival was an acceptable channel for emotions too large to handle alone but too potent to be discussed politely with others.

The language of an evangelical revival called up extreme reactions in Julia. "These were days of emotion, of fervor, of exaltation alternating with abasement," she later recalled.[100] She intensified her religious activity. For example, she began handing out religious tracts in the poorer sections of New York, and she worked for the Orphan Asylum.[101] Apparently she assumed some major responsibility in connection with this institution since she was responsible for writing up an annual report.[102] In this respect, Julia was following in the footsteps of both her mother, who had labored on behalf of this same asylum, and the example of her father, who had poured his time and money into benevolent enterprises. She expressed her religious views, too, by arranging for a cold dinner to be served on Sunday so that no one would have to cook on the Sabbath.[103] At times she vowed to cut back on her social life.[104] She also renewed, periodically, her efforts to guide and teach her younger sisters.[105] She corresponded with various divines on religious topics and kept up her relationships with the conservative clerics to whom her father had introduced her, including the Episcopal divine, Bishop Eastburn, who discussed religious matters with all the Ward girls.[106]

The impact of these solemn conversations was twofold. First, they intensified Julia's sensitivity to spiritual concerns. Second, these religious activities acquainted Julia with the totally masculine nature of church authority. Men delivered the sermons she listened to; men wrote the tracts that she read; men decided the fine points of dogma she heard debated; men trained the supple minds of young women to live in awe of a male God. Although Julia's mental energies were not entirely swallowed up by the task of pleasing male clerics, she did devote time and energy in bending her thoughts and imagination in the directions they suggested.[107] She was carried along a jet stream of conservative doctrine that emphasized male authority.

None of these activities relieved Julia's depression; in fact, they served only to increase her anxiety. She lived in a "moral and religious pressure cooker of religious feeling."[108] Yet Julia did not experience the kind of conversion the revivalists pressed on her. Although she behaved soberly, Julia did not take the big emotional plunge into evangelical faith.[109]

Finally, her depression lifted. The anguish of melancholy loosed its grip and the anguish of religious doubt no longer seemed so penetrating. Julia returned to her old sources of fulfillment—study, writing, and friendship with Mary. First she turned to her favorite outlet, poetry. Not only did this provide a release for her anguish, it also provided a reassuring sense of competence.[110] Writing poetry was something she did well, something she took pride in. Her verses reflected not only skill, but also according to Margaret Fuller, who read and criticized them, "genuine inspiration," "great fulness and sweetness," and "the utmost delicacy of passionate feeling." Julia had met Margaret Fuller on one of her visits to Boston, but they were not such good friends that Fuller would praise Julia merely out of affection. To have this admirable teacher and writer commend the "steady light in her eye" was the sort of support Julia needed. It renewed Julia's self-esteem. Now she could think of herself instead as a worthy individual whose thoughts and feelings showed merit and value. Fuller had even gone so far as to say that Julia had "a capacity for genius" and had urged her to publish her poetry.[111] Here was reassurance indeed.

In 1841 Julia began to read Goethe's *Matthias Claudius*. This work posed the question: "Is not [God] also the God of the Japanese?" At first the suggestion shocked Julia, but the thought intrigued her.[112] It was Julia's first brush with liberal Protestantism; the possibility that one God looked over all people opened an intellectual window for her. The closing passages of Milton's *Paradise Lost*, ironically, also turned Julia away from orthodox Christianity. Julia was puzzled by the impossible contradiction of Satan's lasting opposition to God and God's omnipotent power. This she resolved by rejecting the whole idea of hell. "I threw away, once and forever, the thought of the terrible hell which till then had always formed part of my belief. In its place I cherished the persuasion that the victory of goodness must consist in making everything good and that Satan himself could have no shield strong enough to resist permanently the divine power of the divine spirit."[113] Later Julia described the influence of reading and thinking independently in this way: "I studied my way out of all the mental agonies which Calvinism can engender and became a Unitarian."[114]

Her friendship with Mary Ward helped sustain Julia, too. Mary urged Julia to quit attending the Bible class and to "Quietly go your own way through the winter and keep clear of all extremes." Her sensible advice combined with her sincere and loving expressions of admiration and affection to comfort Julia. More important, Mary sent Julia material to read. "I send you a sermon (not a 'Bible lecture') of Mr. Channing's on 'the Church' which as explaining Unitarian views and as taking a high stand in the discussion which is ever going on, cannot fail to interest you. . . . I want you to step out of the religious atmosphere in which so much of your life has been passed, and for a moment at least, to look abroad upon the Church Universal towards which the spirit of the age and of the best and most enlightened men of the age, is so strongly tending."[115]

Whatever specific points of doctrine these materials discussed, they all conveyed to Julia one important fact: that the "Church Universal" was hardly a unified place, but was instead an extraordinary collection of different—and disagreeing—minds. The Unitarian Church itself was torn by challenges both to theology and to authority. Channing was one of the Unitarian ministers who had criticized the leaders of the Unitarian Church for their intolerant handling of the arguments of the Transcendentalist ministers.[116] This disunity and challenge to authority might have been confusing, but to Julia it had a freeing effect. If distinguished men, trained extensively in Protestant doctrine, could disagree among themselves on fundamental points, then strict submission to clerical "authorities" mattered less than she had thought.

Transcendentalist ideas, too, built up Julia's power to resist the pull of strict evangelical Calvinism. Here again, Mary Ward was responsible, for it was she who had introduced Julia to Ralph Waldo Emerson. Transcendental theory stressed the immanence of God, God's presence in every human spirit, and God's accessibility to everyone, even children. Emerson, Alcott, Ripley, and Convers Francis taught, in contrast to Bishop Eastburn, one of her father's favorite clerics, that the Bible need not be taken literally and that one's intuition could lead to an understanding of God.[117] It was an optimistic, romantic creed, well suited to Julia's own sensitive romantic style. It freed her of dependence on clerical exegesis and encouraged her to seek the heavenly grace she wanted by following her own thoughts and instincts. Julia would read, listen, and study extensively before her own faith crystallized in the 1850s, but from 1842 on, her religious imagination bore the stamp of the Transcendentalists.

By embracing the creed of the Unitarians, and to some extent that of the Transcendentalists, Julia had experienced a deconversion, a religious crisis that

51

resulted in a decision to turn away from conventional dogma. In her old age, Julia described her experience this way.

> I was once counted for a time among those worthies [Calvinists] to whose ranks a wave of religious sympathy drove me in my early youth. It seemed a great relief, afterwards to have escaped from their dreary phraseology, their set pattern of conviction, their stereotyped way of salvation. The domain of nature was doubly sweet to me after such an estrangement. I threw myself on the lap of my mother earth & cried: oh you sweet mother of flowers, lambs, & children, you feeder and breeder of multitudes, why have I scorned and scoffed at you as a vale of tears, the scene of a pilgrimage of days few & evil?[118]

Perhaps Julia embroidered her experience when she recalled it a few decades later. Even if she did, her embellishments signify her attachment to that event, the importance of that moment when she knew she could resist and turn her back on the creed of her father, aunts, and uncles. Like Saul on the road to Damascus, Julia was knocked flat, at least in her remembrance, by God's power. But this was no act of abject submission to an awful, fearsome God. Instead it was a voluntary embrace, a romantic clasping of the earth and, by extension, all Nature. This was in harmony with the Transcendentalist view of God's pervading qualities, and Julia's embrace of the earth was symbolic of her intellectual embrace of that religious view.

Julia's story reveals how she blended the elements of a traditional conversion with the new, less familiar elements of liberal Protestantism. The latter had been on the periphery of her consciousness until, in the depths of her depression, she encountered them once again through Mary Ward. This time, the ideas seized her imagination, and she found in them an acceptable solution to her spiritual dilemma. She translated these new elements into the experience of orthodox conversion, the physical impact of belief pressing her to the ground, with odd results. Julia now had a new set of ideas with which to approach adulthood.

It would not be a simple matter to hold on to these views. Everyone in her family disapproved of Julia's Unitarian leanings, and so her loyalty to them would be both challenged by loved ones and strengthened by having to defend such ideas. In middle age, she was still having to endure criticism from Louisa about her religious views, and this hostility gave her the opportunity, once again, to articulate her allegiance to them.[119]

Julia had, by her own means and under her own power, resolved her conflicts and found a new center. This achievement had several ramifications.

First, it freed Julia so that she could extend her focus from herself to the larger world. Second, it gave her incentive to continue with her studies. Study of religious philosophy had helped her reach the moment of inner harmony when she felt reconciled to God's creation; she would continue to use reading and studying as a way to re-create that moment. Her religious experiences encouraged her to continue making her own decisions about right and wrong, good and evil, especially when it came to the behavior of women. She had handled the most difficult problem of her young life without the interference of elders, freeing herself of her earlier dependence on the authority of conservative male clergy. Now she had both a new religious value structure on which to rest her sense of herself and a strengthened confidence in her own abilities and judgment.[120]

So confident was she, in fact, that she took a batch of poetry to W. T. Ticknor, of the publishing house of Ticknor and Fields in Boston, during the spring of 1842.[121] Ticknor declined to publish the poems, but Julia remained determined. Her wit and zest for life had returned.[122] With them returned her desire for society, company, and a household of her own. These ideas were on her mind in that same spring when, gazing out of an upper-story window of the Perkins Institute for the Blind, she spotted a handsome man on a black horse dashing across the fields in her direction.

FOUR

Marriage, 1843-1846

A great grieved heart, an iron will,
As fearless blood as ever ran;
A form elate with nervous strength
And fibrous vigor—all a man.

A gallant rein, a restless spur,
The hand to wield a biting scourge;
Small patience for the tasks of Time,
Unmeasured power to speed and urge.

He rides the errands of the hour,
But sends no herald on his ways;
The world would thank the service done,
He cannot stay for gold or praise.

. . . .

One helpful gift the Gods forgot
Due to the man of lion-mood
A woman's soul, to match with his
In high resolve and hardihood.

The "noble rider on a noble steed" whom Julia saw galloping up to the Perkins Institute was its director, Samuel Gridley Howe.[1] He was, at age forty, a distinguished physician, well established in his career as a teacher of blind children. He was tall and athletic, with thick, wavy hair and deep-set blue eyes. A portrait reveals a bushy beard, long straight nose, narrow lips, and ruddy complexion. The face is dignified, although perhaps it would have been a trace less so had not his long hair covered his enormous ears.[2]

His character is somewhat suggested in this portrait: serious, forceful, energetic. Everyone who knew him described him as driving, restless, constantly in motion. "My father was through life subject to fits of unaccountable restlessness. . . . Change was the breath of life to him," recalled one daughter.[3] Emerson described him as "Built of furtherance and pursuing/Not of spent deeds, but of doing."[4] Longfellow said he was as "painfully conscious of the passing of time, as if life itself were slipping from under his feet. At the asylum, a bell rings every quarter of an hour—a constant *memento mori*; and wherever he goes he hears this melancholy bell."[5]

Chev was opinionated and domineering. He disliked opposition; he barely tolerated competition; and he craved admiration and obedience from his subordinates.[6] As far as he was concerned, his wife fell into the latter category. Chev was, as well, singularly lacking in humor. Julia's jokes and pranks did not amuse him; in fact, he was pained by what he perceived as insensitivity at worst and wasting time at best.[7]

The man Julia would marry came from old New England stock. His father, Joseph Neals Howe, owned a ropewalk in Boston. The family enjoyed prosperity until the War of 1812, when Howe accepted worthless federal money in exchange for his rope. Business must have improved, however, for young Samuel matriculated at Brown University and then, in 1924, at Harvard Medical School.[8]

Samuel Gridley Howe, although blessed with a fine mind, never stood well in his class. His energies poured over repeatedly into escapades of mischief and even vandalism, and he was put back in the standings. This passion for action and adventure propelled him, after graduation from Harvard, into the midst of the Greek Revolution. Although he suffered injuries from enemy attacks, he involved himself in combat very little. Instead he concentrated on logistical matters—securing funds, distributing supplies to the military and civilian population, building internal improvements including harbor improvements at Aegina and, increasingly, administering relief to the suffering Greek population. He returned to Boston in 1830, bearing the Greek honor of Chevalier of the Order of St. Savior for his five years of service.[9] This honor earned him the nickname "Chev."

The adjustment to a more settled life in the United States proved difficult. "The task of finding a permanent position was hard indeed; a combination of idealism, the urge to lead a useful life, and lingering immaturity kept him in a sea of indecision." After a brief stint as a journalist, Chev accepted the directorship of the New England Asylum for the Blind. Immediately he laid plans to return to Europe to study the latest methods for educating blind children. His European travels came to an abrupt halt in January 1832 when the Prussian government arrested and imprisoned him on charges of smuggling funds to Polish insurgents. Released in March, Chev continued his studies until July, when he returned home.[10]

Chev's major contribution lay in his very American insistence that everybody—even the disabled—should work. This meant that the blind children under his care were taught to read and do arithmetic, as well as take care of themselves, their clothes, and their surroundings. Chev trained them to perform tasks that could provide them with an income. This was a revolutionary concept; even the most "advanced" institutions in Europe never intended to make their wards self-sufficient. Impressed by Chev's plan, one Colonel Thomas Perkins donated a mansion in South Boston to house the institute in perpetuity, thus providing it with its lasting name. Chev raised sufficient additional private funds to provide raised-letter books, musical instruments, and tools for the mechanical crafts.[11] A $2,000 annual salary was offered him at this time, putting Chev on sound financial footing at last.[12]

Perhaps the most notable student ever to enroll at the Perkins Institute was Laura Bridgman. Deaf, blind, and mute, Laura came to Chev's attention in 1837. In October of that year her parents entrusted the seven-year-old girl to his care.[13] Her remarkable progress became a topic of wide interest; Charles Dickens included a chapter about her in his *American Notes*. Julia was as intrigued with the tales of this young woman as everyone else, and she was delighted to accompany Charles Sumner on a visit to the institute in order to meet her. It was on this visit that she saw Samuel Gridley Howe for the first time.

Their friendship blossomed. The relationship quickly assumed a paternal aspect, as Chev referred to Julia as "the child."[14] Since there was a difference of nearly eighteen years in their ages, Julia may indeed have seen in Samuel Gridley Howe some of the qualities of her deceased father. He was tall, confident, stern, and dedicated to the sort of benevolence that had interested Ward. A poem of the period, however, suggests that Julia missed not only her father, but also Henry, and that she hoped Chev would replace them both.

> But when my eyes unclosed again
> I felt I was not all unblest
> I slept upon my brother's bier
> I waked upon my husband's breast.[15]

As Chev squired her to parties, danced with her, and talked with her until the wee hours of the morning, Julia hoped she had found at least an evocation of her brother.[16]

Chev was as taken with Julia as she was with him. To his friend Charles Sumner he confided: "Here I am in the very central bower of Paradise . . . I am so happy that I am really frightened. What does it mean? Is it not some illusion? . . . I never saw anything like it before; no one ever did, for as for all the happiness they tell you about in novels, it is humbug; the authors were never here in this library."[17] To Longfellow he wrote, "You can perhaps form some faint idea of the rapture with which I pour out my long pent up affections for her . . . gushing over with tenderness and love."[18]

There were thorns among the roses, however. The first was money. After Chev announced his intention to marry Julia early in 1843, Julia's male relatives drew up a prenuptial contract that left control of Julia's money in the hands of Sam and Uncle John. This device was a hoary tradition among America's wealthy families, but Chev took exception to it. He disliked the implication that he was not to be trusted with Julia's money. (As events later proved, he should not have been.) After a little testiness on all sides, the matter was resolved, temporarily at least.

Julia's estate was substantial. She owned in her own right a number of stocks, bonds, mortgages, and other securities. More significantly, she owned a good amount of New York City real estate, including land on Pearl Street, Exchange Street, Beaver Street, Sixtieth Street, Third Avenue and Fifty-Eighth Street, and Second Avenue and Seventy-Sixth Street. She shared an interest in houses at 17 Maiden Lane and 26 Broad Street. In addition, she owned with her sisters and brothers the entire block between Eighth and Ninth avenues and Thirty-Fourth and Thirty-Fifth streets. An annual income approaching $2,000 was to be made over to Julia in quarterly installments, and the couple could call upon $10,000 whenever they decided to build or purchase a house. Beyond this $10,000, Chev was not to touch a penny of Julia's property. All her assets and the proceeds were to be kept "free from the debts, control, or engagements of her said intended husband."[19] Chev agreed to this stipulation, and the young couple was satisfied.

Another thorn appeared in early April 1843. One morning Sam found Julia in the family library "with a melancholy expression to which her countenance had long been a stranger." Julia had received a troubling letter from Chev, and she persuaded her brother to write him a reply. From Sam's letter, it is evident that Chev was having second thoughts: Did Julia grasp the nature of her new responsibilities? Was she not somewhat unprepared to manage a household? Would her passion for poetry and literature divert her attention from her husband? Was she ready to pour all her talent and energy into his causes and welfare? He would not, he averred, allow her intellectual interests to rival him for her attention. Sam's soothing reply defended Julia stoutly if conventionally. "I think it fortunate when intellectual occupations, strengthening the mind and refining the taste, fill up those lonely hours, so often consoled by scandal and romances, and render the woman a fitter companion for the man," he stated. He went on to assure Chev that love and gentle guidance would "naturally modify" Julia's behavior.[20]

Chev was fundamentally ambivalent about Julia. He admired her energy and intellectual power, but he resented her abilities when they were not focused on him. He desired a wife of unusual talents who would devote herself exclusively to his wishes, his causes, even his whims. He did not get one, and his response was to criticize Julia for not living up to his ideal of a perfect wife.

Another thorn lay hidden deeper. Chev, a mature man in his forties, had never spent much time with women. His youth was spent in all-male institutions where women appeared only as cooks or maids. After graduation from medical school, he devoted himself to war and relief work, two fields dominated by men. He had no women coworkers or correspondents. His situation in Greece prevented him from meeting women socially, and Chev, in spite of his gay whirl with Julia, disliked parties. He knew few women socially. As a consequence, Chev had not the least idea of what women were like. He idolized his mother, Patty Gridley Howe, and thought that all women could and should behave exactly as she did, or, more exactly, as he *thought* she did.[21] Drawing an analogy from his perceptions of his mother, Chev believed that women were happiest when married and surrounded by children, devoting themselves to domestic tasks and service to their husbands.[22] That a married woman might seek other interests or hope for some diversions seemed to him preposterous. When Julia once chided him for encouraging Florence Nightingale to pursue nursing while forbidding her to pursue anything, he replied, "if he had been engaged to Florence Nightingale, and had loved her ever so dearly, he would have given her up as soon as she commenced her career as a public woman."[23]

Chev's closest friends were men—Longfellow, Sumner, Cornelius Felton (professor of Greek at Harvard and later its president), and George Hilliard. Of these, Sumner was his most intimate friend. Horace Mann would soon come to rival Sumner for first place in Chev's heart. His loyalty to and sympathy with his men friends were so marked that Julia felt, after a few years of marriage, that Chev loved Sumner more than he loved her.[24]

In 1842, however, Julia was delighted with Chev's friends. Never had she known such an interesting collection of intellectuals. Although their erudition intimidated her somewhat, she thought them representative of the new and exciting world of liberal ideas that she had just uncovered. They made marriage to Chev even more attractive.

The wedding took place on April 23, 1843, in Samuel Ward's house. Louisa and Annie had made most of the arrangements since Julia was not inclined toward practical details.[25] Four days later, Julia and Chev sailed for Europe, accompanied by Annie Ward. Her health had been a source of family concern, and everyone hoped a trip abroad would do her good. In a parting letter to her Aunt Eliza, Julia made the first independent stand of her married life. "You will not be sorry to learn that my name is to be 'Mrs. Julia Ward Howe' and not 'Mrs. Samuel Gridley Howe'—my family wish me to retain my maiden name, and I am myself very attached to it."[26]

Julia's experiences abroad were of two kinds. On the one hand, she enjoyed a measure of social success in England. Chev was a "lion," as she herself expressed it, because of his work with Laura Bridgman.[27] The Howes found many doors opened to them; invitations to breakfasts, teas, and balls arrived constantly. Julia was new enough to this sort of life to find it a source of real pleasure. So impressive were her encounters with the likes of Sydney Smith, Charles Dickens, Thomas Carlyle, Reverend Menckton Milnes, Lord Lansdowne, the duchess of Sutherland, and Lady Carlisle that she recalled them in detail fifty-five years later. Equally delightful were the evenings of opera, ballet, and theater that she and Chev enjoyed together.[28] These once forbidden amusements thrilled her, and she became a devotee of the stage from then on.

Her social life gave Julia's sharp tongue and lively wit plenty of subject matter. To Louisa she described a party where she

> . . . did not know a soul—Annie frightened—I bored—got hold of some good people—made friends; drank execrable tea, finished the evening by a crack with Sir Sydney [Smith] himself, and came off victorious, that is to say alive. Sir S. is very like old Mrs. Prime, three chins and such a corporosity![29]

In fact, Julia's sense of humor helped her survive less cheerful moments as well. Aboard ship, Julia had a difficult time finding her sea legs. "I have had various tumbles," she wrote Louisa.

> I confess that when the ship rolled, I generally made for the stoutest man in sight and pitched into him, the result being various apologies on both sides, and great merriment on the part of the spectators.[30]

At other times, however, Julia felt less jolly. It was, after all, Mr. Samuel Gridley Howe, not Mrs. Julia Ward Howe, whom people most wanted to see. Julia frequently felt snubbed or left out. Charles Dickens whisked Chev away on expeditions, while she and Annie stayed at home, bored and restless.[31] Even when she accompanied Chev, the excursions were not always pleasant. A trip to Edgeworthtown to visit Maria Edgeworth, author of the "Harry and Lucy" stories for children, was one such disappointment.[32] While Chev and Edgeworth discussed Irish politics, slavery, and Dickens, Julia talked "with a charming Spanish woman. . . . Miss E said to me what one says to little women in general, this (children) was all my share, and I took it quietly. I am much accustomed to that non-committal conversation, in which one expresses neither thought nor feeling. I weary of it in my heart."[33] When the Howes departed, Edgeworth presented Chev with an engraving inscribed, "From a lover of truth to a lover of truth."[34] Julia was miffed to be left out of this exchange.

In her melancholy moods, Julia turned to poetry. A great deal of revealing verse, contained in little notebooks dated 1843-1844, appears among Julia's papers. Clearly the first months of marriage were not entirely happy ones. Julia wrote "The Present is Dead" only a few weeks after her wedding:

> I feel my varied power all depart
> With scarce a hope they may be born anew
> And naught is left, save one poor loving heart,
> Of what I was—and that may perish, too.
>
> Come nearer to me, let our spirits meet
> Let us be of one light, one truth possessed;
> Tis true our blended life on earth is sweet,
> But can our souls within one heaven rest?[35]

Her sense that Chev did not want or need her intellectual and spiritual companionship led to a desperate sense of having no one to love.

I stifled it in babyhood
The love that struggled at my heart,
Its plaintive waiting I subdued
Controlled its very start.

And when my task of life is o'er
Yielding into the spirit's thirst
I'll open the sealed grave once more
And from its depths shall burst

A fount of tears that cannot cease
A fount that ages cannot dry.
Thus I will pass away to peace
In mine own agony.[36]

Julia began to fear that she had made a mistake.

Hope died as I was led
Unto my marriage bed.
Nay, do not weep—twas I
Not thou that slew my happiest destiny.[37]

Recognizing that she had no power to amend matters, she resolved to try to please her new husband.

When once I know my sphere
Life shall no more be drear
I will be all thou wilt
To cross thy least desire shall be guilt.[38]

Chev's inquiries and connections took them to Scotland, Ireland, and back to England. From there the couple, with Annie in tow, journeyed to Prussia, Switzerland, Austria, and Italy. At length they reached Rome. Julia found the city cold and dismal. It was saved from utter cheerlessness by the arrival of Louisa, who had been packed off to Rome in hopes that she would recover from an ill-fated romance and a cruel domestic row.[39] The Astors had suddenly closed their doors to all the Wards. Margaret Astor disapproved of her erstwhile son-in-law's plans to remarry, and she had snatched little Maddie, Sam's daughter, back to the Astor mansion to live. Louisa had been a second mother to this lonely girl, and she minded the loss of Maddie's childish company more than the exclusion from Astor society. Forlorn and perplexed, Louisa delighted in the reunion with her sisters as much as Julia did.

Julia found Rome depressing. "The Rome I saw then was medieval in its aspect. A great gloom and silence hung over it." Even at parties, the ladies sat quietly and the gentlemen spoke in an undertone. Julia could not endure this for long, and she set about befriending Italians and Americans alike. Artists such as Thomas Crawford and Luther Terry frequented their apartments, as did the banker Prince Torlonia.[40]

Her gift for making friends first emerged here in Rome, but it did not entirely compensate for the discomforts and disappointments Julia suffered. She was ill, she complained, and no one took her symptoms seriously. When the "illness" turned out to be pregnancy, she was gripped with the fear that she would die in childbirth as her mother had.[41] The death of her dear sister-in-law, Emily Astor, in childbirth in 1842, reinforced this fear. A few days before her child was born, she wrote a poem about death in childbirth.[42] No older female relative, not even an experienced English-speaking midwife, was nearby for comfort or advice. Although her husband was a physician, he could be of no help; the medical schools of his generation offered no courses in gynecology or obstetrics to their students.[43] She faced her first confinement terrified and lonely.

When Julia finally left Rome in the spring of 1844, "it seemed like returning to the living after a long separation from it."[44] Certainly part of her relief was the safe arrival, after eight hours of labor, of her first child, Julia Romana, or Dudie, on March 12, 1844. Traveling with sisters, baby, and husband, Julia enjoyed a leisurely return to Boston by way of Naples, Paris, and England. When Julia finally saw the Perkins Institute again, she was looking at the place that would be her home for the next twenty months. Carrying her six-month-old baby, Julia tucked up her skirts and proceeded up the long flight of stairs to the "Doctor's Wing."

Julia was determined, regardless of the unsettling moments she had suffered in Europe, to become a good wife to Chev now that they were home. "The Chevalier's way is a very charming way," she wrote to Sam, "and it is henceforth to be mine."[45] She believed that marriage was "the destiny of women," and set about trying to live up to conventional ideas of conjugal bliss. "We are learning to live for others more than for ourselves," she wrote Louisa, "and in following thus the guidelines of Providence, we have acted more wisely than we should have done in marking out any eccentric course of our own and adhering to it."[46] In obedience to what she perceived as Chev's wishes, she renounced all activities of which he did not approve. "I firmly resolved to admit no thought, to cultivate no taste in which you could not sympathize," she wrote Chev.[47] To Sam she wrote, "His true devotion has won me from the world, and from myself. . . . I am perfectly satisfied to sacrifice to one so noble and earnest the dreams of my youth."[48]

Sacrificing her dreams of literary fame and her hopes of an emotionally and spiritually close relationship with Chev, while trying to live up to Chev's idea of the perfect, well-organized, self-denying wife, cost Julia dearly. During the next ten years, Julia suffered four major, identifiable depressions.

Her misery grew, like a poisonous plant, from the soil of married life. A difficult husband sapped her morale. Servant problems, financial worries, and the cares of child-tending left her exhausted. Physical and emotional isolation compounded her unhappiness, leaving her numb and demoralized. Depression wiped out energy and imagination, depriving Julia of the emotional resources she needed in order to tackle her problems. During her worst spells, Julia dragged herself through her days, choking back tears and contemplating suicide. Sometimes she collapsed into hysterical fits. This was the desperate behavior of a woman who felt trapped, used up, and hopeless. It is also the pattern of someone whose depressions manifest serious illness. To Julia's illness Chev was largely insensitive. He did, however, contribute substantially to its onset and its persistence.

The first episode of depression, beginning in April 1845, seemed to let up in the spring of 1846. This respite was short, however, and the first depression really lasted until the fall of 1846. The second episode lasted from May of 1847 until March 1848; the third, from the fall of 1849 until the spring of 1850; and the last, from November 1852 until November 1854.

All four clearly identifiable depressive periods share most of the following characteristics: First, the onset of winter, with its promise of cold, dark, and physical isolation, had a depressing effect on Julia. Indeed, three of her four crises began in the autumn. Pregnancy usually figured in as well. During the depression of April 1845-June 1846 and her relapse in the fall of 1846, she was either pregnant with or nursing her second baby, Florence. The depression of May 1847-March 1848 began before Julia knew she was pregnant with her third child, Henry, but deepened as she realized she had not escaped another childbirth. Julia was depressed from October 1849 to February 1850, a period that coincides exactly with the latter half of her pregnancy with Laura. The depression beginning in the fall of 1852 is the only one that does not coincide neatly with a pregnancy, but it worsened when Julia realized she was pregnant once more, this time with daughter Maud.

Typically, two things signaled an end of Julia's depression. The arrival of her "unwanted" babies always pleased Julia immensely. She rejoiced in the beauty of her infants, in their appetites, in their affection for her. She was relieved to have survived the threat to her life. With the exception of Flossy's birth, which provided only a short respite, the arrival of her new babies released Julia from her bonds of gloom. This was certainly the case after Henry's birth in March 1848, after Laura's in February 1850, and after Maud's in November 1854.

Another event that helped her was a change of scene. The long depression from April 1845 until December 1846 let up a little in June 1846, when Julia moved into Green Peace, and vanished in the winter of 1846-47, when she moved to Winthrop House in the center of Boston for the season. The third depression loosened its grip on Julia in the spring of 1850. Not only was Laura born then, but Julia was also planning a trip to Rome where she would be reunited with Louisa. Maud's birth in November 1854 seems to have ended the last big depression, although a sparser correspondence from that period makes judgment difficult. In the spring following Maud's birth, Julia convinced Chev to abandon the plan of housing the family at the institute, and once again a new residence brought renewed hopes.

These emotional episodes soaked up a great deal of Julia's mental and physical energy. Far from producing the spectacular literary masterpieces she had dreamed of, Julia found herself struggling to cope with everyday life. Becoming a model of wifely submission and tact was no easy task, Julia discovered. The problems she encountered with Chev revolved around her methods of housekeeping, servants, money, Chev's demands, and Chev's moodiness.

The place Chev had picked for them to live, the Doctor's Wing of the Perkins Institute, made Julia miserable. The building was thoroughly inconvenient; cold, gray marble corridors threatened everyone with chills and drafts. Endless spiral staircases challenged the endurance of mother and servants alike as they trudged up and down between kitchen on one level, parlors on another, bedrooms on another, and still more bedrooms on another. The building was dark and damp, with high-studded rooms and echoing galleries. Moreover, it stank of waterclosets.[49] Julia could not help noting, as she climbed up and down the stairs, that there was no room, not even a corner, she could call her own. The sunny comfort of the New York study with curtains of yellow silk was a thing of the past.

This lack of privacy was compounded by the presence of Chev's sister, Jeanette Howe. "Ponderous" and "inarticulate," Jeanette had devoted her adult life to her brother by serving as his housekeeper.[50] She disliked competition. When Julia proposed to entertain friends at dinner, Jeanette simply disappeared, leaving Julia to fend for herself among unfamiliar shelves and cupboards.[51]

Jeanette was not the only peculiarity in the doctor's old household. Chev, eager to acquaint the older children under his charge with the nature of domestic tasks, assigned them jobs in his own household. Julia then had to contend with children whom she scarcely knew and whose handicaps somewhat put her off.[52]

Victorian literature, especially the short stories in women's magazines, stressed the delights of homemaking for young brides. Typically, the heroines were free to embellish their modest houses as they saw fit, to arrange the furniture according to their liking, and, by dint of constant hard work, to create a cozy domestic circle that reflected their own interests and tastes. Although they might not participate in affairs outside their homes, young wives could reap satisfaction from the decoration and the management of their own houses. Julia was learning that she might not be allowed to do this.

A poem written during this difficult period of adjustment reflects Julia's lingering doubts about her marriage. In fact, it hints that neither husband nor child could offer her the true "home" of solace, comfort, and companionship that she wanted.

> Oh thou, who when I lost my home,
> Didst call me to another.
> Forgive me if I sometimes mourn,
> My father and my brother.
>
> If while my child's angelic voice,
> My heart with rapture owns.
> It feels a strange sad yearning still,
> For those familiar tones.
>
> Forgive, for I have learned to seek
> A father's love in thee;
> And when I leave this world, my home,
> In thine own light shall be.[53]

Julia struggled on despite these obstacles. She really did wish to become a good housekeeper. With a dash of merriment characteristic of her high moods, she boasted to Louisa of her successes with the soap fat merchant and the rag man. "Both of these were clever transactions. Oh, if you had seen me stand by the soap fat man, and scrutinize minutely his weights and measures, telling him again and again that it was beautiful grease, and he must allow me a good price for it—truly, I am a mother in Israel."[54] In addition, she practiced making various puddings, including blancmange, which she described as "first rate."[55] When Catharine Beecher's book on domestic economy appeared, Julia bought a copy to study.[56]

Julia's dreams of managing her household like "a Mother in Israel" were unrealistic. During her youth she had managed to ignore not only the secrets of puddings and yeast rolls, but also the whole question of getting along with cooks and nurses. "I am entirely too easy a person to get along with my servants," she confessed to her sisters. "They are not good and require the strong arm of authority. . . . I must, I think, get some nice, active, conscientious woman to keep the rest in order. . . . My cook is miserable—do you know of a first-rate one, who will also assist in the washing—the work is very light."[57] Since this paragon of cook-laundress was not forthcoming, Julia adjusted her expectations and outlined a new staff that would suit her needs. Ideally, she wanted four servants: a cook, a nurse, a chambermaid, and a man to do the outdoor work.[58] This she never quite managed; her letters reveal that she was always looking for new people.[59]

Upset by Julia's failure to set up a smoothly running household and goaded by his own perfectionism, Chev decided to take a hand in things. He was so emphatic about her uselessness that Julia began to echo his judgments. To Louisa she wrote, "The longer I live the more do I feel my utter, childlike helplessness about all practical affairs. . . . For everything that is not soul, I am an ass, that I am."[60]

Chev's intervention not only prevented Julia from learning, but it also confused matters. For example, he liked to take a hand in the hiring, so Julia was required to send prospective servant girls to him for an interview. As an enthusiastic phrenologist, Chev was confident that he could predict the honesty of his servants by examining the contours of their craniums.[61] One of his favorites, however, left the household with several of the family's valuables in her possession.[62] Another choice, a girl from the Idiot School, presented a different kind of problem: she could count only as high as seven, after which she said "many."[63] Occasionally he convinced Julia to fire the cook, resulting in a frantic period of looking for someone new while eating only vegetables and hasty pudding.[64]

Chev felt free to fire servants, too. He thought nothing of dismissing the whole staff, from nursery to kitchen, when Julia was out of town and unable to offer any opposition.[65] This interference tried Julia's patience. In exasperation she wrote to Annie, "Chev wrote to you about Fanny Jarvis, last night—entre nous, I am not greatly pleased with the idea of bringing her. I had rather bring Lizzy and the baby's nurse, but Chev's will be done in Bordentown as it is in Boston."[66] When the departures of servants left Julia shorthanded, she then managed as best she could, doing a little cooking, all the baby tending, or perhaps some "chamber work" as required.[67] Chev did nothing to make up for the havoc he caused. The resulting fatigue depressed Julia's spirits, as did the frustrations and annoyance that Chev's interference caused her.

Life was made even more difficult by a sudden change in her finances. Chev began to smart from the blow that Julia's trust agreement had dealt to his pride, and he decided to do without its proceeds. He was prompted to take this drastic step by what began as a misunderstanding. Sam Ward, believing that Chev was requesting the trust income for inappropriate purposes, refused to honor a £200 debt the Howes had contracted in Europe.[68] Chev fumed and wrote to his lawyer, Charles Sumner, to see if he could overturn the trust: "pray write and let me know for if I have any legal right to take any part of her property out of *his* [Sam's] hand, I shall do it without the loss of an hour."[69] Chev was confident that Julia disliked the agreement as much as he did, vowing she would "tear up the document" if she could.[70] A painful correspondence ensued between Chev and Sam with Julia frantic to smooth things over.[71] The Wards refused to abandon the agreement, but Sam did step down as trustee in deference to Chev's feelings. Dr. James K. Mills, the physician to Perkins Institute, took Sam's place on November 9, 1846.[72] Since he was a close friend of Chev's, Chev was able to keep a close eye on Julia's funds from that date onward.

Still Chev chafed at what he perceived as the Ward family's insulting refusal to let him handle his wife's assets directly. Convinced that Julia would live "ever so lowly" rather than see her husband receive "dolings out of rents, etc." from Sam, Chev devised a plan whereby Julia turned over all her income automatically to him.[73] This money Chev refused to receive, turning it directly back to the trust. "Next January, & as many January's as I am in life, I shall ask her to do the same," he told Uncle John, "& I trust she will ever love me enough to prefer to live with me in poverty than ask me to submit to humiliation."[74] Sam wrote back sternly, telling Chev that the recent check for $450.70 and the $1,000 in stock certificates were not his to dispense with, but Chev held fast to his plan.[75] Apparently Julia was not as enthusiastic about the reduction in income as Chev had expected.[76] Certainly her description of the arrangements to her brother were perfunctory and not in the least sympathetic to Chev's position: "I am sad today & will not write any more about this affair."[77]

Chev was hypocritical about all this. He was willing to abjure the trust where actual income was concerned, but he could not resist it where real estate was involved. In July 1845 and in January and May 1946, Chev requested and received parts of the $10,000 that had been set aside to pay for a house.[78] With this money he bought and improved a dilapidated old farm located near ·the institute in South Boston. Chev also agreed to accept Julia's share of the profits when Uncle William's estate, The Grange, was sold.[79] Unbeknownst to Julia and with no interference from James Mills, Chev embarked on another real estate speculation, this time using Julia's interest income. To do this he simply failed to return to the trust the quarterly checks that he had forced Julia to make over to him. Beginning in 1845, he started to buy from Micijah Pope various lots of land in South Boston. The land he bought was vested in his name alone. Hence, he had managed, even while the Wards were in titular control of the trust, to commingle Julia's funds with his and to claim as his property the real estate purchased with Julia's assets. He had, in effect, overturned the trust designed to keep Julia's assets "free from the debts, control, or engagements of her said intended husband," in the space of two years.[80] Clearly the issue for Samuel Gridley Howe was not simply one of humiliation under the terms of the trust, for the "doles" to which he objected were perfectly bearable as long as they concerned real estate and went directly into Chev's account. What was at stake was his wife's potential independence of him. This Chev could not endure.

Now Julia had no money of her own. To tide herself over, she began to write for money. Her daughter Florence claims that her mother did clerical work during the summer before her birth to earn money for baby clothes. Although there is no evidence of this in her letters, she did send short pieces to local magazines in hopes of publication, and she made a little money this way.[81] No matter what Chev claimed, Julia was not content with this new restraint on her life.

In particular, the changes in the trust income meant that Julia had to spend less on clothes. Clothing, especially for herself, had always delighted Julia. Principally Julia ordered her clothes, hats, and fabrics from New York. Boston was still a provincial city in many ways, and New York offered a greater selection of styles at competitive prices. As a consequence, both Annie and Aunt Eliza received regular requests for clothing in their letters from Julia.[82] Julia liked to look pretty; it gave her confidence to wear something new. She preferred rich fabrics, including lace, silk, and velvet, and she selected fashionable French designs whenever her purse could afford it.[83] Although she later advocated dress reform and opposed expensive dress, Julia had no hesitation about indulging in fashionable and costly clothing during the 1840s. Such expenditures not only boosted her ego, they also helped her link up, at least visually, with the aristocratic class she had abandoned in marrying Chev. Since the social status of a professional reformer was not high in antebellum Boston, Julia had to establish her right of entry into elite circles in ways other than along bloodlines. Expensive, stylish clothing, she thought, would help her do this.[84]

Turning to New York for dresses had a reassuring effect, too. There people recognized her as a member of one of New York's distinguished families. Merchants willingly extended her credit since family money sometimes bridged the gap between purchases and Julia's ability to pay.[85] Here again was the comfortable sensation that whatever else went wrong, Julia still had a claim to distinction, in her own right, as a Ward.

Nevertheless, Julia needed to compensate for the decrease in income by wearing plain hats and washable muslin dresses.[86] Only rarely did she model the beautiful clothing she loved. What she did buy was paid for by accumulated small sums that she coaxed out of the household budget. Chev's financial decision was restricting indeed.

Julia was discovering that Chev was difficult to live with in other ways and that his "way" was not always "charming." He demanded unstinting admiration and attention from his wife. To Louisa he prescribed a "long session" in perfect wifehood: "Women are apt . . . to think all they have to do for a lover is give him first their heart and then their hand. Think you not so, but begin to love tomorrow & love on more and more until you die; in this alone never say die."[87] Cloaked in this formula for marital happiness is the essence of Chev's central wish—a devoted wife who would love him to the exclusion of everyone and everything else. Such selflessness was impossible for Julia, who craved attention, affection, and company for herself.

Furthermore, Chev had internalized the view of womanhood that had emerged in the first few decades of the nineteenth century in New England. He wanted not only a self-denying wife but a creature of domestic perfection who would maintain a serene and happy home far from the perplexing and alienating world of work.[88] Julia, on the other hand, entertained no such notions. She clung to a much broader view of her role. After all, just as this view of women's work had been taking hold, she had been growing up without a mother. Julia had had no examples before her of this role, for while Aunt Eliza provided decent care for her young nieces and nephews, she had not reflected any of the refined notions of elevated wife-and-motherhood. Because she had been so sheltered from the society around her, Julia had little chance to observe other women and to absorb the new value system from them. Besides, New York society was not like that of New England. The New York women of Julia's circle took their cue from the "cavalier" society of the South, and New York women emulated the ideal of the leisured aristocrat more than that of the domestic matron.

This huge gap in attitudes was complicated by other, more ordinary factors. Chev was frequently grumpy and intractable. He was subject to violent headaches several times a year. Whether migraines or emotional in origin, it is difficult to tell, but they made life hard for everyone. Julia was required, on these "black days," to hurry about with cracked ice and hot "fomentations" in an effort to ease Chev's agony. His lamentations during such crises were sufficient, apparently, to convince a casual visitor that he was dying.[89] In addition, Chev was as subject to depression as Julia, and like her, his moods responded to the weather.[90] He suffered several breakdowns, at least two of which occurred shortly after the birth of a new baby.[91] This meant that just as she was starting to feel better and to assert herself, Chev pulled her away from her own pursuits to minister to him.

These conflicts with Chev were like buckets of cold water on Julia's flickering hopes for a happy marriage. Her once glorious convictions about wifely dignity and importance diminished; she began to see marriage in terms of duty and resignation.

Marriage, like death, is a debt we owe to nature and though it earns us something to pay it, yet we are more content and better established in peace when we have paid it.[92]

71

Life goes harder with us *matrons* than with single women, and we have some heavy burdens to bear, but matrimony teaches us many precious lessons & I am sure I would not give up one of the important truths it has taught me.[93]

As Chev became increasingly involved in state politics and work for the blind, Julia began to feel neglected, even cheated. It was ironic that he threw himself so completely into the defense of society's downtrodden while ignoring and even trampling on her needs. Chev simply assumed that Julia would share his interests and that she would not question his tendency to elevate philanthropic causes over his marriage. She made a few attempts, attending a dismal meeting of the Prison Discipline Society with him, for example.[94] Despite these brushes with benevolence, Julia could not take such causes to heart. When an old friend, Francis Lieber, announced that he was coming for a visit, she sent him a "list of the subjects of conversation prohibited in my presence":

> All insane hospitals, idiots, educated or otherwise, and madness of every description. (Liebe ausgenommen). All prisons, prison disciplines, prison societies, prison reforms, secretaries of prison discipline societies, every form of legal imprisonment (der Heiraten ausgenommen). Philanthropy—philanthropic enterprises, workhouses, relief and vigilance committees, interests of the African race, disgusts of the Mexican War, every kind of philanthropy—every description of philanthropist (der Lerfel ausgenommen). In literature, free discussion on any topic will be allowed, and the criticism and commendation of every book, author, in prose and in verse (ausgenommen Longfellow's poems).[95]

In her scrapbook, Julia analyzed the situation. "My husband has scarcely half an hour in twenty-four to give me. So, as I think much, in my way, and nobody takes the least interest in what I think, I am forced to take an imaginary public, and to tell it the secrets of my poor ridiculous brain. While I am employed with fictions my husband is dealing with facts, but as we both seek truth which lies beyond either, we do not get so very far apart as you might think. At least I know what is in *his* mind if he does not occupy himself much with mine."[96]

Knowing what occupied Chev's mind was not much help since Julia neither liked it nor would do much about it. In fact, there was really no clear way for Julia to link herself to Chev's interests unless it was to give him the unstinting admiration he needed. Other male occupations often did have a built-in role for the wife that enabled her to share her husband's work and to bind them together in a common aim.[97] A farmer's wife tended livestock and kitchen garden; a minister's wife could aid him as comfort giver; a businessman's wife abetted his fortunes by her role as hostess. But Chev was none of these. His business was benevolence; his work was agitation. It would have been difficult for Julia to aid him without becoming a public figure herself, something Chev would never tolerate. As a consequence, she turned inward, focusing on her family. She was bitterly disappointed to have to do this, as she told Louisa. "My babies are all the poetry and beauty that I can see in life. If I had them not, I should quietly die of inanition. Dearest Wevie, what is this problem? . . . Is it selfish, is it egotistical to wish that others may love us, take an interest in us, sympathize with us in our mature age as in our youth? . . . What shall I do? Where shall I go to beg some scraps and remnants of affection to feed my hungry heart . . . my husband? May God teach him to love me and help me to make him happy."[98] She wrote to Chev, outlining her regrets and her plans for coping with them. "I will not expect too much from you. I will enjoy all the moments of sunshine we can enjoy together. I will treasure up every word, every look of yours that is kind and genial, to comfort me in those long, cold wintry days when I feel you do not love me."[99]

Unfortunately, driven by his own concerns and impatient with Julia's, Chev was not often around to spread moments of sunshine. Julia knew, underneath her brave pose, that marriage was not the idyllic meeting of sympathetic minds that romantic literature had led her to expect. The solemn advice in ladies' books did not match her experience. After struggling with this disappointment, Julia had pared down her view of marriage to a simple system of mutual duty and responsibility. Banker's daughter that she was, she now viewed her bond as a contractual one that set forth obligations on both sides. She did not, as she might have, respond to the Declaration of Sentiments issued by the first woman's rights convention that met just five years after she began to realize that marriage could be a form of imprisonment. Even if their ideas appealed to her, she could not pursue them. Her marriage was in turmoil; the last thing she needed was a set of ideas that would shake it up further, and so Julia proved resistant to the whole movement for several years.

As she tried to cope with her prickly husband, Julia suffered from a lack of role models. Her mother might have showed her a good many things: how to blend determination with the pose of a "true woman" in order to get her way; how to assert her spiritual and intellectual independence in the context of a marriage; how to combine domestic cares with literary work. Without this example, Julia was at a loss as to how to manage.

Her response was essentially a personal, nonpolitical one. She retreated to the small circle of books and babies. One consequence of this was that Julia was even more susceptible to depression; one consequence of the ensuing depression was that Julia had neither the emotional nor the physical energy to turn outward. The nurturing of small children, four of which were born in the space of six years, also turned Julia's thoughts inward, both literally and figuratively. She found, like many mothers, that she had no time to focus on matters outside the daily circle.

Yet books and babies served Julia well in some ways. Her children could be a source of pride, and her books offered her solace and refreshment. The paradox of her marriage was that while Chev undermined her, the results of domesticity served at times to strengthen her.

FIVE

Children, 1846-1850

This evening, as the twilight fell
My younger children watched for me;
Like cherubs in the window framed,
I saw the smiling group of three.

While round and round the house I trudged,
Intent to walk a weary mile,
Oft as I passed within their range,
The little things would beck and smile.

They watched me, as Astronomers
Whose business lies in heaven afar,
Await beside the slanting glass
The re-appearance of a star.

Not so, not so, my pretty ones,
Seek stars in yonder cloudless sky;
But mark no steadfast path for me,
A comet dire and strange am I.

. . . .

Between extremes distraught and rent,
I question not the way I go;
Who made me, gave it me, I deem,
Thus to aspire, to languish so.

But Comets too have holy laws,
Their fiery sinews to restrain,
And from their outmost wanderings
Are drawn to heaven's dear heart again.

And ye, beloved ones, when ye know
What wild, erratic natures are,
Pray that the laws of heavenly force
Would hold and guide the Mother star.

Julia's children were a complex source of pride and pain. The first difficulty Julia encountered with her babies was the problem of overwork. Julia, who had, as she put it, "floated *en l'air*" for so long, found only herself to rely on when it came to the daily press of business. "The baby must be fed at regular intervals," her daughters remembered, "and she must feed it. There must be three meals a day and she must provide them; servants must be engaged, trained, directed, and all this she must do."[1]

The burdens of having children so closely spaced were substantial.

When you become the mother of two children, you will understand the value of time as you never understood it before. My days and nights are pretty much divided between Julia and Florence. I sleep with the baby, nurse her all night, get up, hurry through my breakfast, take care of her while Emily [the nurse] gets hers, then wash & dress her, put her to sleep, drag her out in the wagon, amuse Dudie, kiss, love, scold her, etc., etc. . . . I have not been ten minutes, this whole day, without holding one or other of the children, and it was not until six o'clock this evening that I got a chance to clean my teeth—at meal times, I have to sit with Fofo on one knee, and Dudie on the other; trotting them alternately, and singing Jim along Josie until I can't Jim along any further."[2]

In addition, steady pregnancy and nursing took a serious toll on her health. "I am not well able to write," she told Louisa. "Writing, sewing, anything that requires attention causes me at once to feel giddy and faint—I cannot even make Dudie's little clothes or work on my worsted work for it makes me feel ill."[3]

The children were frequently sick, always a cause for anxiety and more sleepless nights.[4] Even teething, with its accompanying fever and diarrhea, could be dangerous if it were summer and dehydration threatened. Nursing her sick children was something Julia did well, but it was one more task to sap her energy.

A life confined by the demands of pregnancy, nursing, and small children not only was hard on Julia's health, but it was also a bit dull.[5] She longed to spice her existence with evening parties and musical afternoons. But any hopes Julia had of extending her social success in London to the halls and parlors of

Boston were fading. Likewise, her chances of setting up a salon where music, philosophy, literature, and benevolence could mingle dwindled rapidly. "Dearest old absurdity that you are—am I to write to you again? is my life not full enough of business, of flannel petticoats, aprons, and the wiping of dirty little noses? Must I sew, and trot babies, and sing songs, and tell Mother Goose stories and be expected to know how to write?"[6]

Not only were the babies an impediment; so were her parlors. Situated in South Boston, the Institute was a long drive from Beacon Hill. An omnibus ran between the two locations, but it appeared only once every two hours.[7] Julia was simply too far off the beaten track to attract many visitors.

Another dimension to the problem was the tightly knit quality of Boston society. She was no longer a novelty, and Julia quickly discovered that an imported New Yorker, married to an unsociable philanthropist, did not have much drawing power. These circumstances erased the automatic social status that she had claimed in New York. She found herself in the midst of a city that felt intolerant, narrow, and conservative. Gone was the access to liberal Unitarianism that she had enjoyed with Mary. Julia now confronted a different Boston. "The fashion of the time was conformity," Julia remembered later. "Woe to the man or woman who should be detected in raising a new issue or in manifesting [as Chev did] the smallest tendency to be held at variance with the popular standard."[8] Under these circumstances, invading the formal parlors of the "Puritan cousinhood" was no easy matter. The most prestigious circles consisted of interrelated families, some of whose members might not be on speaking terms with the others of their clan.[9] Julia felt herself "wondering and floundering" as she tried to get a foothold on Boston's strange social ladder.[10] She found her neighbors essentially cold, critical, and inhospitable. One day, while passing the Charles Street Charitable Eye and Ear Infirmary, she read the name aloud and remarked to her companion, "Oh, I did not know there was a charitable eye or ear in Boston!"[11] Later she remarked to Louisa, "I cannot swim about in this frozen ocean of Boston life in search of friends—I feel as if I had struggled enough with it, as if I could now fold my arms, and go down."[12] Not even her friend Mary Ward could help. She had married a Bostonian and settled in the city, but she and Julia had drifted apart after Julia's marriage. Family responsibilities made visits difficult, and, as Mary became less interested than Julia in religious philosophy, the two found themselves with little in common.

Compounding her troubles was Julia's lack of experience in giving dinner parties. She forgot to serve the rolls, or she lost the ice cream, or the lamps, long neglected by the cleaning rag, blew out during dinner.[13] Her gift for friendship that would later embellish her life could not overcome her lack of skill or her status as a "stranger." This was a blow to Julia, for social success was one of the few avenues of achievement open to women and one of the few things she desperately wanted. The demands of children, the nature of Boston society, and her own occasional awkwardness put this dream out of reach.

Julia was fortunate in having two loving sisters to confide in. Louisa's marriage to Thomas Crawford in November 1844, followed by her prompt removal to Rome, deprived Julia of one source of comfort, however. Now her only link to "dear Wevie" was letters, and these took weeks to arrive.

> I miss you more than I can tell—it was too desolate to go into your room last night, after you had left it—too desolate to go to ride, and come back, without the hope of seeing any dear, familiar faces, and then to sit down to my solitary tea.[14]

She dreamt of Louisa at night, glad even for this brief "visit" and teased a little:

> Oh dear old fat Wevie! for one good squeeze in your loving arms, for one kiss, and one smile from you, what would I not give?[15]

In the days before telegrams, telephones, and 747s, the squeeze, the kiss, and the sisterly smile were all but unobtainable. The distance was as complete as if Louisa had lived on the moon. No wonder Julia whispered to Julia Romana one night, "I hope my darling that you will never have a sister who will go away to Rome and leave you."[16] Her letters did, at least, give Julia a chance to vent her disappointments. She confessed her sense of failure as a wife. Her heart was aching, she wrote, with the realization that she had "given up all else on earth to make one man happy and have yet failed utterly to accomplish this."[17]

> My dearest, dearest Wevie, I hardly know what in my little, small, quiet life, may be deemed of sufficient importance to tell you. I still live the same subdued, buried kind of life which I used to live when you were with me. . . . My voice is still frozen to silence, my poetry chained down by the icy hand of indifference.[18]

By April 1845, despite the arrival of spring, Julia's first long depression began. A sense of numbness, insignificance, and hopelessness soaked through her usual cloak of cheerfulness. "I have been in a sort of frozen sleep—scarce knowing or feeling anything." She felt herself sinking into "dimness, nothingness and living death."[19] Her heart she described as a "burnt ship," her life as "resemblant unto those famous Sodom apples—round and rosy without but ashes within."[20] "God only knows what I have suffered from this stupor—it has been like blindness, like death, like exile from all things beautiful and good. . . . I pray that I may die rather than relapse into that brutal state of indifference."[21]

This indifference abated in June 1846, when the Howes moved into their first real house. This was the old farmhouse that Chev had bought in the winter of 1846 with Julia's money. Renamed Green Peace, it would house Julia and her family intermittently until 1881.

At first Julia was enchanted. She secured a little space for herself. "My spirits have risen wonderfully since I left the Institution," she wrote Louisa. "My little corner is so green and pretty, so quiet and hidden from all."[22] The rural quality of her new home pleased her. She rejoiced in her flower beds, the abundance of trees, her endless supply of strawberries, even in her productive little cow.[23] She began to spend time outdoors. She even boasted, "I have been transplanting trees and digging in the earth."[24]

The house was not large. A sitting room, kitchen, and side room constituted the first floor, and there were four small bedrooms above. The house had required considerable repair, and even with the addition of a dining room, conservatory, more bedrooms, and a greenhouse, the building could never be considered attractive. Nonetheless, it was Julia's first real home, and she was delighted with it throughout the summer.[25]

In her new surroundings, all sorts of domestic tasks seemed more pleasant. She wrote to her sisters about her children, delighting in their beauty, their good health, and their new accomplishments. With the aid of a "useful little receipt book," she began preserving some of the fruits that Green Peace produced in such abundance. Housekeeping was so much easier in her new "snug corner."[26]

By fall, however, the faults of the house became more apparent. It was damp, drafty, and subject to leaks. Biting east winds tore across Boston harbor and whipped the orchards and shrubbery. And it was just as isolated as the institution. To her aunt, Julia commented that "Sumner is the only unmarried man who ever visits me, and he does not come oftener than once a month."[27]

A lack of bachelors made the Howe parlors unattractive to Boston's eligible daughters. An invitation there was easy to pass up, especially if other receptions were available where young men were likely to appear. Julia, so fond of company and conversation, found herself utterly alone. "Yesterday was my first Friday at home, and I dressed myself quite nicely, opened the two parlors, and remained from twelve till two o'clock in readiness to receive visitors—none came but the Everetts, nor do I expect ever to see many people at my receptions."[28] It was during this period of isolation that Julia wrote in desperation about her situation. "I have had nothing but myself to write about—for four months past I have seen and heard only myself, talked with myself, eaten and drunk myself, made a solemn vow to myself every morning, and condoled with myself that I was about to be left to myself for another day. Oh cursed self, how I hate the very sight of you! do stay away one day, and send me somebody else's self to keep me company!"[29]

The new location did not solve Julia's other problems either. Servant troubles persisted; Chev was grumpy and overworked; constant nursing was "pulling down" her health. Julia wrote to her sisters in a minor key, confiding her loneliness and Chev's coldness: "it has been so long since anyone loved me."[30] She fought the numbness and indifference that characterized her depressions by consciously putting on a cheerful face, but the winter blues gripped her as hard in 1846 as they had in 1845.[31]

Julia found it a great relief when, in the winter of 1846-47, she moved herself and her two children to Winthrop House, a fashionable boarding hotel in the center of Beacon Hill. Here was the freedom from housework and from Chev's critical eye. More important, here Julia found people to sing with and women friends to walk with. Chev took her to the theater. Best of all, she found a successful way of entertaining at last; she invited heterogeneous groups to Saturday evening parties featuring music, dancing, and ice cream.[32] Her affairs were not fashionable, but they were a stepping stone to greater success.

Chev encouraged Julia's "little parties," especially as her group broadened to include some prominent Bostonians. Not only were Chev's old friends the Longfellows and the Feltons in attendance, but also Carys, Motleys, and Storys. Frequently Greek, Italian, and French names appeared on Julia's guest list as political changes in Europe sent small waves of liberals to Boston.[33] A mysterious flirtation emerges from her accounts of these happy days: "*my dear beau*, almost always makes two appearances," she told Annie. "I dress with care every day, make my hair very smooth, and clean my teeth with powder—from this you may gather that my smiles are somewhat more in request than formerly."[34] To Julia, who appreciated the attention of men, this recognition of her existence had a bracing effect. Whatever Chev might say of her inadequacies, Julia felt reassured by admiration.

Julia returned to Green Peace in the spring of 1847 in high spirits. She had recovered from a bout of scarlet fever in February, she had fitted up a new study for herself, and she could now make use of a carriage and horses, which freed her of dependence on the Boston omnibus.[35] She basked in the feeling that Chev loved her; she felt he was more interested in her pursuits than he had been previously.[36] When she left South Boston in April to nurse Annie through her first confinement, she wrote to Chev with great affection. "I cannot, cannot tell you, my darling husband, how I long to be once more under the shelter of your wing—my heart has ached ever since you left me, though I have tried somehow to dream away the time."[37]

Julia felt happier about her children, too. Florence amused her with her toddler antics.[38] Of Julia Romana she wrote, "We shall never, never have such a beautiful child as she is, no, not if we went through our whole alphabet."[39] Best of all, rejoiced Julia to her sister, "Flossie is nearly twenty-two months old and there is, as yet, thank heaven, no prospect of a successor."[40]

Julia's good spirits began to wane once more during the fall of 1847. In fact, as early as May of that year, her recently acquired composure had begun to slip. The old longings for a literary career asserted themselves, despite the pleasure her children brought her.

"Is not your heart fully satisfied with such a sight you will ask me. I reply, dear Wevie, . . . that I am glad, in the midst of all my comforts, to feel myself still a pilgrim in pursuit of something that is neither house, nor lands, nor children, nor health—what that something is I scarce know."[41] These inchoate feelings, without form or outlet, pulled down Julia's spirits. As the fall began, she entered another season of "oppressive melancholy and sorrow" compounded by the loneliness of her "utter seclusion" at Green Peace. She was pregnant with her third child, Henry Marion, or Harry, and the prospect discouraged her. Her letters complained of physical discomfort, the trials of night nursing, and the intellectual stagnation she feared would accompany the months following the baby's birth.[42] Chev's irritation at her handling of ordinary household matters fretted her, as did her lack of time for study. To Louisa she snapped, "I have spoiled a good student to make an indifferent wife."[43]

To Annie she confessed, "Dudie [meaning herself] has not been well and her natural insanities have returned upon her with more force than usual, so that she has been utterly sad and disposed to silence." Her mind was restless; she dreamed of ghosts and spirits. "Oh do you know how beautiful that austere vision of death looks to one quite bewildered with the perplexities of life, how consoling, how soothing the thought of that sleep of the new creation. All the gifts of God are good—were it not strange if he kept not the best for last?"[44]

Part of Julia's unhappiness came from an increasing sense of isolation from her family. Louisa was still in Rome, tied to her household by two new babies; Francis Marion was in New Orleans, and his death of yellow fever in September 1847 came as a shock to Julia. Manny had always sustained the greatest interest in the welfare and comfort of his sisters. Julia, tied down by family responsibilities, to say nothing of a third pregnancy, could not attend his funeral or burial. Denied the consolations of ritual, she put her loss into poetry.

> I am modest, I am mournful
> Thou mayest crush me 'neath thy feet,
> I'll not even say, tread lightly,
> Death itself from thee were sweet.[45]

Annie, too, was no longer at hand. After drooping through two dreary winters in New York, Annie had brightened at the attentions of dashing Adolphe Mailliard, adviser and cousin to Joseph Bonaparte of France. In June 1846 this wealthy, handsome young man married the youngest Ward and whisked her away to Bordentown, New Jersey. Here he served as caretaker for the Bonapartes' American villa and stables.

Certainly New Jersey was accessible, but Annie could no longer visit Julia at the drop of a hat any more than Julia could count on instant hospitality from Annie. Husbands presented complicating factors; Chev thought nothing of changing travel plans on a whim.[46] Julia wrote longingly to Annie, "Oh! dear hot water bottle, if you were only here—I think of you as one of my greatest earthly comforts."[47]

Even dear Sam, always her champion, could not be counted on. Owing to a series of financial mishaps, Sam was no longer welcome in South Boston. The problems began at the end of 1846 when the Wards and the Primes forced out their partners, Gracie King and James Gore, for encroaching on the firm's profits.[48] The firm reorganized as Prime, Ward, & Company, with Sam as partner. He then invested in a good deal of unsecured commercial paper. By the end of 1847, the firm was bankrupt.

Sam was widely blamed for "very extravagant speculations in flour" and for buying up large amounts of insecure debt. Julia felt, with Sam, that he was not entirely to blame, since the more sober and senior partners in the firm had assented to these ventures.[49] Nevertheless, family bitterness fell on Sam's shoulders. No one welcomed him, least of all Chev. Julia remained loyal to her brother, exhorting her sisters to forgive him and explaining away some of his peccadillos. "Let us think tenderly of him, he is our only brother," she wrote.[50] She advised him about Boston publishers who might pay him for his work, and she pleaded with Chev to lend him some money.[51] Despite these efforts to soften the family's hard feelings, Julia had to wait a full year before Sam was accepted in her house.

Sam was not the only Ward affected by the upheaval. Uncle John, too, felt its aftershocks. Although Chev did not condemn him for the disaster, a certain shift in relations took place. Uncle John seemed old and frail; the bankruptcy had shaken him to the core.[52] He no longer could claim the superior wisdom with which he had justified his management of Julia's trust. When Chev suggested, in the summer of 1848, that he resign his trusteeship, Uncle John made no protest.[53] Chev had himself made trustee in Uncle John's place, thereby achieving more control over Julia's assets. He hoped, too, that his maneuver would make his purchases of South Boston land in 1845 fully legal.

At the time of the change, Julia's assets were still considerable. Sam had avoided mingling his sisters' funds in his speculations, so the chunks of Manhattan real estate remained secure. Convinced that this land would never bring a good return, Chev began to sell it off. The profits he put into more South Boston land, confident that this chilly peninsula was going to be the next Beacon Hill. (The filling in of the marshes behind Charles Street had not begun, so Chev had no way of knowing that the expanding city would push out into the harbor rather than south.) Chev's gamble was a losing one. Frequently taxes and repairs cost more than rents brought in. Chev's investments, all made with Julia's money, swallowed up her great income.

Chev's control over the trust, his real estate ventures, and his moral victory over his in-laws did not soften his feelings toward Julia. His treatment of her continued to be erratic. Letters from the period reflect her frustration and bewilderment at Chev's behavior along with her desire to understand and love him. To Louisa she wrote: "[My unhappiness] is partly, sweet child, the result of an utter want of sympathy in those around me, which has, like a winter's frost, benumbed my whole nature." "I had some good quiet days with Annie before the others came, and had time to penetrate somewhat into her condition of mind. Like all of us, she has had to sacrifice many illusions—marriage is not what she expected and men still less. Like us, after dreaming of perfect union of minds, intimate sympathy, etc., she will have to fall back somewhat upon her own resources."[54]

The two most difficult things for Julia to endure, surrounded as she was with young children, were Chev's dislike of any physical contact (except that which was likely to produce pregnancy) and his stony silence when he was angry. The first was hard for Julia because she would have loved cuddling, especially if it did not put her in danger of conception. Although she never relaxed into the unabashed sexual frankness of her parents, she clearly delighted in physical affection and complained from time to time of Chev's reluctance in this regard: "Chev is the same old Chev—sometimes a little grumpy, never fond of kissing, yet I hope and believe, truly fond of me."[55] She dared not ask for the affection she wanted. "I long for the sound of your voice, for the sight of your face, I would say, for a thousand kisses, were I not afraid of vexing you and making you say 'get out you beast.' "[56]

When he was angry, Chev rebuked Julia by refusing to say a word to her. This was an especially harsh treatment for Julia since her eyes, burned by lime confetti in an accident in Rome, could not function in artificial light. On long winter nights, when she could neither read, write, nor knit, she sat miserably while her husband ignored her. To her aunt she wrote: "What I would not give for a little cheering from you tonight! . . . I have been alone all day with my husband who, being out of sorts, has hardly spoken one word to me in twelve hours."[57] A letter to Annie conveyed Julia's jumble of confused feelings. "Chev is better than when you saw him, and is most kind and very dear to me. . . . Crawford [Louisa's husband] thinks I am afraid of him, and so I am, inter nos, but that does not keep me from being tenderly attached to him."[58]

Although the lack of improvement in her marriage was a source of great unhappiness to Julia, more unwelcome still was the third, unwanted, pregnancy. Julia had wanted just two children; she could hardly rejoice as the string of siblings grew longer and longer.[59] "Anna Shaw (Mrs. Green) called the other day and asked me if I was not delighted at the prospect of a third child. I could not say that I was. I am wicked enough to hope that my child will be a girl, that she may bear the name I have long ago given her, that of Dolores."[60] She wrote along similar lines two years later, when she was pregnant with Laura. "When the unwelcome little unborn shall have seen the light, my brain will be lightened, and I shall have a clearer mind. The time wears on—thank God, that even this weary nine months shall come to an end and leave me in possession of my own body and my own soul. . . . I cannot bear to think of the child—do not make it anything—it will be a monster or an idiot, I fear."[61] Four and one-half years later, a miserable Julia confessed her dismay at a fifth pregnancy, telling Louisa she did not even want to see the baby when he or she was born.[62]

Julia dreaded the pregnancies for a combination of reasons. She still worried that she would die in childbirth. She regretted the loss of mental strength and resiliency that accompanied her pregnancies, and she dreaded the numbing fatigue that characterized her days and nights when her children were infants. The physical discomforts of pregnancy plagued her, too, rendering her temper "not heavenly."[63]

Most of all, Julia desired work independent of her family circle. She thought she had more to offer the world than just her offspring. "It is a blessed thing to be a mother, but there are bounds to all things, and no woman is under any obligation to sacrifice the whole of her existence to the mere act of bringing children into the world. I cannot help considering the excess of this as materializing and degrading to a woman whose spiritual nature has any strength—men, on the contrary, think it gratification enough for a woman to be a wife and mother in any way and upon any terms."[64]

Added to these considerations were the annoying Victorian conventions about behavior proper to pregnant women, in particular that expectant mothers should not reveal their new proportions in public. Julia put up with these dicta to an extent. "I have grown dreadfully out of shape. . . . I still adhere to corsets, but with difficulty, and am going to have some [made up] with elastics, and without a bone in front. I keep out of sight as much as possible, and make myself as genteel as possible when I do go out."[65] But in fact she entertained no intention of staying cooped up indefinitely with her noisy brood. Nor did she suffer much from false modesty. She went out in her carriage, sometimes driving herself. She took the children on picnics and even went bowling. Just before Laura was born, she took the omnibus to South Boston, "climbed up to the Wrights, at the top of the Institution, and afterwards walked over to Green Peace to see Donald" and back to Chev's office.[66] In all, this was a drive of some five miles and a two- to three-mile walk.

Julia's large family implies that she did not use birth control. Julia seems not to have heard abut the methods some women employed to limit their fertility; if she had, she would likely have communicated this information to her sisters as she did information about chloroform.[67] The main obstacle to family limitation, however, was Chev: he had no sympathy with it.[68]

This left Julia with the one method of contraception she did understand—abstinence. She used nursing as her excuse. "I have utterly excluded poor Chev from my chamber à coucher, am I wrong? I will *not* run any risk of being obliged to wean my baby, for I have seen, with my own eyes, the difference between a child teething with the breast and without it."[69]

Julia's perception of the link between nursing and pregnancy is interesting. Historians and breast-feeding advocates claim that nursing prevents conception. Julia's experience had been the other way around—pregnancy with Flossy had ended the nursing of Julia Romana—and she did not wish to repeat the experience. Hence abstinence, not nursing, looked like the best possible contraceptive. To this end Julia not only requested Chev to stay out of her bedroom, but she also kept babies in bed with her.

> Oh little rascal [Florence], can all the pangs of dentition constitute a sufficient excuse for the manner in which you kick, pummel, scratch, claw, and roll over your mama, from night until morning, not to mention sundry libations of exceeding warm water, which make the bed exceeding cold, and constitute a pleasant surprise for mama, when, turning over from a newly-made puddle, she plumps into the old wet one of the temperature of zero, and trying to find some dry thread to draw about her, finds that baby has been entirely impartial, and that neither nightgown nor chemise can complain of having been neglected.[70]

Chev disliked this policy. He could not understand why Julia did not want to have more children. The fear of childbirth he dismissed as "wrong & wicked. . . . The pains & perils of childbirth are meant by a beneficent creator to be the means of leading them [women] back to lives of temperance, exercise, and reason," he assured Louisa.[71] As a consequence, Julia went on bearing children until she was forty. Ultimately, her best form of contraception was menopause.

Although the pregnancies were unwelcome, the babies themselves were loved as soon as they were born. In letters to Annie and Louisa, Julia recounted her childbirth experiences with directness and delight. "I suppose Annie wrote you of my ridiculous accouchement," she wrote Louisa after Harry's birth.

I took two walks on the day of the child's birth—I wrote with a pillow at my back, all the morning, but feeling a slight twinge now & then, I put my writing safely away, & got all my things ready. . . . I thought I would have my tea upstairs, but Sumner came in & I was called down. I had not sat in the parlor ten minutes before the real labor pains came on—I got upstairs as well as I could—threw the india rubber sheet on my bed, myself on it, and *wished* for the chloroform—Chev coming in, I sent the maid for some, & Sumner for Fisher or the nurse—Chev & I were alone in the house but the child was born, after half an hour's labor, without any assistance. I suffered very little for the head, but as Chev did not know how to assist me I had to make a tremendous effort for the shoulders & gave one horrid scream, the only one of which I was guilty. Chev soon gave one himself: oh Dudie! it's a boy! I couldn't believe it—we both cried and laughed. . . . I had very severe afterpains. Now I am well and even very stout for me—I have a quantity of milk and the boy thrives on it wonderfully.[72]

·To Annie she wrote of Laura's birth:

It was the easiest I have had yet . . . got up at seven and went to breakfast—staid at home all day for the first time this winter—thinking that I should not have another dinner for some days to come, I ordered a capital one and did justice to it. . . . I went down to tea and after tea sat in the parlor, entertaining Theodore Parker. I began to get worse, and at half-past nine concluded to send for the nurse, and went upstairs to get ready. . . . Chev was summoned but refused to remain. "I shall hear you downstairs before you shall want me," he said and descended to the library to finish a letter to Mr. Mann. I sent for him again, however, and after half an hour of severe pain, the child was born. I had resolved not to scream, and did not. Indeed, it was scarcely worth while, for such short suffering. I had no physician, and did not mean to have one. Chev tied the baby and everything was just right. The baby was of the smallest pattern—six pounds & a half in weight—she looked like an insect. I supposed she had been exercised half to death—her arms and legs looked as if they had been parboiled. This was because there was such an unusual quantity of water. She was born with a good appetite, began immediately to suck her fingers, and in the space of an hour began to cry so lustily that I was forced to put her to my breast, where she thought fit to remain all night.[73]

Whatever her regrets during pregnancy, Julia always loved her newborns. She thought them the dearest, the prettiest, and the hungriest of all babies, and described them fondly in her letters.[74] She also seemed happier when she was actually nursing her babies than when she thought about it.

You complain that no one tells you about Florence. Oh! she is a perfect angel. . . . She is much more robust than Julia was at her age—she eats nothing but me, and has as much tittie as she can accommodate, and often rather more. . . . I cannot leave my Florence for more than two hours at once, and I will not have her fed, while I have milk for her—everyone says that I am an excellent nurse, for the child has grown tremendously, and does not have any colics, though I eat whatever I like.[75]

Julia recommended to both her sisters that they try nursing their children, advising them to rest, drink plenty of water, eat plain food, and be patient. She was equally direct and just as full of advice when it came to weaning. "I believe that there it is not thought safe to wean a child as late in the spring as May—in Rome I should think the beginning of April as late as one would dare do it." Describing her own success in that department, Julia wrote to Louisa: "These darling children, they are growing like weeds—it seems quite strange to me to have no baby, but Flossy often asks to see her 'Tittie' and pulls it out and kisses it."[76]

As with all other aspects of baby care, Julia was ready to talk about and offer advice concerning toilet training. "If it would not be very naughty I would tell you, too, that when she [Flossie] want to make pipi, she cries out to have her didi taken off, and to be held out, in Wardie's fashion, which being done, she performs in the most satisfactory manner."[77] Since Wardie was a male cousin, this was an original method for training her daughters.

The birth of her third child, Harry, brought Julia a surge of energy and the relief from her typical depression. For the next eighteen months, she enjoyed family, friends, and a sweet taste of literary success.

In May 1848, Julia made a visit to Bordentown with Julia Romana and infant Harry in tow. Annie was expecting her second baby when she invited Julia, and Julia was delighted to comply. They spent three congenial weeks together, with visits from Sam's second wife, Medora, and his young daughter, Maddie, to round out the family party. Julia and Annie sipped caudle, knitted and sewed, and talked endlessly of marriage and children. Julia returned to Boston with a newly clarified perception of marriage, which helped, for a time, to salve her disappointment about her own marriage. "Marriage is not an affair of happiness," she wrote Louisa. "It is a contract . . . it is a relation in which we assume grave obligations to other people and it is quite as important that we should make them happy as to be happy ourselves." Julia admitted that she had been "bitterly and dreadfully unhappy" at times during her marriage and that "vast and painful longings of my soul" lay unsatisfied. Nevertheless, she hoped to cultivate a "spirit of humility, of gratitude, and the love of *uses* upon which my Swedenborg so insists." By focusing on duty and action, Julia believed she could overcome ill feeling. She planned to set her marriage on a new plane of obligation rather than on "hopes of the perfect union of minds, intimate sympathy, etc." Furthermore, as she said bluntly, "If I could be free tomorrow, it would be difficult for me to find as kind a guardian, as pure and noble a man."[78] Practically speaking, Julia decided to settle for her debilitating marriage because life without Chev would not be any easier.

Philosophically, Julia still held herself, as a wife, responsible for the success of her marriage. Yet throughout the letters of this period are glimpses of new thinking, bold rejections of the conventional roles of wife and mother. Julia was not yet ready to rewrite the script of women's lives, but beneath her determination to please Chev lay conflicting impulses that could not be shoved aside for long.[79]

Nevertheless, Julia returned to South Boston in good spirits, ready to reconcile with Chev and to revitalize her social life. She had already masterminded one successful affair, a banquet in honor of Horace Mann, before her visit to Bordentown.[80] Now she was ready to build on her success. She presented "a neat little dinner" for Chev's friends, consisting of "soup, salmon, sweetbreads, roast lamb and pigeon with green peas, potatoes au maitre d'hotel, spinach and salad. Then came a delicious pudding and blanc mange, then strawberries, pineapple, and ice cream, then coffee, etc." In addition, she entertained her friends Mary Ward, Jeannie Belknap, and Sarah Hale.[81] To Annie she boasted of another successful party, illuminated by gas lamps with lots of food, musicians, and "polking." A party for the Wormleys complemented this success, and Julia prepared for a busy social season in town.[82] At last the Boston matron was enjoying a little of the social life she had craved as a young girl in New York and had tasted as a bride in London.

This social success was all the sweeter because literary success accompanied it. A few of her poems were published in *Lays of the Western World*, as well as in Griswold's *Female Poets of America*. Publication in Griswold's volume was a source of great satisfaction to Julia. She could bask in the knowledge that not all her talents were hidden under a bushel, even if she did not have sufficient funds to buy herself copies of these volumes.[83]

These small successes were the results of some writing she had attempted during the spring of 1847.[84] She wrote a series of poems concerning "Eva and Rafael," two characters that would reappear in later efforts. She did most of this for her own amusement, intending that no one should see them except herself.[85] Her success with Griswold, however, encouraged Julia to continue writing for the public. After Harry's birth, she determined to "give up the world and cut Beacon Street" in order to study and write, and from that point onward Julia produced a steady stream of poetry, plays, and stories for both private and public consumption.[86] Among these were children's plays to be acted out in the nursery, just as *The Iroquois Bride* had once been performed by the Ward children. *Beauty and the Beast* and *The Goose and Golden Eggs* were two of the folktales Julia adapted for her children. She wrote as well a more serious play, *Telma*, dealing with the First Crusade.[87]

Julia had something more, in the spring of 1849, to interest her. Trailing her daughters Annie (age three) and Jennie (age two), Louisa had landed in New York for a long family visit. Apparently the sisters shuttled back and forth between New York, Bordentown, and South Boston to see one another. At length, Louisa came to stay with Julia during the late fall of 1849 and early winter of 1850.

By this time, however, Julia's spirits were again sliding downhill. As usual, Chev's behavior seemed timed to torment Julia. In October she described her predicament to Annie. "Louisa has had but a humdrum time of it, I fear—you know how gloomy the house is. . . . Chev sits in the library—Crawford and Louisa in the dining room—I flit from one to the other, quite uneasily, having nothing to bestow any where but my tediousness. We are all heartily glad when bedtime arrives. . . . I am too, too sick at heart, it seems to me, to do more than vegetate anywhere. The pressure of an endless discontent which weighs upon me from without is enough to break a spirit stronger than mine."[88]

Winter brought no improvement. Julia was now seven months pregnant and could not avoid the fact that a fourth child would soon fill the nursery. She was so unhappy that she feared she would affect her unborn baby. This fear of "marking" her child was the first of its kind for Julia and, as such, a measure of the depth of her discouragement. She went on to confess to Annie that she no longer felt like "the old Dudie." "In her stead a spirit of crossness and dulness, insensible to all the gentler influences of life, knowing no music, poetry, wit, or devotion, intent mainly upon holding on to the ropes and upon getting through the present without too much consciousness of it."

Chev continued to fret Julia. At Christmas he berated her in a "long and most painful talk." Julia was overcome, and she cried herself "almost ill."[89] She suffered acutely thinking that "Chev almost hates me, and I wish I could cut my throat. He is dissatisfied because I try to study a little, & do not teach the children—he is perhaps right, but my mind is much too confused and puzzled to decide upon anything. I only feel as if my death were the one thing desirable for his comfort. . . . I should like to know how it feels to be something better than an object of disgust to one's husband."[90]

Chev persisted in thrusting his ideas and methods into the domestic routine. With obvious self-interest, since Julia would not allow sexual intercourse while she was nursing, he advised her to end the nursing period earlier than she intended.[91] Although his pressure was not effective, it was another strong signal that Julia could not count on control of any matters conventionally within her sphere, even the most personal ones. Chev continued his earlier attempts to control the education of the children, a field that was generally considered the province of mothers. His plans fluctuated wildly: first a German nurse, then a governess to teach French and Italian, then a school, then Julia to function as teacher, then another school.[92] This frustrated Julia; she never knew from one month to the next whether she would be presiding in the nursery, instructing in the schoolroom, or enjoying some time to herself.

There was a total lack of shared interests and sympathies. As Chev moved increasingly into abolitionism, Julia turned increasingly inward. Julia tried showing Chev her poetry, but he only passed it on to his friends to review. Their "cold praise and ardent criticism" was more than Julia could endure and she found "the comparison with Longodingdongo (Longfellow) utterly insufferable."[93] She vowed to keep her efforts to herself from now on.

Nothing, not even the addition of their son and heir, Henry Marion Howe, in 1848 had done anything to change the old patterns of anger and misunderstanding. By 1850 Julia continued to think she was generally inadequate and stupid in the face of household responsibilities, and Chev reinforced this with scoldings and threats.[94]

To survive, Julia sought relief in the sort of stories and articles that had brought her pleasure after the birth of Harry. She continued to read, especially Swedenborg. Reading and studying not only provided a respite from Chev's torments and the children's demands, but it also suggested a way that Julia might regain the sense of competence, relief, and integration she hadn't experienced since the spring of 1842. Study had broken down the walls of depression then; perhaps it might do so again.

However, as Julia pressed on with the studies that helped her survive psychologically, she annoyed Chev further.[95] In response, he continued to press his influence over the household. This created an unfavorable imbalance of roles. Julia could not claim the power and respect deeded the mistress of the house since Chev claimed responsibility for domestic arrangements. Her status as a hostess, though much improved, was not significant enough to improve her prestige with Chev. All she had left was the shaky ground of literature and publication. Since she feared the description of "bluestocking" for herself, Julia could not adopt that role definition either. All that was left to her, as she saw it, was the physical fact of motherhood and the responsibility for rearing small children.

She rejoiced when the older girls could go to school, writing to Louisa that it was an "immense relief to have them out of the way for a little while."[96] While Julia certainly cherished her children, she had her limits. It was not until she was an old woman, enjoying her grandchildren with a mixture of physical distance and emotional detachment, that she waxed ecstatic about the virtues of mothering. While she was engaged in that busy role, she longed for some relief.

Julia was no lady of leisure despite her middle-class status and her several servants. Every moment of study, thought, writing, or self-improvement was wrung with difficulty out of an exhausting schedule. "My house plagues me, my servants neglect, my husband scolds me."[97] No wonder the fourth baby in six years seemed so discouraging. Yet when Laura was born in February 1850, "parboiled insect" though she appeared, Julia once again enjoyed the sensations of delight that her babies always inspired.

The news that she was to accompany Chev on a trip to Europe also gave Julia's spirits a boost. This trip would include a long stay in Rome with Louisa's family. She hoped that this would improve her prickly relationship with Chev and that they could draw closer together.[98] Also, although it pained her to leave behind her older girls, the prospect of a reduction in family size, combined with the hope of inexpensive Italian nannies, cheered her up considerably.

After a flying visit to New York to say goodbye, Julia buckled down to the task of packing. With the surge of energy that had characterized the spring following Harry's birth, she tackled "the piles of things that can't be done by any possibility! The baby's shirts and nightgowns not ready, the house in town not sold, the country house half-rented! Was there ever such a man as Chev? Still, one lives through many things, and all this week of worry and discomfort seems little compared to those wretched days in which you saw me so overcome with sorrow."[99]

The question of caring for the children was a vexing one. Ultimately, Chev decided to leave Julia Romana and Florence with the Edward Jarvis family in

Concord, hoping that they would be happier together than if they were left in different families.[100] This plan had one flaw, however. The Jarvises maintained a school for retarded children in their home, and Julia Romana and Flossy were uncomfortable there. They could hardly wait for their parents to return home.[101] Harry and baby Laura were to go with their parents to Germany, where Chev would take a water cure for his headaches. From there the family would travel south, settling down for the winter in the Eternal City.

Late in 1848, Julia wrote thoughtfully to Louisa, "I am myself much changed, but it is time I were, for next spring I shall number thirty years. Thirty years—some of them have been good, and some very evil—God give us all rest."[102] By the time Laura was born in 1850, Julia was nearly thirty-one and had no reason to change her assessment. Some of her days were indeed good, others unpleasant. The seven years of marriage had been complicated, with a difficult husband, four children, a constantly shifting series of servants, and a succession of dwellings to adjust to. Julia had battled at least two serious depressions and one other period of discouragement and unhappiness. Growing social success had provided some diversion, but the more important fields of marriage and domesticity lagged far behind social success as achievements that Julia could point to with pride. Even motherhood was a mixed success, for it took an enormous toll on her health and spirits. "God help me," she wrote Louisa, "if all my life is to be like [the last four years]."[103]

Yet these years had taught Julia a great deal. The strong bonds among the sisters sustained Julia through many difficult times, and she valued them more than ever before. "Of all womankind," she wrote them, "you are nearest and dearest to me."[104] So they would always remain, even as Julia broadened her contacts with other women after the Civil War. They had taught her the value of womanly company in general, and it was their support that provided the model for Julia's later relationships with women. "Sisterhood" began with Louisa and Annie, and it eventually stretched to encompass women from Minneapolis to New Orleans, from Italy to San Francisco.

Julia learned, too, during these years of marriage and motherhood, of the particular usefulness of writing. Earlier she had poured her excess religious anxiety into poetry; now she released her disappointment and thwarted affections through various letters. For the rest of her life, Julia turned to plays, poetry, fiction, and letters to help identify, catalog, and release her feelings, particularly her negative ones.

Although poetry and plays were obvious vehicles since they allowed Julia to fiddle with reality and create an emotionally satisfying world, even her letters show a propensity toward emotional release. At the same time, by articulating her woes, Julia was able to put her emotional life in better order. It was no wonder that Julia believed that her pen, her closest ally and consolation, would be her ticket to popular acclaim.

Julia's writing had not, so far, produced the great work she hoped one day to leave to posterity. The first seven years of her marriage, given over entirely to Chev and to babies, had seen very little writing, except for her letters.[105] The second seven years would build on those early efforts, however, producing dozens of poems, a novel, and a play in addition to various other scraps of writing. Julia spilled her emotions onto paper, tried out various ideas, and earned a measure of public recognition. She would no longer have to turn exclusively to Chev for sympathy or pleasure.

SIX

Passion Flowers, 1850-1854

To my fiery youth's ambition
Such a boon were scarcely dear
"Thou shalt live to be a granddame,
Work and die devoid of fear."

"Now as utmost grace it steads me,
"Add but this thereto," I said:
"On the Matron's time-worn mantle
Let the Poet's wreath be laid."

The years 1850-1854 were transitional ones for Julia. They had several characteristics in common with the seven years of marriage that preceded them, including difficulties with Chev, money troubles, depression, and the demands of young children. Yet beginning with her second trip to Rome in the winter of 1850-1851, Julia began to make some changes in her life. She lived on her own for a while in Rome; she developed a small network of male friends; she published a book of poetry; and she reestablished her presence in Newport. None of these things gave Julia the strength to reclaim the power she had lost to Chev or even to confront him with the emotional agony he was causing her. She continued to turn inward and to look to herself for solutions. Yet these small steps enabled Julia to begin defining what she needed most, some sort of emotional and intellectual life independent of Chev.

The second trip to Europe gave Julia her first opportunity to enjoy such a life. Julia and Chev stopped first in England. From there they journeyed to Paris, picking up Louisa's husband along the way. Their next destination was Boppard-am-Rhine, where Chev sought relief from his headaches. From there they went to Heidelberg to meet Louisa and her two daughters, as well as Annie and her one child. Babies, nurses, mamas, and their accompanying paraphernalia filled up two-thirds of an entire diligence. Customs officials did not even try to inspect them. "Baby baggage," one muttered as he waved them through.[1]

As the family group headed for Italy, Chev dropped out of the party. Julia and he had enjoyed some pleasant moments: "rambles upon the hillside, musings among the ruins, and jaunts upon the waters."[2] Nothing, however, could induce him to travel to Rome. He could not leave the Institute for more than six months, and he was too restless to enjoy the prospect of drifting through another Roman winter.[3] Julia's hopes of a leisurely vacation in which to rebuild ties of loyalty and affection with her husband came to an abrupt halt. Chev returned to South Boston, rescuing Florence and Julia Romana from the peculiar care of the Jarvis family. The girls were grateful; they would always feel a special loyalty toward their father for his early return to them.[4]

Julia, Louisa, and Annie arrived in Rome in late October. Julia found a small apartment not far from Louisa's home at Villa Negroni and immediately set up the kind of informal housekeeping that suited her. The artist Edward Freeman lived above her, and Mrs. David Dudley Field lived below. Whenever any of them entertained, a great swapping of lamps and teacups occurred since no one could boast a fully outfitted pantry or parlor.[5] Once she had secured a grand piano and a winter's supply of firewood, Julia felt ready to renew her acquaintance with Rome.

Italy was a "paradise for intellectual women" in the mid-nineteenth century.[6] Margaret Fuller, whose example of womanly talent and achievement stirred many of the intellectual women of the time, had led the way to Rome in 1847. Julia, who wished intensely to emulate Fuller's literary success and to claim some of her stature among the Boston-Concord Transcendentalists, must have seen the parallels between their two cases. Obviously Julia's marital status was different, but both encountered Rome without husbands, and both hoped to find physical independence and intellectual freedom in the Ancient City.

Opportunities for artistic and philosophical conversation abounded in Rome. Julia seems not to have been adopted by any particular circle, perhaps because her political ideas were beginning to take shape along the lines of Chev's liberal views. Rome had just entered a period of reaction against the liberalization of Pope Pius IX, and liberal politics were in disrepute. Julia's pointed questions about the pope's retrenchment and her readiness to argue about Italian politics may have made her difficult company. Nevertheless, she found herself drawn into Roman-American circles as the sister-in-law of Thomas Crawford. She attended the balls given by artists, intellectuals, and socialites, and she formed friendships with members of this group.[7] The social freedom was delightful. "After the privations entailed by maternity, the weakness and physical discomfort, the inevitable seclusion . . . I found myself free and untrammeled. . . . I was absolutely intoxicated with the joy of freedom and used to dance across the great salon in my sister's apartment, singing 'Liberty, Liberty.' "[8] Julia's liberty caused gossip, some of which inevitably reached Chev. Most likely the heart of this gossip centered around a young man named Horace Binney Wallace. A poet and writer, Wallace was exactly the sort of free spirit who appealed to Julia. She quickly fell in love with him.

Actually, there was nothing impressive about him, at least not outwardly. Friends described him as "slim, but not tall," "refined, high-bred, and delicate," and "not handsome." He was distant and shy toward most people. His intimates, however, found him "frank, cordial, and communicative," and they praised his intellectual abilities and sweetness of disposition.[9]

Julia Ward Howe and Horace Binney Wallace seem to have liked each other instantly. Perhaps both felt the pull of a kindred spirit. Wallace's upbringing and education had been urban and conventional, as had Julia's. His emotional life was as troubled as hers was; his biographer describes him as a "solitary melancholy youth of morbid sensibilities," subject to severe emotional disturbances. Both were in Rome seeking retreat, Julia from Chev, and Wallace from the depressions that he feared were driving him insane.[10] Both were lonely, poetic, sympathetic. To discover one who had suffered on the verge of insanity, as she felt she had, was a great relief to Julia. They spent hours together discussing her poetry, Wallace offering the most helpful criticism Julia had yet encountered.[11]

Her *Reminiscences* talk of rambles over the city and of Wallace's jest that "the highest effort of nature is to produce a rosso."[12] But these sedate sentences hardly reflect the emotions that churned within her. In a poem of the period she describes the elation and despair of having her capacity for love rekindled by an attractive young man.

> If thus it be sin to love thee,
> Tis hers who has given thee birth
> Tis God's who flung down for the jousting
> A gem of his own to earth.

Oh! Mother, twas not for our comfort
Thou madst him so heavenly fair
Oh! God didst thou set him to hallow
The brink of unloved despair?

Torn by the responsibility toward Chev and love for Wallace, Julia questioned the forces that had drawn them together. How bitterly unfair it was to find a soul as philosophical and poetic as hers—and out of reach! In poetry she imagined a resolution.

And yet it seems to me a time must come
When every morn shall find me at they side
When placidly toward our celestial home
Together down life's stream our barks shall glide
When my sad soul unfearingly may drink
Joy from the deep light of thy lustrous eye
Nor deem that joy a crime, nor start and shrink
Lest poison in those stolen glances lie.[13]

In actuality, no such resolution offered itself.

This friendship occasioned a bitter correspondence between Julia and Chev, most of which Julia later burned. Certainly the reports of Julia's relationship with Binney had unraveled further the already tattered fabric of Chev and Julia's marriage. Chev's suspicions were high and his dignity wounded, while Julia's feelings had been wrenched by conflicting loyalties. In a letter to Louisa, however, Julia recalled some of the feelings that attended these days of accusation and retort. "When you remember me in Rome, dear sister, try to remember how much there had been to unsettle my mind, how utterly I seemed to have been cast adrift, and given up to the caprices of fate. I felt sometimes the pleasure of a naughty child in being bad. I had been much tormented—I liked perhaps to torment others."[14] There is a suggestion here that Chev demanded his wife's return, at the price of his own faithfulness and their marriage. Julia resisted this pressure, but at length her days of independence could be prolonged no more. In the summer of 1851 she sailed home, stopping briefly in London, where she befriended journalist Edward Twisleton and his wife, Ellen. From England she sailed home, leaving behind her life of independence and encouragement.

Julia never saw Horace Binney Wallace again. Despite plans to meet in New York at the end of 1852, their paths did not cross; Wallace left for Paris before Julia could make the journey down to meet him.[15] Julia was forlorn:

"I miss you so much and life is so short and friendship so precious." At a loss about her poetry, Julia needed his direction. More than that, however, she wanted a friend. "I need to be practically reminded that Love is a Religion of Life, and who can bring us back to its standard if it be not one who is dear to us? . . . You must not forget me. I am too lonely, too helpless, too orphaned to be deserted by you, my brother. Life brings us too little occupation for the heart—he must prize and make the most of any *dear* relation it brings us, for indifference lies widely all around and in us."[16] Julia never sent this letter. Word reached her, shortly after she finished it, that Wallace had committed suicide.

When Julia returned to South Boston in September 1851, however, she had no reason to think that her friendship with Horace Binney Wallace would end abruptly just sixteen months later. Her spirits were high. Travel, freedom, love, and work had had a bracing effect. Julia felt resilient and confident. Furthermore, Chev seemed genuinely glad to have her back. "Chev is kind . . . my absence has been the best thing for both of us. I feel stronger than I did and bear all things better than I had been able to some time before I left," she told Louisa.[17] To Annie she wrote, "My nerves are steadier and my temper more tranquil than of old."[18] Her Roman trip had given her "a little firmness and independance"; she felt "calmer and more self-sustained."[19]

Julia had not given much thought, during her absence from Chev, to the connections between her depressions and Chev's treatment of her. She had learned to write better poetry, and she had found that she could indeed run a household on her own. She refrained, however, from using these accomplishments as weapons with which to challenge Chev's constant criticism of her. Instead she put all the responsibility on herself, vowing to try harder and to do more to please her husband.

By assigning herself full responsibility for the welfare of their marriage, Julia avoided a confrontation with Chev as well as a confrontation with the social ideals and values that contributed to and justified Chev's domination. She did not yet challenge the popular stereotypes that prescribed self-denial and self-sacrifice for wives, but not for husbands. She avoided these confrontations in part because she was so isolated. She had no one with whom to share her discontent; even her sisters failed to understand the sources of her dissatisfaction. She also genuinely wanted to make her husband happy.

Whatever his faults, Chev had many fine qualities, Julia believed. His courage in championing the neglected and downtrodden segments of society appealed to her, as did his dedication to all causes that fostered progress. In her private writings, occasional comments suggest that she admired him in spite of their differences. "He is much led by flattery, and prizes above all a certain obsequiousness which always implies a want of character in those who show it. . . . He is yet *un des hommes du bon Dieu*. I have told all his faults in these few lines, but if I should begin to speak of his perfections, many pages would not suffice."[20]

When he was kind, Julia enjoyed the company of an energetic husband whose mind and interests ranged widely, who was consistently kind to their children.[21] She told herself that marriage was "not simply an affair of happiness" and that she should be grateful to Chev "for many kindnesses, for much that embellishes and elevates my life."[22] In a poem published in 1857, she wrote the most romantic thing about Chev that she ever composed.

> Let it content thee that I call thee dear—
> Thou'rt wise and great, and others name thee so.
> From me, what gentler tribute wouldst thou know
> Than the slight hand, upon thy shoulder laid,
> And the full heart, high throbbing, not afraid.
>
> No, not afraid—of manly stature thou,
> Of power compact, and temper fervor-tried—
> Yet I, a weakling, in thine armour hide,
> Or, sick beyond the medicine of Art,
> Hang on the healthful pulses of thine heart.
>
> In waking dreams I see thine outstretched arms
> That conquer night and distance for my sake
> Like the brave swimmer who was wont to break
> The crystals of the deep in shivering light,
> To bless his Ladye with his radiant sight.[23]

Determined to please Chev after her taste of independence in Rome, Julia confined herself to a simple domestic routine of studying, writing, and caring for children. "I do not intend to go at all into society, this winter," she told Annie, "but shall devote myself to my children, my studies, and the care of my health."[24] Hydropathist that she was during these years, Julia faithfully took a vigorous nighttime walk and a cold bath every day.[25]

This was certainly a recipe for staying out of trouble with Chev, who disliked parties and wanted Julia to devote herself to domestic duties. It was also the old recipe for depression, especially since Chev quickly began to resume old patterns of behavior very quickly. The kindness and patience that had greeted Julia when she returned home began to wane. By the fall of 1852 Julia and Chev were in conflict again. "Chev's sourness of disposition becomes too dreadfully aggravated by any success of mine," Julia wrote to Annie. "He was miserably sick every time he came to Newport [where Julia had gone for a short August visit] and fearfully cross—would not go out anywhere, and was strangely indignant at my enjoyment of society, which was indeed, very moderate."[26]

Chev seemed firmly opposed to Julia's doing anything except caring for the children. Perhaps the memory of Julia's Roman winter and her flirtation with Wallace reinforced his reluctance to see Julia shine at social functions. More threatening than Julia's appeal to other men, however, was a sudden spurt of social success. Julia had been hobnobbing with intellectuals and dancing with nobility while abroad. She found it easier to attract people to South Boston, and she received invitations to social functions.[27] This was an avenue to power for upper-class white women of the time, and Chev could see Julia beginning to progress up the ladder. In November 1852, when Julia was showing off her social flair by hostessing a lavish dinner, Chev sabotaged the affair. He refused to assist Julia with any detail, and when the dinner was served, he forbade any wine at the table. In answer to Julia's protests, he conceded that she might entertain a few friends once a week at tea and whist. "What an ass he must take me for! Do you think that Giant Despair ever gave tea parties?"[28]

Chev's mean-spiritedness began to take its toll on Julia's good humor. "Having lost the elasticity produced by my pleasant Roman life, I feel worn out and weighed down just as I used to feel before I went away."[29] His treatment of Julia also contributed to her melancholy.[30] Their antagonism was aggravated by Julia's delay in weaning Laura. At twenty months, Laura still slept in her mother's bed, which meant that Chev did not.[31] Chev responded with familiar devices, which intensified Julia's melancholy. For example, Chev resumed his practice of not talking to her in the evenings. In a poem of the period she described their relationship.

> Between us the eternal silence reigneth
> The calm and separation of the tomb;
> Though still thy face thy ruddy hue distaineth
> Where whiteness would astonish, but for bloom
> We'll keep a silence words shall never waken
> A severance no changing time can join
> Each thinks as each, apart and joy-forsaken
> Each pledges each in uncongenial wine.[32]

The collapse of Julia's spirits continued during the winter of 1853, with news of Wallace's death contributing substantially to her already large burden of unhappiness. At first she was merely numb. To Annie she wrote, "My sensibilities are much exhausted—I shed few tears for him—it was rather like having had a limb amputated while under the influence of Chloroform, and then waking up and feeling the loss in the *want*." Never had she had a companion so completely in tune with her feelings and tasks since she and Harry had rambled the Catskills.[33] Now, just as she had found Harry's death difficult to accept, she found she could not easily deal with Wallace's suicide. As the year wore on, Julia's numbness gave way to grief. She wore mourning on his account and she confided her anguish to Annie. "Oh! my dear—this sorrow departs not from me, day or night. I always loved him, but I did not know how much until I lost him."[34] Later: "This is a loss which rends my life apart."[35]

Julia's gloominess increased. "I cannot remember any period, even in my worst days, in which my nerves have been so completely worn down. . . . I am devoured with discontent, the feeblest, wretchedest form of misery."[36] Julia complained of depression and a constant struggle against a "constitutional discontent."[37] She began to worry about madness, recalling her terrifying brushes with the "spirit world" that had plagued her in the late 1840s. The news that a Beacon Hill friend, Susan Bigelow, had succumbed to insanity touched a chord. Now two of her sensitive, poetical friends had been pushed over the brink by a cold, indifferent society. One was insane and the other was dead. To her friend Edward Twisleton she unfolded her bitter analysis of the cause of their—and her—misery. "How she [Susan Bigelow] did reprove that cold undemonstrative [New England] temperament, content with loving (if at all) in the most distract manner, leaving those who claim affection to determine its existence, if they can, by logical and scientific tests, not showing it daily and hourly, in its simple and genuine form."[38]

Julia's melancholy during 1852 and 1853 had another familiar component. As in the past, money problems complicated both her relationship with Chev and her own sense of well-being. Chev had, within three years of signing the prenuptial contract, effectively overturned it. But he was not content. Perhaps Julia's Roman venture was a signal to Chev that he did not control his wife; as long as she was still theoretically claimant to a large fortune, he never could. In February 1853 Chev convinced James Mills to turn over his trusteeship of Julia's property. The receipt from this transaction reveals that Julia was a wealthy woman, with capital totaling almost $60,000. All of this was invested, with the exception of around $3,000, in notes, bonds, stocks, and, of course, the disappointing South Boston land.[39] Julia could get her hands on none of it. Chev had thoroughly and completely transferred the entire control of Julia's property to himself.

The real sting in this was that the Howes were strapped during 1853 by a lack of ready cash.[40] Chev impressed upon Julia the meagerness of their resources. This hurt Julia particularly because lack of funds endangered her newfound social acceptance. She noted that the Coolidges of Beacon Hill snubbed her for want of money and that she received very little notice at balls because of her shabby dress.[41]

Julia attacked the problem with good business sense. She knew of a legacy under the control of her cousin, Charles Ward. To her sisters and to "Cozie" himself she wrote, ferreting out the interest he had withheld.[42] In July she recovered $375 of this money, which she lodged in the hands of her old friend, Samuel Grey Ward, Mary Ward's brother. Complaining that Chev had "greatly distrained our pence in these latter times," she assigned him the care of her money, intending perhaps to pay off (quietly) any bills that she might decide to run up without Chev's knowledge.[43]

Julia's direct approach to Charles Ward about her legacy and her decision to entrust Samuel Grey Ward with it were bold steps. Never before had she fought back when Chev had tried to control her money. If her year in Rome had not forced her to recognize Chev's role in her depression, it at least taught Julia that she could cope on her own, and this lesson survived even the renewed attacks of despondency.

Julia counterattacked Chev's moves to curb her autonomy in other ways. After the death of Horace Binney Wallace, she began to seek alternative sources of male approval and guidance. Her friendship with Wallace had shown her that some men, at least, would take her seriously. She had also learned the dangers of gossip and the pitfalls of romantic attachment. From now on, her relationships with men would be purely intellectual and above reproach.

Gradually during the mid-1850s Julia turned to the great Transcendentalist minister Theodore Parker. Julia probably heard about Parker soon after her arrival in South Boston.[44] The parishioners of his church, the Twenty-eighth Congregational Society, were a blend of working people and middle-class reformers who agreed with Parker that true Christians should take an active role in reforming society. Parker invited Julia to his Sunday evenings at home, where she met all of Boston's important thinkers. Theodore Parker and Julia

Ward Howe exchanged books, sent each other German translations, and debated points of philosophy.

Henry Wadsworth Longfellow, too, became her friend. In the 1840s Julia had resented the praise heaped upon him. Now she abandoned the passive role of envy to make friends with the poet. She began to write regularly to "Longo" for advice about her poems. It was he who helped her edit the poems for *Passion Flowers*, her first book of poetry. He also assisted her with various aspects of its publication.[45] Since Chev disliked the theater, Julia attended performances with the Longfellows, for which they secured the tickets.[46] Longfellow was a good enough friend that Julia could talk to him about her health and could even banter with him. "Won't you write something about me, as an offset to Whittier's lines on Chev? The Heroine would do as well as 'The Hero.' Chev, Whittier says, was merciful to a wounded Greek, but have I not been merciful to all men in only marrying one?"[47]

Wallace, Parker, and Longfellow all supported Julia's first efforts at independence. As established men of letters, they could advise her about the intricacies of editors and publishers. Julia knew of no women who could provide equivalent advice. She did, however, continue to turn to her sisters for support in other areas of her life. She continued to write to them both, freely pouring out her anxieties and woes. Her special treat was a journey to Bordentown, where Annie pampered and consoled her. And in 1856 the three sisters enjoyed a more satisfactory reunion in New York and Boston.[48] The moral support of Annie and Louisa, combined with the guidance of male mentors, strengthened Julia's determination to resist the financial and marital pressures besetting her.

In the summer of 1853 Julia's spirits improved somewhat. A boost to her morale came from an unexpected source, her husband. Chev had undertaken at the beginning of 1853 the editorship of a struggling abolitionist journal, the *Commonwealth*. He had hoped this new position would help ease his cash-flow problems, but he found instead that it paid irregularly while soaking up all his time. He deputized Julia to do what editors of nineteenth-century journals did so often—fill up his columns with reviews, essays, and editorials.[49] She told Twisleton that the job was a grind and that she was writing a good deal of "trash." Journalism, she decided, was a "Bad School."[50] Of course, Chev had no objection to all this writing. When she wrote at his bidding, for his purposes, and under his supervision, he had no qualms about Julia's authorship. Some of Julia's "trash" got good reviews.[51] This experience confirmed for Julia that she could write for a popular audience, and the taste of acclaim was sweet.

In addition, Julia had the year before found another resource with which to bolster her spirits and steady her self-confidence. In the late summer of 1852 she returned to Newport for the first time in thirteen years. She renewed her acquaintance with the town and in particular with her father's old Newport house. She romped with her children during the day; at night, she went to parties escorted by Albert Sumner, her husband's friend and Charles Sumner's brother. These were "particularly happy" days; Julia was in her element socially.[52] Touching base with her distinguished Rhode Island heritage helped her, too, strengthening her resolve to lead a "real, vigorous life," as she believed her ancestors had.[53] Furthermore, the trip had boosted Julia's hopes for a place among Boston's intellectuals. Assembled with her at Cliff House were Henry Wadsworth Longfellow and his wife, Fanny; Fanny's brother, Tom Appleton; George Curtis; the Freemans; G. W. Coster; and Count Adam Gurowski, a political refugee from Poland, then the pet of Beacon Hill.[54] Gurowski gave the literary company the title "Hotel de Rambouillet"; Julia was their Madame de Sévigné.[55]

Newport life was an alternative to the drudgery of South Boston. At Newport Julia's recognized place as intellectual and aristocrat provided an antidote to Chev's constant efforts to master her independent spirit. And because its climate was renowned as healthy, Julia could claim frequent visits as essential to her well-being. Indeed they were, for throughout the rest of her life, Julia would draw strength and comfort from the old seaport. When Julia set off to Newport again in July 1853, the climate and the company worked their usual magic on her. Fortified by this summer excursion, Julia forged ahead with a daring plan, one that would realize a childhood ambition: she decided to publish a volume of poetry. She proceeded without telling Chev, fearful he would halt her project if he knew about it.

Longfellow suggested that Julia publish anonymously and that she give her book the title *Passion Flowers*.[56] To Ticknor & Fields she confided her manuscripts, pledging them to secrecy.[57] Intrigued by the anonymity and by the surprising passages of strong imagery in the poems, Ticknor & Fields agreed to publish.

All during the fall of 1853, Julia led a double life. She poured over her poems as they metamorphosed from handwritten scraps to galley proofs. She hid all evidence of her literary career from Chev in hopes that he would never find out about her authorship.[58] Finally the work was done. In December 1853 Julia saw her first volume of poetry appear in print.

Passion Flowers was a success, running into a second edition almost immediately.[59] Its anonymous authorship tantalized the public, especially since the offices of Ticknor & Fields had let slip the rumor that the author was one of Boston's own matrons. The poems stirred interest in their own right as well. Their romantic and religious themes fit neatly into the mainstream of popular taste, and the occasional surprising personal revelations titillated Beacon Hill.[60] Friends gossiped about stanzas like these:

Often at midnight, on the cold stone lying,
My passionate sobs have rent the passive air,
While my crisped fingers clutched the pavement, trying
To hold him fast, as he had still been there.

I called, I shrieked till my spent breath came faintly,
I sank, in pain Christ's martyrs could not bear;
Then dreamed I saw him, beautiful and saintly,
As his far convent tolled the hour of prayer.

The voice fled heavenward ere its spell was broken
I stretched a tremulous hand within the grate,
And bore away a ravished rose, in token
Of woman's highest love, and hardest fate.[61]

May I turn my musings to thee
In my wintry loneliness?
May my straggling measure woo thee,
May my deeper thought pursue thee,
Till thy sunlight, striking through me,
Pause to fertilize and bless?

I, methinks, could speak, unfearing
Fault of blemish to unfold,
Blots, the soul's deep beauty blearing,
Tortuous scars, the frail heart searing—
In such wise and gracious hearing,
Life's arcana may be told.

. . . .

Friendships fragile and diurnal
I have wrought me in my time,
Out of sympathies most vernal,
Dreams that charm Life's childish journal,
Images of loves eternal
Broken in the play of Time.

But these gifts of Nature's lending
We should hold to permanence;
Loftier growths, more nearly bending,
Heart more nobly heart befriending,
Eyes that in their deepest blending
Cannot lose their heavenward glance.

Fate's pure marble lies so whitely,
Formlessly, between us cast,
I have wrought and studied slightly—
Thou who knowest all things rightly,
From my heart's love, but not lightly,
Mould a Friendship that shall last.[62]

Chev was outraged when the rumors he had heard proved true.[63] He could scarcely believe his wife would seek "notoriety" by publishing, especially when she knew he did not approve of it. During the first months of 1854 he refused to speak to Julia at all except to criticize. Her fragile emotional balance, which she had recovered sufficiently in the fall of 1853 to publish her poetry, disintegrated.

Her eyesight, always painful, was aggravated by her tension; she could hardly scribble a legible hand.[64] To Twisleton she wrote of a recent diagnosis of her difficulty, calling it a "nervous debility," which it certainly was. "When I write with intensity, I feel a compulsive rigidity throughout my face and hand."[65] Only bed rest could calm her.

Poems of the period suggest the intensity of her depression. "The Shadow That Is Born With Us" describes "the weight that hangs upon my soul." Another dismal poem describes a mother who, while singing to her children, is overcome with grief "Till the breath of song was stifled,/And tears burst forth instead."[66] In both poems, the woman described is not only sad, she is inexpressibly so, burdened by sorrow that she can neither articulate nor relieve.

"Sadly lowered in spirits," Julia struggled not to cry lest she further damage her eyesight.[67] In May she suffered a "crise de nerfs" brought on, she believed, by her efforts not to cry and by Chev's extreme unkindness.[68] She described her "horrible depression" to Annie: "I had at that time one fit of raving hysterics, I was perfectly mad, and rushed from room to room like a wild creature. Chev happened to be at home, and was thoroughly frightened. I became calm at length, but had to go to bed, and finish the day there. I had been having these crises for some days—ever since then he has treated me very kindly, and has not done anything to plague me."[69]

Julia's "fits of hysterics" succeeded in capturing Chev's solicitous attention for a while.[70] To Louisa she wrote in July, commenting that having "nearly driven me to insanity, so horribly did he behave," Chev was now "much less unkind." This improved relationship was temporary, however. Julia returned to her old view that the responsibility for maintaining a good marriage was hers. She tried hard to please her husband so that his "fits of perverseness" would abate.[71]

Julia had other reasons for feeling miserable; she was expecting her fifth child.[72] This baby had been conceived in 1854 as a result of Julia's efforts to placate Chev. In the spring of that year, Chev had requested a divorce so that he could marry a more devoted young woman. Julia either had to renew sexual contact with him or lose Chev, and, by his demand, two of her children. In a painful letter to Louisa, Julia described her feelings.

> After three years of constantly increasing unkindness and estrangement, no alternative presented itself before me, but that of an attempt at reconciliation or a first separation. The latter had been all along in Chev's mind, and was so favorite a project with him that he would bring it up even in our quietest hours when there was nothing whatsoever to suggest it. His dream was to marry again—some young girl who would love him supremely. Before God, Louisa, I thought it my real duty to give up everything that was dear or sacred to me, rather than be forced to leave two of my children, and then the two dearest, Julia and Harry. In this view, I made the greatest sacrifice I can ever be called on to make. . . . I am no Fanny Kemble—I can suffer and die with my children, but I cannot leave them.[73]

To keep her marriage intact, Julia renewed sexual contact with Chev, with predictable results.

The summer brought no relief to Julia's oppressed spirits. Chev now advanced a plan for selling the Beacon Hill house where Julia had spent her winters and returning his family to the Doctor's Wing at the institute. Chev knew how Julia dreaded its cold, damp halls, and she must have wondered if this was not some form of punishment. In the absence of complete financial records, it is difficult to tell if poverty or perversity forced the family back to

South Boston. Perhaps the real estate transactions of 1853, when Chev purchased most of the South Boston lots, had already begun to drag on the family income, and Chev really did feel pinched. Whenever funds were low, Chev liked to rent out all the property he owned and to move, rent-free, into the Doctor's Wing.

If money were the problem, then Julia could not help but regret Chev's decision in the summer of 1852 to buy a rundown farmhouse in Portsmouth, Rhode Island, near Newport. This was Lawton's Valley, and in order to make it livable, Chev had to pour thousands of dollars into it, thus impoverishing the family. Julia had no particular attachment to the place at that time, except as an "experiment worthwhile to try."[74] She could not figure out why Chev was so determined to have it when it was not convenient either to his friends or to his workplace.

In fact, Chev continued throughout the middle years of their marriage to move Julia around a great deal. Their daughter Maud attributed this tendency to his "restless temperament." "As far back as I can remember," she wrote, "our family life was diversified by frequent movings. . . . We moved perhaps every six months from one habitat to another. There was, besides, the regular hegira to our summer home, Lawton's Valley." The inconvenience in all this was substantial. Although Julia did not usually have to move furniture, since the institute and Green Peace were furnished, she did have to make arrangements for servants, food, linens, wardrobes, books, toys, and the grand piano that went wherever she did.[75]

Chev expected Julia to take all his decisions in stride and to accept them cheerfully. After all, he would have argued, he was head of the household and entitled to make such decisions. Julia would not have attempted to contradict this assertion; indeed, she did not expect to have the final word on choosing a residence. But she did expect to be consulted. Middle-class women, even her own mother, had traditionally enjoyed this "right-of-consultation."[76] Chev did not grant this privilege to Julia, however. His rapid and independent method of selecting residences left her entirely out of the process, even when it was her money that made the transactions possible.

Even if Chev did not consciously intend to harry his wife with abrupt changes of plans and peculiar investments in real estate, his "passion for change" and his independence of Julia's judgment worked to his advantage. Constant change meant that Julia had little incentive to improve her skills and only strengthened her inclination to ignore housekeeping. Why bother to reorganize or redecorate if the future was uncertain? Moreover, as Julia lost both access to her money and control over her living arrangements, Chev cemented his power. He wanted to be the undisputed ruler of all he touched, and Julia, unsure both of her income and of her domicile, could not challenge him.

Chev's motives seem to have been a mixture of his desire to keep Julia off balance and a restless desire to buy, sell, speculate, and make money on real estate. In 1854 Chev told Julia he planned to sell Green Peace. This had been the only house she could call her own, and whatever its faults, Julia was horrified at the thought of losing it. She begged Chev to give up the Newport house rather than sell the South Boston property, a plea she expected would be useless.[77] (Actually, her protests were not in vain, and the family returned to Green Peace in the spring of 1855.) Nevertheless, Julia felt once again, as Chev threatened the roof over her head, that her husband was utterly without sympathy for her. She still could not admit what she would acknowledge later, that Chev needed to control every aspect of her time, energy, body, and money.

Julia had no place to turn during these perplexing, troubled times. Her friends were still few, especially in Boston. There were not yet any women's clubs or places where she could go for diversion. Despite some social successes after her return from Rome, Julia felt that her life was once again sinking into monotony. So boring was her existence that she signed her letters to Annie, "A Blighted Being." The sameness of each succeeding day, exacerbated by her inability to work in artificial light, oppressed her.[78]

To compound her troubles, Julia faced in the early summer of 1854 the probability that Chev was unfaithful to her, despite her efforts to mend relations. "Chev is cold and indifferent to me as a man can be—I sometimes suspect him of having relations with other women and regret more bitterly than ever the sacrifice [her pregnancy] which entails upon me these moments of fatigue and suffering."[79]

Julia believed she was sacrificing her health, her studies, and her leisure to write with this fifth pregnancy, and she had done so at the behest of a man who clearly cared little for her. His suspected adulteries knocked the last prop out from under Julia for a while.[80] She could not claim a successful literary career, control of her household, control of her body, or even exclusive union with her husband. She was wretched.

Julia's despair, combined with her denial of the outlet of crying, brought her close to the "madness" she feared. Portraits of Julia painted in the mid- or late 1850s depict a morose woman clothed in black, with large, dark eyes downcast, head tilted in the manner typical of depressed people, hair drawn back severely, and mouth closed and pensive.[81] The 1850s was a sentimental decade, and perhaps the portraitists were carried away with the gloomy possibilities of Julia's physiognomy. More likely they painted what they saw, a woman worn down by maternity, financial worry, and marital discord.

Yet Julia was more resilient than ever she realized. Her resources for overcoming depression were better than ever before. To an extent she relied on the things that had tided her over during the summer of 1852. She went to Newport; she wrote to her sisters; she composed verses; she made friends; and despite the burdens of her pregnancy, she began to enjoy her children.

When the fifth child, Maud, was born, somewhat ahead of schedule, Julia was, as always, delighted. Julia came quickly to love this new arrival.

When Maud appeared in the nursery, she was confronted with three sisters and a brother, ranging in age from ten to three. Julia Romana was the oldest, intelligent and serious. She was the family favorite, beloved equally by Julia and Chev.[82] High-strung as her mother had been, she had bedeviled her mother as an infant and would prove to be a difficult adolescent. At age ten, however, she was generous and kind to her little sisters and brothers. She wrote stories and poems for them and took them on long walks. With her newest sister, Julia Romana formed a special attachment.[83]

Flossy, eighteen months Romana's junior, was the "flaxen-haired doll," small, quick, and inventive. She made paper dolls, collected pins with the sharpness of a young entrepreneur, and with Romana invented a secret language called Patagonian. Next came the nursery's inseparable pair, Harry and Laura. Six-year-old Harry, two and one-half years younger than Flossy, was the family scamp. His mischief was renown: he put boots down the chimney into the fire, nailed shoes to the closet floor, and once, after he had been put in a closet as punishment, passed the time by snipping all the pockets out of the dresses hanging there. Laura came next, less than two years behind Harry. Almost five when Maud arrived, she was old enough to play games with her brother.[84] Laura was the tender, thoughtful child. After riding her mother's foot until it had become tired, she stopped, patted it, and said, "Poor foot."[85]

Both Julia and Chev appeared to have enjoyed their offspring a great deal. The children served, too, to keep the shaky marriage together. As virtually every conceivable topic—sex, money, housing, ambitions, careers—widened the gulf between them, the children served as links between two unhappy parents.

The three daughters and one son were too dear for either of them to abandon: "What a point of union they make," Julia observed.[86]

Both parents took the children for walks and for swims in the ocean at Newport. Together they concocted plays and charades for the family to enact together, and they gave wonderful children's parties.[87] Once a year, in the spring, Julia invited dozens of children and their parents to Green Peace.

> A donkey carriage . . . afforded great amusement out of doors, together with swing, bowling alley, and the Great Junk. While all of this was going on, the Hales, J. Sumner and I prepared a theatrical exhibition of which I had made a hasty outline. It was the story of Blue Beard. . . . Our play was very successful, and immediately afterwards came supper—there were two long tables for the children, twenty sat at each. Ice cream, cake, blanc mange, and delicious sugar plums—and oranges, etc. were served up in style. We had our supper a little later. Three omnibus loads went from my door—the last, the grown people, at nine o-clock.[88]

Julia devoted part of each day to the children, usually in the afternoons when they read, sang, or danced. The dancing was no ballroom affair, but vigorous, rhythmic activity in which the children acted out stories, using kindling wood as props. Gory tales, particularly *Macbeth* and *Julius Caesar*, were favorites. Julia taught the children foreign songs and nonsense verses of her own devising. Sometimes she played the piano and sang to them.[89]

In the middle of this, Chev was likely to come bounding into the room, full of high spirits. "Sometimes he would put on his great fur-coat and come into the dining room at dancing time, on all fours, growling horribly, and pursue us into corners, we shrieking with delighted terror," Laura remembered. Chev read to the children from his favorites, Scott, Byron, and Pope. He apparently had endless patience with children, even if he did not with his wife, for he allowed them to tag after him at any time of the day or night. He took them horseback riding, or into the orchards he was cultivating at Green Peace, or to the institution to observe the workrooms, or up to his room where they plowed through his bureau drawers looking for old bits of junk that he had collected on his travels.[90]

The company of her children became increasingly valuable to Julia in the mid-1850s, especially since her lack of funds and her return to isolated South Boston kept her out of Boston's social whirl. She found the older girls especially rewarding, and they were often the only sources of enjoyment she had. Beginning in 1852 her letters to her sisters sound the theme over and over again: "The children amuse me more than they did." "I am studious and stay much at home, seeing nothing of the world and little of anyone but the children. They are more and more to me, and atone for many wants and deficiencies of life." "I am full of courage, and very devoted to my two great objects, my children and my studies." "Julia has become my constant companion—she shares my lonely walks and is like a very young sister to me." "I find more comfort and pleasure than of old in the society of my children."[91]

Of course, not every moment was delightful. "The five children seem always waiting, morally, to pick my bones, and are always quarreling over their savage feast. . . . The baby keeps me awake, and keeps me down in strength. Were it not for beer, I were little better than a dead woman, but blessed be the infusion of hops, I can still wink my left eye and look knowing with my right, which is more, God be praised, than could have been expected after eight months of Institution."[92]

The children's poor behavior may have been owing to their inconsistent upbringing. Julia held no strong views about the education of her children, but she did worry about it. Theoretically, Chev controlled these matters, but he never settled on one plan for very long. Sometimes he ordered Julia to do the teaching. Sometimes he did it. From time to time, Chev employed various political emigrés who caught his fancy to tutor his children.[93] Sometimes music and dancing masters—including John Sullivan Dwight, the dean of Boston's musical life—were brought in. The children attended, in addition, schools run by Caroline Willay, Susan Hale, Lucia Peabody, Elizabeth Peabody, and Henry Williams. They also went to the Hilliards' School and the Stevenson School at various times.[94] This sporadic approach bothered Julia. "I am so anxious to place them at a first rate school. He [Chev] will and will not. He will teach them a little. I shall teach them a little—meanwhile, if one believes the old notions, the devil may be teaching them a great deal."[95]

Nowhere in her writings did Julia develop any theory of child-rearing. Clearly she wanted all her children educated, regardless of sex, and she later would develop theories about the proper curriculum for women in higher education. (She advocated courses in religion and the Bible, literature, languages, mathematics, astronomy, and the biological sciences.) In the 1850s, however, Julia had few rigorous notions about the training of her children. She allowed them a good deal of freedom, not only to express themselves in the heavy dramatic roles that had not been permitted in her nursery, but also to roam around the city. Maud recalled that she and her siblings rambled over Beacon Hill freely as children, playing in the streets and even entering the unlocked vestibules of trusting residents when a game of hide-and-seek required it.[96]

Perhaps Julia, remembering her dislike of the restrictions put upon her as a girl, went to the opposite extreme with her own children. Perhaps she did not care much for the sort of mothering then prescribed, believing that if she were going to contribute to the moral regeneration of society, she would do it through her own activities and not through the rearing of children. Or perhaps she was just absentminded and forgot to keep track of all the bodies under her care. (Her forgetfulness *was* legendary. Family tradition has it that Harry once came into the parlor repeatedly while Julia was entertaining guests to ask his mother for some favor. Julia said no each time, but he persisted. Finally she asked the boy why he kept pressing the issue. Harry replied it was because Flossy had told him to. His sister figured that if Harry asked often enough, Julia would forget to say no and say yes.[97])

The friendship of small children, however pleasant, did not satisfy Julia's yearnings. Her problems were too complex to dissolve in the company of Julia, Flossy, Harry, Laura, and Maud. To cope with the currents of anger, ambition, and alienation that surged through her, Julia needed other resources. She turned, once more, to study and writing.

SEVEN

Student and Writer, 1854-1857

Can you read the song
Of the suppliant Bee?
Tis a poet's song
Asking liberty.

In the mid-1850s Julia was in her mid-thirties. She had been emotionally buffeted by Chev for ten years; she had survived by small expedients and by writing frequent letters to her sisters. Julia had begun to assert herself in the recovery of her trust funds from Charles Ward and in the publication of *Passion Flowers*. Now she returned to studying in a serious manner. Studying had been her route out of depression and into a joyful sense of reconciliation and renewal in 1841. Study consequently seemed to Julia a good path to inner harmony. When she resumed her habit of daily study, she chose once again to pursue philosophical and religious questions.

At this time, Julia also wrote more items for publication. These allowed her to release her intense and often unhappy emotions, and they gave her an opportunity to experiment with some ideas about women's status, women's role, and gender identity. Even more interesting than her published works are a group of manuscripts written for personal use, in which Julia expressed herself freely and openly. In all this writing, Julia was not only establishing her independence from Chev, she was also writing to establish an independent inner life. Her writings and her studies enabled her to enter a world of work, thought, aspiration, and reward that Chev could not control.

Her books were essential to Julia. Sometimes, she confessed to Annie, her studies were all that kept her going.[1] Ironically, Chev's encroachment on her domestic sphere helped Julia devote a good deal of time to study. He had, while Julia was absent in Rome, hired a housekeeper named Stanwood to manage the household. When Julia returned, he refused to let Stanwood go;

Stanwood kept Chev abreast of everything concerning the household, and Chev liked things that way. Julia disliked Stanwood, finding her messy and insolent.[2] Chev ignored Julia's protests.

Although this arrangement undermined Julia's already weak status in the household, it did free her from burdensome tasks. The loss of sovereignty in domestic matters was a stiff price to pay, but the compensation was a chunk of time every day to employ as she wished. She chose to study. She developed a systematic approach: "When she had finished her housekeeping duties and taken her morning walk, she went straight to her desk, and spent the morning, and often the greater part of the day, in study and composition. . . . We were not allowed to interrupt my mother's study hours unless there was some good reason," recalled Laura.[3] This was Julia's "precious time," nicknamed "P.T." by her unimpressed family.[4]

Julia also took care to carve out a corner of her own to use as a study. For years this was the landing of the attic stairs at Lawton's Valley, where she could find both quiet and north light and, on occasion, unwelcome yellow jackets.[5] This was a far cry from her girlhood room in New York, lined with yellow silk, where Julia had begun her program of studies, but it was distinctly her own. Julia also experimented with renting rooms, once from a disreputable character, Albert Cornell, the "Old Bachelor of Newport." Not surprisingly, Chev quickly put an indignant end to these arrangements.[6] Whatever her situation, Julia persisted in her studies.

In these studies, Julia sought a religious philosophy that would allow her to cast off permanently the doctrines she had grown up with, while still allowing her a basically Christian orientation. Of orthodox Congregationalism she wanted no part, but atheism could not appeal to her either. In addition, she searched for some explanation of the individual's role in life. What were her responsibilities to God, to a society that had given her the cold shoulder, to a husband who was hostile and even unfaithful? Of the choices she saw before her, which ones were best? How could she justify her choices, once made? These explorations would last for a decade, as Julia moved closer to an articulation of individual moral responsibility that would ignite all her allegiances to reform, particularly to the advancement of woman's place and status in society.

Julia began by focusing on strictly religious issues. She had abandoned a great deal of her childhood training, especially the belief that "all mankind were low, vile, and wicked." She had come to the conclusion that God was a tolerant deity who loved all people, regardless of the religious forms they chose. She had also decided that there could be no hell and no evil force so great it could overcome the "divine power of the divine spirit."[7] She had recognized the male power that had perpetuated the old views, and early on had steeled herself and her sister Annie to resist it. "Do not let Bishop or Uncle or anyone frighten you into any conceptions—tell him, and all others that, even if you agree with them in doctrine, you think their notion of religious life narrow, false, and superficial—you owe it to truth, to them, to yourself, to say so. . . . While your life is the true expression of your faith, whom can you fear? . . . For those duties which concern your own soul, you are accountable to God alone."[8] In the 1850s Julia studied in order to expand her religious understanding from this small base.

Theodore Parker's tutelage opened new worlds to Julia. He introduced her to new ideas that formed the basis of her enduring religious faith. Transcendentalism linked together several modes of Christian expression, at least as Parker saw it. From him Julia learned that in a genuinely religious life meditation and study could be complemented by social criticism and altruistic activity.[9] Parker taught her that to love of God must be added love of justice and love of men.[10] Like his perfectionist friend Samuel Gridley Howe, Theodore Parker believed that the right kind of education—an "*intellectual, moral* and *religious* education"—would prepare society for its redemption. People would "learn to trust their consciences and act on them."[11] To Parker, social activism necessarily accompanied a Christian conscience.

An activist faith of this sort was helpful to Julia. Here was a religion that could help her, in part, to understand Chev. Parker taught that religious passion must flow into channels of activity, into crusades for social betterment. This was also Chev's philosophy, and so, at a time when they otherwise had no intellectual life in common, Parker's version of Transcendentalism linked Julia and Chev together.

The second major influence during this time was Swedenborg. Julia had begun taking an interest in his work in 1847, but it was not until her return from Europe in 1851 that she began to read *Divine Love and Wisdom* seriously.[12] Emanuel Swedenborg was associated with social and religious radicalism. Every sect from the Millerites to the Communitarians claimed some link with him.[13] This was racy intellectual company for Julia to keep. But beyond this, Swedenborg had a great deal to offer her.

There is no existing record of Julia's reaction to the "doctrine of correspondences," the core of Swedenborg's thought. Much of his theory, however, fit into her growing framework of belief. Swedenborg believed in a

117

benign deity, as she did; he saw redemption as a gradual process available to all introspective individuals, as did she. His reformulation of the doctrine of the fall as an expression of self-love and pride, rather than as total sinfulness, made sense to her. She also appreciated Swedenborg's perceptions of religion as a part of one's total life, not merely a set of special obligations practiced at certain times. Like others of her generation, including the senior Henry James, she welcomed the departure from the doctrines of her Calvinist childhood.[14] The honesty, industry, and benevolence that Swedenborg stressed complemented Parker's belief in the practical application of Christian belief, and Julia liked this, too. One of the more curious aspects of Swedenborg's theories was his belief that spirits of all kinds moved freely about on earth and that human beings could talk with them. Julia, who had recently felt that "ghosts" or "the spirit world" were close by, was comforted by this, for it drew off some of the terror they had held for her.

From her close attention to Swedenborg, Julia gleaned another powerful lesson. Christ had chosen a career on earth and dedicated himself to it despite temptations to do otherwise. In this he had relied on God's inspiration and guidance. It was to God's word, and no other, that Christ listened. In this interpretation of Christ, Julia found justification for those independent souls who felt called to follow their own self-defined vocation. People were required to follow the dictates of their own consciences, Julia decided, for those dictates were divinely inspired. She took seriously the Old Testament admonition to heed the "still, small voice" because she believed that it was the voice of God speaking through individual conscience. Julia arrived at the conclusion that American women from Anne Hutchison onward had similarly arrived at: no temporal authority, whether governor, minister, or husband, could tell her how to conduct herself spiritually. Only God could give this direction. Furthermore, this theory could justify disobedience of temporal authority if it interfered with divine orders. Julia did not instantly turn her back on Chev, but she gained courage by listening to her "inner voice."

In later works, Julia could articulate with confidence and clarity the convictions that were growing within her in the mid-1850s. In an undated sermon of the 1890s, she preached that "the still, small voice tells us that God believes in us." We may experience anguish and upheaval as a result of listening to that voice, she warns, but eventually our confidence in God's word will be rewarded by periods of clarity and calm. Julia explicitly equates conscience with the "still, small voice."[15] In another sermon, Julia refers to the voice as "the inner voice who has bidden me to do the greatest thing I could do, to rise to the greatest height I could attain."[16]

In addition to her study of Swedenborg, Julia began to study German philosophy. She had taken her first steps in this direction under the tutelage of Joseph Green Cogswell when she still was in her teens. Now she picked up Hegel, whose *Aesthetik* and *Logik* she struggled with for several years.[17] Into her commonplace book she poured passages she liked, combined with her own observations and criticism.[18] No doubt her study of Hegel confirmed her view that the religious doctrines of her youth were insufficient; it also helped her understand Transcendentalism. Hegel's discussion of the "universal soul," for example, appears in her notes.[19] On the whole, however, Julia found Hegel too obscure to be of much use. "I became convinced that the obscurity of his style was intentional, and left him in some indignation."[20]

Her notes of the time indicate other authors whose works appealed to her, including Michelet, Schleiermacher, and Fichte.[21] She also studied Auguste Comte. Wallace had introduced her to Comte's works during their conversations in Rome. She followed his *Positive Philosophy* with great interest. "The objectivism of his point of view brought a new element into my too concentrated habit of thought," she observed.[22] Comte stressed three stages of thought: the "theological," the most primitive; the "metaphysical," which was somewhat more advanced; and the "positive," the most highly developed. In this last stage, people sought not divine inspiration or any proofs of divine existence, but instead confined themselves to understanding scientific and moral laws. In this connection, Julia picked up the study of astronomy. Apparently neither this science nor Comte's doctrine held her interest for long. Julia was still casting around for an intellectual resting place.

In the spring of 1854 Julia wrote her friend Edward Twisleton that she had dropped Swedenborg and Comte. She disliked Swedenborg's "cumbrous symbolism" and Comte's "atheism."[23] She now turned to Fichte and Spinoza. Spinoza she read "with great interest," becoming "for a time almost intoxicated with the originality and beauty of his thoughts."[24] He remained her principal study for the remainder of the decade, until George Bancroft turned her attention to Kant. Later she would confess that these studies were "rhapsodical rather than systematic," but she found them fascinating during the mid- and late 1850s.[25] If nothing else, the peace of her study and the pleasure of mental discipline bolstered her flagging spirits.

Writing was Julia's third solace, after children and studying. Her literary output during the middle 1850s was substantial and, interestingly, entirely

119

unrelated to her philosophical studies. She wrote to order her feelings and to try out some new ideas. Some of these feelings and ideas emerged in the form of plays or verse. Others were rambling, formless pieces, sometimes in the form of conversations with herself, at other times in the form of addresses to others, and at still other times, in the form of discussions with her alter ego, Sybil.[26] They lack the control of her usual phraseology; tense, person, and topic change rapidly in almost stream-of-consciousness fashion. These private musings, written on sheaf after sheaf of copybook paper, are undated, but evidence points to the 1850s as the time of composition.[27] The dating is important, for the manuscripts reveal a great deal about Julia's state of mind when she wrote them. Most of them reveal a profoundly angry, unhappy, restless woman.

The essay "Universal Truth Cures Special Sorrow" provides a case study.[28] Rambling and digressive, it moves back and forth between first, second, and third person, picking up and dropping various topics with no relation between them. The references are usually veiled, but the overall effect is one of great hostility and disappointment, probably toward Chev. "You and I have had our moments of magnificence and of meanness, our yearling compromises between duty and convenience, our fervent prayer, our dear vision and flaming zeal, our dullness, darkness, concupiscence, and disgust. . . . We have substituted the wretched trash of life for our birthright of integrity." Another section seems directed to the guardians of her youth. "What is your trouble today, dear friends. Your daughter, who had a fit of saintship, two years ago, wise and virtuous beyond her years, has taken to the world again, or indeed, for the first time? insists on dresses, parties, and attentions, and can even confront you angrily with these fair eyes which used to contemplate heaven? . . . This forces you to one conclusion, her religious experience was not genuine, nor of the right kind." This paragraph, written a decade after her first steps toward religious independence in 1841, suggests what Julia's determination had cost her. Ten years later, she was still dealing with anxiety and guilt caused by her defiance of her family.

Bits of unconnected anger float out of the essay. "It would not really inconvenience you so very much if you should sometimes cultivate a little goodly sorrow for a few of the very worst things you do, which might possibly bear the construction of sins. But far be it from me to importune you, gentlemen."

Julia's effort to explain her life, to find the touchstone that would clarify its purpose to her and would justify its direction to others, emerges too. "In all my bad ways, and they may have been worse than yours, I have felt something within me that gave a good clear sound when I did what was honest, generous, or thorough, a muffled uncertain sound when I lost sight of the better motive or intention. . . . And by and by it grew so strong that I was forced to give it my unwilling hand and to say, let nothing in life or death part us. Since that time I have walked in much greater peace." The imagery of the passage is important, in part because of the symbolic marriage ("to give it my . . . hand and to say, let nothing in life or death part us") between Julia and the inner voice ("a good clear sound"). Since a life devoted to Chev was inadequate emotionally and intellectually, Julia invented another partnership to fill the void. Thanks to the guidance of Parker and Swedenborg in the early 1850s, Julia had no doubt by the end of the decade that the sound was divinely inspired and that she should obey it.

Two other pieces, less forceful but equally rambling, deal with Julia's desire for a successful literary career. In "To Write a Book," Julia debates whether she should write novels or sermons. "Olympia's Letters" is full of reflections about publishing. Written after she had suffered two literary failures in 1857, these sets of fictionalized letters vented some of Julia's bitterness about the treatment she had received at the hands of critics.[29]

Another significant manuscript dating from this period is an unfinished novel entitled *Eva and Raphael*. Apparently it was begun as a play in the 1840s, possibly around 1847. After several false starts, Julia gave it up until the 1850s, when she changed the cast of characters. The play then became a novel and a minor character, Laurent (or Laurence), became the protagonist. Although this work is incomplete, the remaining fragments are sufficient to provide a rough story line. The tale concerns not Eva and Raphael so much as Laurence/Laurent, an androgynous character, reared and educated as a man but renounced, at the age of twenty-two, by his father for his sexual inability to perpetuate the family name.[30]

An outcast both because of his sex and by the decree of his family, Laurence begins a series of wanderings. His adventures all revolve around his ambiguous sexual attraction. In one, Emma, a mature and beautiful widow, believing Laurence to be a man, falls in love with him and attempts to seduce him in a scene remarkable for its candid portrayal of feminine sexual drive. When Emma appears in his room at midnight, she pleads with him for love. "I am here alone in your room, in your power, at dead of night—you cannot misinterpret this," she urges.[31] Distressed at this turn of events, Laurence begins a long

121

journey, the difficulties of which reflected the inner turmoils of his/her soul. At this point Laurence becomes Laurent.

During these solitary wanderings, Laurent endures a series of crises, each of which is followed by "an interval of exhaustion and repose." The story ends on a note of crisis. Roland, an adolescent who befriended Laurent earlier, has come to believe that Laurent is a woman. After a dueling scene in which he is stabbed, a bleeding Roland staggers into Laurent's room and attempts to rape him. On this highly charged note, the novel comes to an abrupt halt.

This is exactly the sort of novel that a Victorian (or any) father might forbid his daughter to read. One taboo subject after another appears: seduction, rape, madness, confused sexual identity, sodomy, and that particularly Victorian horror—the burial of a person still alive. The whole tone of the novel is highly emotional, written almost entirely at a fever pitch. The characters are always wrought up—the father is outrageously cruel and unfeeling; Laurent's spiritual visions are ecstatic; rival lovers are passionately jealous; a sensitive musician suffers because of his intense absorption in music; suffocating loneliness alternates with oppressive madness. Ghosts and spiritual encounters are as much the stuff of everyday life as the people in the novel.[32]

The scenes of seduction and rape reveal a strong sexual nature. Clearly the novel offered an opportunity for Julia to express the sexual feelings that were stifled in her life. But if sexual drives came bubbling up in her writing, this was not because of an unreasonable repression of sexuality. Julia denied herself sex in part because she feared becoming pregnant. With Julia, as with countless other women, sex meant pregnancy. Pregnancy, in turn, meant not only the loss of time and mobility, but the threat of depression and, more important, death. Complicating Julia's situation was Chev's disdain for the sort of sex she could enjoy, the cuddling and embracing that would have been an outlet for her passionate nature.

The attempted rape and the seduction scenes bear special mention not only because of the sexuality they symbolize, but also because of the power relations between the sexes that they depict. The rape is a failure, but the message is clear—men are brutal and violent. Roland enters the scene fresh from a duel in which he has been wounded, and he then turns the attack on Laurent. With his "virginity" despoiled, Roland is ready to deflower his feminine companion. The other men depicted in the story have violent natures, as well. The cruel father is hasty and intemperate with Laurence; Laurence's rivals at college steal from and lie to one another.

The only woman character is much more appealing. A widow, Emma, combines learning, virtue, and worldly experience in such a way as to make her irresistible to all the young men of Laurence's circle. She is the very embodiment of feminine sexual power; she knows "what it is to be a woman," in Julia's words. How Julia, in the sexual maturity of her thirties, might have yearned to be in Emma's place. Both of them, however, suffer rejection and frustration, Emma because her chosen is not a true man and Julia because her husband, in addition to threatening her autonomy, held out the alternatives of abstinence (accompanied by his infidelity) or constant pregnancy. In Julia's fantasy world men either disappoint women or threaten them physically.

The novel gives Julia other opportunities to dwell on the virtues of womankind. In a scene where several of his classmates are debating Laurence's sex, Julia turns the direction of the conversation to a defense of women. She has one student insist that a woman's power of feeling is more highly developed than that of a man; another grants women the faculty of instinct. Women's intellectual powers, they agree, are more subtle than those of men. To these qualities, Julia has her characters add modesty, purity, dignity, and adherence to duty. A later scene provides Julia with the opportunity to claim, through still another male character, that the faults of women are merely those that derive from a defective education; if women's intellectual training were not neglected, these weaknesses would fade away. In defending women in general, Julia was also mounting a defense of herself. By asserting the fine qualities of women, she was establishing her own self-worth, in contrast to Chev's constant belittling of her.

As she worked out the theory in her novel, the possibilities for someone with a dual sexual nature began to look distinctly unattractive. She saw in store for the ordinary mortal whose sexuality was ambiguous nothing but loneliness, misunderstanding, and pain. The ultimate lesson, reinforced by everything around her, was that gender defined role. Without a clear gender definition, a person had no place in society. He or she was condemned to a life of "solitary wanderings on earth." Anyone who stepped outside of a gender-based role definition was doomed. To a woman with high ambitions, this was a sober conclusion.

The novel also suggests some of what it was that plagued her when she thought she was close to insanity. Laurent describes various stages of "madness" in the course of the story. "When the passionate music and the angry discords of life have been hushed and silent enough for the soul to hear other sounds than those of earth, then the holy dead, the living dead, have walked with me, have spoken with me, and my heart and life have borne the record of their heavenly messages." Ghosts had always been a torment to Julia, and her concern about the ghost and spirit world was heightened during times of depression. The religious training of her girlhood had planted the seeds of this anxiety, for although she had consciously abandoned the idea of hell, she was not sure about the soul's outcome after death; even her study of Swedenborg had not entirely reassured her on this point. "They still live, but where, but how? Are we wholly parted from them, are they forever lost to us? . . . Anxiously and earnestly do we strive to follow their unseen flight through regions imagined . . . until that ancient solemn voice from olden time enters our hearts: 'he shall not return home, but I shall go to him.' "[33]

Indeed, it was death that still gnawed at her soul, a fear that tormented her during every serious depression. That she would duplicate her mother's tragic life and that her children would replay the unhappiness of her own childhood haunted her during her pregnancies. The deaths of her father and brother, which had plunged her into her first major depression, still affected her fifteen years later. In a sense, she had never become reconciled to them, and as she continued to mark the anniversaries of Harry's birth and death in her letters and journals, she kept alive the embers of that painful loss.

Repressed sexual yearning, the beginnings of feminist thinking, and anxiety about death informed the fantastic story of Laurence/Laurent. These same themes appear in other manuscript fragments of the period. An appendage to the story of Laurence/Laurent concerns a family of four grown children: a brother, Berto, and his sisters Briseida, Gigio, and Nina. (Laurence appears in this manuscript, too, but it is not clear whether Julia intended this to be a part of the other work, or whether it was merely a spinoff from it.) Berto allows Laurence to dress as a girl and to join his sisters in their secluded Roman house for the purpose of discovering how a woman's mind works. Berto hopes, too, that Laurence will spy on his sisters and tell him if they have any liaisons. He is also curious to find out if his sisters think Laurence is a man or a woman. Since Laurence is in his male mode in this segment, the whole scene is one of sexual restraint, of sexuality held in abeyance, of true sexual natures disguised, undisclosed, undiscovered.[34]

Throughout the segment there is a titillating overtone—what if the women discover there is a man in their midst? Will Laurence suddenly be seized with masculine urgings, to the destruction of the sisters' virtue and reputation? Nothing of the sort occurs, but the theme of rape appears in several forms in the story. First, the girls tell the story of Eleanora, a virgin, whose lover seduced and abandoned her. Later, they all see a ballet in which the heroine is threatened with "ravishment"; she must spurn the advances of dissipated men. Ultimately she falls in love, submits to her suitor, and dies.

In equating love and death, Julia articulated not simply a common psychological connection, but a very real and present fear. As she had learned from her mother, sex could bring death. In this fragment also, Julia developed her ideas about womanhood. Once again, she defends women. She portrays them not only as constantly threatened by men, but also as unreasonably bound and constrained by them. Men deny women a full education; they prevent them from going out and exploring on their own; they insist on admiring only the most cumbersome clothing in which women cannot move freely. They hold out to women only the dreariest choices—poverty (the result of male carelessness with money), exhaustion through maternity, or a life of dubious morality while they are supported by "reprobates." The character who provides most of this dreary—and angry—analysis is Briseida. She vows never to marry, instead to retain some control over her fate. Of all the sisters, she is the most interesting and determined, a woman who knows her own mind and who dares to be different. She is, perhaps, modeled on the noble women of Goethe's *Tasso*, a work that Julia appears to have studied.[35]

None of these manuscripts were intended for publication. They did not have form or polish enough to win an editor's approval, and they treated indelicate topics. But in this private and protected world of unpublished writing, Julia was able to give voice to new ideas and to enjoy some release of emotion. And in the case of *Eva and Raphael*, Julia had given herself a chance to work out several ideas and characterizations that would appear in her first published play, *Leonora, Or The World's Own*.

This play, produced in 1857 at Wallacks Theater in New York, caused a sensation. It was a five-act drama, with well-known players, Matilda Heron and Edward Askew Sothern, performing the leading roles. Although Julia later admitted that it was "full of literary merits and of dramatic defects," she was enthusiastic about it at the time.[36] When the critics attacked it, her feelings were hurt, though she wrote to Sam about them in a bantering tone. "Much of the abuse bestowed on it should go far to convince you of its merit. . . . 'For so treated they the poets that went before me.' So I am satisfied and gratified even with abuse, though the whole thing naturally makes me grave."[37]

Again seduction and the relationship between the sexes is the theme. Leonora, an innocent country maiden, allows herself to be seduced by the evil

125

Lord Lothair, believing that an exchange of rings between them has sanctified their love. Lothair then abandons her, and the gossiping women of the village revile her until Leonora leaves the village. Lothair, in the meantime, boasts of his conquests to a company of soldiers. One of them, Lorenzo, is so offended by Lothair's treatment of women that he challenges Lothair to a duel. Lothair survives, however, and goes on to marry a woman named Helen. She bears him a baby. Leonora, meanwhile, has given birth. This baby, too, was sired by Lothair.[38]

In the last act, Leonora is revealed as utterly transformed by her experience. No longer innocent and trusting, she emerges as cold-hearted and duplicitous. She contrives a plot to reveal Lothair as a traitor to the prince, hoping that he will hang for this crime. Whatever his faults, Lothair is not traitorous, and his wrongful death leaves his innocent wife and child helpless. Finally, Leonora's brother Edward appears and convinces her of the evil of her ways. Leonora stabs herself and repents her cruelty as she dies.

Although *Leonora* was considerably toned down in comparison to *Eva and Raphael*, it still dealt directly with sexuality. When Leonora is convinced that she and Lothair are betrothed, she throws her arms about him and says, "Take then my love, my soul, my breath of life." When Leonora asks Lothair why he has brought her to a secluded corner of the woods, he replies:

> Ask every thrilling tendril in your bosom
> Ask every pulse that fills your woman's heart
> Ask Nature's mystic priestliness that fills
> This hour with deepening awe . . .
> Or ask these lips that would not speak in words
> But press their burning answer back on yours
> On yours that said, I love thee. I am here
> To claim the bond of your sweet promising,
> To breathe my soul's fond passion on your breast
> And in your kiss receive another soul.

We know the result in a later scene, when he boasts that he left Leonora in the village, "Not leaving all the treasure that I found."

The candid language and frank acknowledgment of sexual passion outraged New York, or at least its male critics. Sam told Julia that these were hypocrites, unable to endure a woman's depiction of passion and portrait of male infidelity. He also acknowledged that her portrayal of the balance of power between the sexes, however truthful, offended some people.[39] Not only did her play stress the power of men to destroy the lives of innocent girls, but it depicted a woman who dared to step out of her sphere to retaliate, a woman who refused to accept the blame for the incident and who did not pine away from shame. Had Julia's heroine suffered the passive, lingering death of regret and submission that was popular in Victorian literature, perhaps her play would have been granted wider acceptance. Instead, Julia portrayed a more uninhibited woman, full of sexual longings, angry at her unjust treatment, and determined to get revenge. Indeed, a long passage in the play defended the dignity and honor of women, even those "frail creatures" that "pay your [male] pleasure with her sacrifice."

> . . . You fling a jewel
> Where wild feet tramp and crushing wheels go by;
> You cannot tread the splendor from its dust;
> So in the shattered relics, shimmers yet
> Through tears and grime, the pride of womanhood.

The twin themes of sexuality and women's rights were too much for her audiences to accept. After a short run, the play closed. Ordinarily Julia would have been seriously discouraged by this reception, but she was not. With the encouragement of Charlotte Cushman, she plunged ahead with another drama, *Hippolytus*.[40] Although she did not finish it for several years, her willingness to begin another play suggests Julia's resiliency. To write, to see her ideas take form on stage, to experiment with thoughts entirely independent from Chev's were major steps. To accomplish them was a major gain.

Julia also decided to publish another volume of poetry. This was a particularly bold decision because of Chev's violent reaction to her earlier book. Risking another bout of his displeasure meant that Julia felt stronger and more able to weather his blasts. *Words for the Hour* appeared under Julia's name in late 1857, to less than enthusiastic reviews. George William Curtis praised it in *Putnam's*, but predicted, accurately, that it would not meet with the popularity of her first book.[41] Very little of Julia's complex feelings during the past three years made it into this volume. For those who wanted to think of Mrs. Howe as a domestic soul, there were poems such as "Fanny Kemble's Child" and "Maud," which stressed the duties of motherhood and the comforts of children.

> What ghosts of bitter Fancy
> My child has chased away;

127

First with her helpless pleading,
Then with her fairy play;
A child of consolation
Whose presence fair and pure,
Made in these months of nursing
So much of heav'n secure.

Those who had decided to group Julia with Boston's antislavery supporters got some satisfaction in "Slave Eloquence," "Slave Suicide," and two poems protesting Charles Sumner's treatment at the hand of "Bully Brooks." Another lengthy poem, "Sermon of Spring," was a response to the fighting in Kansas. Foreshadowing in tone her later "Battle Hymn," she linked violence with God's will.

"Oh! thou blue banner of God, with the stars of thy promise,
Wave in thy fury, avenge this usurping and insult!
Crack! thou crystal! let flame from the high empyrean,
Sweep from the outraged earth the vile chief and his
        legions, . . .
Blood he has counselled—not once but again and often
Blood he shall have, poured to God with a holy
        intention—
True blood of seventy-six, that brave men have bequeathed
        us—
Left to be spent as they spent it, freely for Freedom.[42]

Julia included, as well, some of the poems written in the depths of her depression in 1854. None of this, however, saved the book from mediocrity.

Julia's reaction, as was so often the case when things did not go well, was to travel. Her next trip would be a flying one out West with Chev and Flossy. Yet this escape was not the desperately important one that her trip to Europe had been in 1850. In the summer of 1857 Julia was much stronger than she had been seven years earlier. Her studying, while not a well-ordered approach to specific questions, steadied her and gave her a sense that she was doing something to improve her well-being. Her writing also had strengthened her, by allowing her to focus on "the still, small voice" within and by forcing her to shape and develop it. In exploring the intellectual life, Julia was encountering new dimensions in her inner landscape and acquiring new tools for dealing with the larger issues swirling around her.

EIGHT

Civil War, 1857-1862

It was borne in upon me (as the Friends say) that I had much to say to my day and generation which could not and should not be communicated in rhyme, or even in rhythm.

In the late 1850s and early 1860s, Julia's life, like that of the nation, changed radically. While North and South battled to define the political, economic, and ideological future of the country, Julia began to define her own future. The Civil War touched her directly, and in her most famous poem, "The Battle Hymn of the Republic," Julia transformed its bloody work into inspiration. In the process, Julia was herself transformed.

In the spring of 1857 Chev informed Julia that he intended to go on an inspection trip through Kansas and he wanted her to accompany him. Julia decided to go, taking Flossy with her; she thought a rest would do her daughter good. The trip was not restful, however; it was hectic. From New York to Bordentown to Philadelphia to Baltimore to Wheeling to Antioch (for a visit with Horace and Mary Mann) to Cincinnati to Louisville to St. Louis they went. "Heaven knows what I have not been through with since I saw you—dust, dirt, dyspepsia, hotels, railroads, prairies, Western steamboats, Western people, more prairies, tobacco juice, captains of boats, pilots of ditto, long days of jolting in the cars, with stoppages of ten minutes for dinner, and the devil take the hindmost. There ought to be no chickens this year, so many eggs have we eaten."[1] After reaching St. Louis, Julia and Flossy turned back to Cincinnati to visit friends. Chev went on to Kansas. Political violence over slavery in that state had led to the epithet, "Burning Kansas," and Chev, as a vigorous abolitionist, was determined to leap into the fire.

Chev had not always been interested in the abolitionist cause. His support had come in gradual steps. He had initially been inclined to leave the slaveholders alone. During the Mexican War, however, he became a Free Soiler. In 1846 he ran a hopeless race on the Conscience Whig ticket for a congressional seat.[2] He lost, but he remained opposed to the spread of slavery.

129

In 1853 Chev agreed to edit the *Commonwealth*, an antislavery newspaper that presented an alternative to the immediatism of abolitionist journals like the *Liberator*. When the Kansas-Nebraska Act was passed, however, Chev shifted ground. He suspected that the slave power could not be contained and that slavery would have to be abolished in all the states. First, however, slavery could not be allowed to spread into Kansas.

In April 1854 the governor of Massachusetts signed a bill creating the Massachusetts Emigrant Aid Company. Chev was on the board of this organization, whose purpose was to assist emigrants to Kansas while at the same time investing in Kansas land and in other business ventures. In July, spurred by the passage of the Kansas-Nebraska Act, the society sent out its first party of New Englanders to take possession of Kansas soil. Chev contributed money to this party and to subsequent ones. As news of increased violence in Kansas reached Massachusetts, Chev formed a new committee, the Faneuil Hall Committee, to donate clothing and money to the Free Staters in Kansas. In July 1856 he set out with Thaddeus Hyatt, a New York abolitionist, to view conditions in Kansas for himself. Everything he found there reinforced his opinion that slavery had to be eradicated. He spent the rest of the year raising money for the Free Staters. By May 1857, when he left for Kansas with Julia and Flossy, he could bask in a sense of accomplishment. Kansas was calm and dominated by northern interests. He inspected the state with pleasure and left the remaining funds that he had raised with the Free Staters in the Kansas legislature to finance a campaign against the LeCompton Constitution.[3] Chev had one other important financial dealing before he left. With Julia's money, he bought some land in Kansas, adding one more item to his list of profitless real estate deals.[4]

Julia was not an enthusiastic abolitionist. Because her South Carolina relatives were slaveholders, she had been brought up to regard the system as a beneficent one.[5] Her relatives believed that "any pronounced opposition to slavery would be the signal for the general uprising of the slaves, and for a widespread massacre of their former owners."[6]

After her marriage, Julia absorbed Chev's dislike for the spread of slavery.[7] At a Boston temperance festival she asserted her new views publicly by offering a toast "Free soil—free water—free grace."[8] When Chev took over the *Commonwealth*, Julia helped him, but most of her articles dealt with literary matters and not with politics. Although firmly opposed to the extension of slavery, Julia was not an activist.[9]

When Julia returned home from the Midwest, she found her life monotonous and disappointing. Hard work on her first fair helped brighten her spirits considerably, however. This fair, lasting five days and five evenings, was exhausting, but also "an entirely new experience and a very amusing one. My table was one of the prettiest, and, as I took care to have some young and pretty assistants, it proved one of the most attractive. I cleared $426.00 which was doing pretty well, as I had very little given me."[10] All the money raised went to benefit the poor of Boston. Robert Winthrop, the sponsor of the fair, had asked several women of his acquaintance to "take a table," as Julia had.[11] These women were then responsible for obtaining articles for sale, for setting up and decorating their booths, and for acting as sales clerks. Julia had just been introduced to the basics of a system that would absorb her energies increasingly in the next ten years.

Better than the fair was a new opportunity that beckoned in the first months of 1859. Chev had decided to go to Cuba for his health and to take Julia with him. Although she was still working on her new play, Julia agreed to go. She learned that *The Atlantic Monthly* would pay her for a series of letters written from the Caribbean; she hoped her travel essays would appeal to a wider audience than her poems. Another advantage of the trip was that Theodore Parker intended to travel on the same steamer. Parker, too, was in poor health and hoped that the journey would restore him.[12]

Julia enjoyed the trip. Conversation with those on board was pleasant, and Julia stashed away some ideas for her first travel letters. Eventually she collected the letters, publishing them in 1860 as *A Trip to Cuba*.

The tone of most of the letters is amusing and lighthearted. Life in the Caribbean had its drawbacks, however. For example, Julia found she could go nowhere without a male escort. She thought she understood why this was so: "wherever the animal vigor of men is so large in proportion to their moral power . . ., women must be glad to forego their liberties for the protection of the strong arm." Nevertheless, such a life was tedious, and Julia chafed at Chev and his company of like-minded philanthropists who "mounted their humanitarian hobbies and rode them until they were tired."[13] As was the case on her honeymoon, Julia was left out of these activities.

Another unhappy note crept into the letters when she recorded her farewell to Parker. The rough journey had done the tubercular Parker no good, and Julia must have known, as she watched him set off for Italy, that she might not see her old mentor again.

With his assistance we had made a very respectable band; now we [Chev and Julia] were to be only a wandering drum and fife—the fife particularly shrill, and the drum particularly solemn. . . . And now came silence, and tears, and last embraces; we slipped down the gangway into our little craft, and looking up, saw bending above us, between the slouched hat and silver beard, the eyes that we can never forget, that seemed to drop back in darkness with the solemnity of a last farewell. We went home, and the drum hung himself gloomily on his peg, and the little fife *shut up* for the remainder of the evening.[14]

The trip had had its advantages, however. Chev still ignored her, but this gave her time to write her essays. She was earning money and confessing her own views frankly to the public at large. To this pleasure was added the advantage of trading a chilly, unpredictable New England spring for the dependably warm and lush climate of Havana. Julia had not resolved her problems, but she had escaped them for a while.

In her Cuba letters, Julia candidly expressed her ideas about the South, slavery, and abolition. To the first she was somewhat sympathetic. The second she did not think entirely objectionable. The third she found distasteful. About the South she wrote, "I cannot curse the pleasant Southern land, nor those who dwell in it. Nor would I do so if I thought tenfold more ill of its corruptions. Were half my body gangrened, I would not smite or reproach it."[15]

Her reaction to slavery in the Caribbean reflected not only her still cool relation with abolition but also her low opinion of blacks.

The negro of the North is an ideal negro; it is the negro refined by white culture, elevated by white blood, instructed even by white iniquity; the negro among negroes is a coarse, grinning, flat-footed, thick-skulled creature, ugly as caliban, lazy as the laziest of brutes, chiefly ambitious to be of no use to the world. . . . He must go to school to the white race, and his discipline must be long and laborious. Nassau, and all that we saw of it, suggested to us the unwelcome question whether compulsory labor be not better than none."[16]

In other discussions of Caribbean slavery, Julia expressed pity for the slave but little opposition to the institution.[17] Her abolitionist fervor was, in the Caribbean climate, seriously dampened by racism.

Of abolitionists, Julia held a low opinion. She disliked their "self-congratulation and vituperation of their brother man, . . . their moral strainings, . . . the habitual sneer," and their unwillingness to acknowledge the "actual alleviations which often temper the greatest social evils."[18] Julia's hostility was daring. She used her book to condemn Chev's friends and allies and thus, indirectly, Chev himself.

Julia used her coolness toward abolitionism to establish her independence from Chev. It would not have been impossible, by this late date, for her to have been far more committed than she actually was. Not only was her husband intensely involved with the struggle, but so were many of Boston's finest families. Parker had been preaching on the subject as long as Julia had known him. Women like Lydia Maria Child (a distant relative by her aunt's marriage), Abby Kelley Foster, and Maria Weston Chapman provided role models for Julia; their dignified "womanly" carriage suggested to her that not all abolitionists needed to be vituperative or sneering.[19] Yet Julia held out against the cause. It was one area where she could exercise her intellectual freedom and let Chev know it.

Later, in her various memoirs, Julia attempted to shine up her reform credentials by dating her commitment to abolitionism vaguely. She wished posterity to remember her as one of the hardy band of early opponents of slavery who picked the "right" side from the beginning. She also wished to impress other reformers with the important role she had played in the major progressive cause of the mid-nineteenth century. Consequently, she always implied that she had been an early supporter. In fact she was not; her actual switch to abolitionism occurred during the last quarter of 1859.

On October 15, 1859, John Brown staged his famous raid. With his tiny band of twenty-two men, he failed to free the slaves surrounding Harpers Ferry, but he succeeded in shocking the nation. Within hours of the news, rumors began to circulate linking Chev to the abortive insurrection. Indeed, Samuel Gridley Howe was a longtime supporter of Brown's violent work in Kansas, and he was one of the "Secret Six" who had supplied Brown with the funds used to arm the slaves at Harpers Ferry.[20] Soon the proslavery press attacked him, naming him as an accomplice.

Julia and Chev were calm at first. In a letter to Annie, Julia asserted that the newspaper stories did not annoy them. "Of course all the stories about Northern Abolitionists are merest stuff. No one knew of Brown's intentions but Brown himself and his handful of men."[21] Chev had known, however, that Brown had been plotting something like this for nearly twenty months, and while he thought the plan unlikely to succeed, the dramatic gesture appealed to him.

Perhaps because of these connections, Chev grew increasingly nervous as the month wore on. Papers implicating the Secret Six had been discovered, and

Virginia was eager to continue holding treason trials. When his lawyer, John Andrew, suggested that he leave the country to avoid arrest, Chev became anxious. At last he decided to flee, heading for Canada in mid-November. He was, he said, on a mission concerning the education of blind Canadian children. He returned after Brown's execution on December 2, 1859.[22]

Another problem exacerbated the anxiety surrounding Chev's role in the Harpers Ferry incident. Julia was pregnant for the sixth time. The baby was due in late December; this was no time for its father to disappear either to respond to a court summons or to avoid one by fleeing to Canada. Since a conviction for treason in Virginia did not carry with it the automatic right of appeal, Chev did run the risk of death by hanging if he went south to face a jury.[23] By going to Canada, Chev was forced to leave Julia at a critical time. He had always been near Julia during childbirth; now she would have to face the birth and the threat of death without him. Julia saw not only the life of her husband threatened, but also her own life and that of her unborn baby. While she had no desire to see slaveholding southerners as her enemies, the thirst of the proslavery forces for revenge on all of John Brown's associates made a choice unavoidable. From now on, Julia would be an abolitionist without stint.

Making this task easier was her instinctive admiration for John Brown. She had met him once, in 1857, "gratified" by the chance to see someone whom Chev had described mysteriously as a "man [who] seemed to intend to devote his life to the redemption of the colored race from slavery, even as Christ had willingly offered his life for the salvation of mankind." His religious orientation appealed to Julia, and while she doubted the wisdom of his Harpers Ferry plan, she found his attempt "great-hearted." With Victor Hugo, Julia believed that Brown's death would "thence-forth hallow the scaffold, even as the death of Christ had hallowed the cross."[24]

Julia's tone in discussing John Brown suggests another reason for her conversion to abolitionism. Seen as a religious crusade, the movement fit into her growing convictions that individuals must take concrete action to comply with God's will. Her talks with Parker and her reading of Swedenborg prepared her to understand and admire the spirit of a man who believed he was acting according to divine instruction. "I should be glad to be as sure of heaven as that old man may be," she wrote, "following right in the spirit and footsteps of the old martyrs, girding on his sword for the weak and oppressed. His death will be holy and glorious."[25]

By translating the political cause into a religious one Julia could now be a heartfelt supporter. The threat to her husband's life—and hers indirectly—cemented her loyalty. She had begun to see "the glory of the coming of the Lord."[26]

But before the Civil War began to absorb her attention, Julia had something else to attend to. On Christmas Day, 1859, with her husband in attendance, Julia bore her last child, Samuel Gridley Howe. This baby became an instant favorite.

Sammy seemed from the start to belong most to Julia, and she enjoyed his infancy more than those of her previous children.[27] She nursed him for thirteen months, keeping him in bed with her the whole time. Often he slept across her breast, a habit Julia had begun to comfort him when he woke crying in the night. He shared her bed until he was nearly three, sometimes occupying far more than his share. Although his restless ways kept Julia up at night, on the whole she found Sammy a comfort. She took him with her on walks and errands. During her morning study time, she often read in the nursery while he amused himself with his toys. In the afternoons, she played with him; blocks, balls, reading, and music occupied their time. Whenever she traveled to New York or Newport, she took Sammy along.[28]

His "baby ways" brightened some otherwise dark days. Before Sammy was a year old, Lincoln was elected, and southern secession became more than a threat. He was barely walking before Fort Sumter was fired on, making war inevitable. The grim business of battle soon turned both parents to patriotic efforts, each of them choosing highly significant and very different paths.

In April 1861 a group of New York City women responded to the attack on Fort Sumter by forming the Women's Central Association of Relief for the Sick and Wounded of the Army. They turned for advice about the direction of their work to prominent men of their community. These, in turn, sought help and approval from Washington. Thus began the Sanitary Commission, a medical, supply, and relief organization that supported the Union Army throughout the Civil War.[29]

Samuel Gridley Howe was the logical choice for a commissioner of the Sanitary. He had had firsthand experience in the Greek Revolution; he was a physician; popular benevolence interested him. In November 1861, when he went to Washington to sound out his political friends on the subject of the commission, Julia went with him. James Freeman Clarke and John Albion Andrew, now governor of Massachusetts, accompanied the Howes. In Washington, they conferred with Charles Sumner and President Lincoln.[30]

Opposition from the army delayed some of the commissioner's plans, so Congress set to work. It would not be until April 1862 that the reorganized medical arm of the army would accept the presence of the Sanitary Commission in all facets of its hospital and medical supply work.[31]

Chev's political work took time. Julia had ample opportunity to absorb the sights and sounds of military life. She saw the Army of the Potomac encamped around Washington. Ambulances, officers on horses, and orderlies on foot dashed up and down Pennsylvania Avenue in front of the Willard Hotel where Julia and Chev were staying. Sometimes she went off with Clarke as an escort to visit camps or hospitals. She also visited the first Massachusetts Heavy Artillery, commanded by her distant cousin, William B. Greene. Later she went with friends out to Bailey's Crossroads, Virginia, where she watched a review of the troops. These exercises were cut short when a detachment of Confederate troops suddenly engaged some Union soldiers. Julia could hear the sounds of battle as her carriage headed back to Washington. It was during the long, slow ride back from Bailey's Crossroads that she heard the song "John Brown's Body" and that James Freeman Clarke suggested she write some new words for the tune.[32]

The actual writing of the words to the "Battle Hymn" was an intense, exciting experience for Julia, one in which, as she recalled it, she was transformed from a bewildered housewife into an inspired poet.

> I distinctly remember that a feeling of discouragement came over me as I drew near the city of Washington. . . . I thought of the women of my acquaintance whose sons or husbands were fighting our great battle; the women themselves serving in the hospitals, or busying themselves with the work of the Sanitary Commission. . . . I could not leave the nursery to follow the march of our armies, neither had I the practical deftness which the preparing and packing of sanitary stores demanded. Something seemed to say to me, "You would be glad to serve, but you cannot help anyone; you have nothing to give and there is nothing for you to do."

After her excursion to Bailey's Crossroads, Julia had an experience that erased her sense of inadequacy.

> I went to bed that night quite as usual, and slept, according to my wont, quite soundly. I awoke in the gray of the morning twilight; and as I lay waiting for the dawn, the long lines of the desired poem began to twine themselves in my mind. . . . I sprang out of bed, and found in the dimness an old stump of a pen which I remembered to have used the day before. I scrawled the verses almost

without looking at the paper. I had learned to do this when, on previous occasions, attacks of versification had visited me during the night, and I feared to have recourse to a light lest I should wake the baby, who slept near me.[33]

Just as she had awakened while the dark of night was giving way to daylight, Julia sensed that she was emerging from a state of confusion into a state of clarity and accomplishment. She knew the lines were good; she would need to make only thirteen changes. The rush of pleasure accompanying her writing assured her that she had found the right words for the right time.

The verses, of course, did not spring out of thin air. Her own predilection for linking Old Testament violence to contemporary events, evident in "Sermon of Spring," for example, helped decide her choice of images. Her religious background, too, affected the poems. Edmund Wilson has pointed out how much the Old Testament, particularly Isaiah 63:1-6, supplied her with images of an angry God, violent and bloody in his righteousness. The "righteous" sentence, the "winepress," and the "trampling" all come from this passage, as does the idea contained in the third stanza that those who revile God will have to face his angry justice.[34]

More important, Julia was able to draw on images and ideas about the war that had been circulating through the press but that she had not yet fully confronted. New England intellectuals of the period like Orestes Brownson, Henry James, Sr., Charles Eliot Norton, Frances Parkman, Moncure Conway, William Lloyd Garrison, and John Greenleaf Whittier were all sounding similar notes of religion, violence, justice, and retribution. They believed that divine energy informed the course of events and transformed ordinary individuals into instruments of God's will. Garrison thought that Lincoln and the Republicans were "instruments in the hands of God." Whittier proclaimed "the chastisement that Divine Providence is inflicting on the nation." Henry James, Senior, saw the war as the first step in the coming of the millennium. Although it brought terrible agony, the war would, like a tide, wash in the new sanctified era as it washed away the sins of the past.[35]

Julia's genius lay not so much in creating the elements of the "Battle Hymn" but in fusing them together. Her original version, which she later edited, shows her skill in piling up these images.

Mine eyes have seen the glory of the coming of the Lord
He is trampling through the winepress where the grapes of wrath are stored
He hath loosed the fateful lightnings of his terrible swift sword
His truth is marching on.

I have seen him in the watchfires of a hundred circling camps
They have builded him an altar in the evening dews and damps,
I can read His righteous sentence by the dim and flaring lamps
His day is marching on.

I have read a burning Gospel writ in fiery rows of steel
As ye deal with my contemners, so with you my grace shall deal
Let the hero, born of woman, crush the serpent with his heel
Our God is marching on.

He has sounded out the trumpet that shall never call retreat
He has waked the earth's dull bosom with a high ecstatic beat
Oh! be swift my soul to answer his, be jubilant my feet
Our God is marching on.

In the whiteness of the lilies he was born across the sea
With a glory in his bosom that shines out on you and me
As he died to make men holy, let us die to make men free
Our God is marching on.

His is coming like the glory of the morning on the wave
He is wisdom to the mighty, he is banner to the brave
So the world shall be his footrest and the soul of [illegible] his stave
Our God is marching on.[36]

The poem is a powerful assertion about the war. It demonstrates that Julia had not merely heard all the rhetoric, but had also internalized it. Previously the images and metaphors had been at the periphery of her consciousness, but now the agitation of war, seen at such close range, pulled to the front of her mind the ideas she had ignored. As line after line fell into place on that dim November morning, Julia was able to make the meaning of the war crystal clear to herself.

Until that time, she had not understood it. John Brown had translated politics into religion for Julia Ward Howe, freeing her to identify with the major moral and intellectual issue of her age. She was not prepared, however, to accept war as the consequence of commitment to abolitionism. The blood of men and women was a high price to pay for loyalty to an idea. War did not, therefore, provide Julia with the sort of tests that would heighten her dedication to abolitionism. Not only was she grieved to find northerners and southerners fighting, but Julia also felt left behind by the bloody contest. As she recalled in her *Reminiscences*, she could not see how she could relate to the Civil War at all. Because her husband was too old to fight and her sons

138

too young, she could not connect to the war by means of her family. She was too busy in the nursery to help on the battlefield and too clumsy to wrap bandages or to scrape lint. She was saddened both by the fact of war and by her distance from it. She felt discouraged and alienated.[37]

"The Battle Hymn of the Republic" freed Julia from this quandary. In writing her poem, she translated the Civil War into eschatology. She imbued it with ultimate religious purpose, both for individuals and for society as a whole. Those who went to war were not merely marching off to shoot southerners. They were accomplishing the Lord's purpose, fulfilling his promises of bloody justice. They were in the Lord's vanguard; they were evidence of his imminent coming.

To this Old Testament message, Julia added the image of a transfiguring Christ. Just as his death promised new life for all, so the deaths caused by the Civil War would bring society a new opportunity. The work of war was more than fire, blood, terror, and suffering. It was to be an act of individual renewal in which men and women would confront divine justice fearlessly in hopes of salvation. Moreover, the war would be an act of social renewal, wherein the entire state would have its sins trampled and its rebirth assured through the suffering of its citizens.

To have the meaning of the war open itself to her in this way was a surprising help to Julia. The sense of competence, clarity, and light it gave her, and the understanding that accompanied the nearly effortless composition of the poem, had a good effect. If only for a moment, Julia had felt divinely inspired. She hoped she could look for it to happen again.

James Fields published "The Battle Hymn of the Republic" in *The Atlantic* in February 1862. The timing could not have been better. As the fortunes of war worsened for the North during the bleak months of February to April, men and women needed to hold on to some large principle that could explain and justify the war. The "Battle Hymn" offered that expression of principle, a fearless statement of the war's significance. Ordinary folk, of course, did not read *The Atlantic* or listen to Transcendentalist preachers, and an intellectual poem about the war might not ordinarily have trickled down to the eyes and ears of America's farmers, housewives, factory operatives, laborers, and tradesmen. Songs did, however. By setting her poem to the music of "John Brown's Body," Julia made her poem accessible to everybody, and she made it memorable.

In addition to her Washington visit and her writing of the "Battle Hymn of the Republic," Julia had a good deal else to keep her busy. At home Sammy, who was proving as mischievous as Harry, took up a great deal of time. Sammy was especially fond of sharp objects; he required constant observation.[38] The girls gave her great comfort; Flossie's beauty and Julia's sensitive nature touched chords of pride and sympathy.[39] But now Julia Romana and Flossy were old enough to enter society. They required her company as chaperone at various receptions and parties.[40] Illnesses, too, occupied her time. Sammy suffered with a "bowel complaint" in the spring of 1861, Laura was sick throughout the following summer, and Julia Romana was unwell virtually all the time.[41] Even when such crises abated, Julia's hands were full of work. "[I] mend, scold when necessary, and try to keep things up," she wrote.[42] Maud's boots needed repair; cellar and pantry needed filling; someone had to pay the laundress for the fifteen sheets and seven pillow slips that were washed weekly.[43] In the fall of 1862 a weary Julia returned from Newport to supervise a complicated move from South Boston to a rented house at 13 Chestnut Street. This move, from chilly, cramped quarters to a large, sunny Beacon Hill townhouse, was a welcome change, but it was one more demand on Julia's precious time.[44]

Her social life, too, seemed to gather steam. In spite of her stern poem, "Weave no more silks, ye Lyons looms, to deck our girls for gay delights!,"[45] Julia entertained a good deal more than she had in the past. She acquired a superb German cook whose excellent fare attracted Boston's first families. In Lawton's Valley, visitors, mostly Julia's intellectual friends, came in a steady procession to enjoy good food and the Newport air.[46] During the winter, Julia gave many dinners and several evening parties at her new house.[47]

Despite her new house and social successes, Julia recalled the late 1850s and the early years of the war as a troublesome time. Her life was flecked with difficulties. Julia Romana, who had suffered a nervous breakdown in 1859, was still unwell. Julia took her to Washington in 1863 to brace up her health, but this did not solve her daughter's problems.[48]

Chev, too, was a continuing source of worry. His health was not good, and illness did not improve his disposition.[49] He and Julia still quarreled frequently. One scene occurred when Julia criticized Chev "for making Flossy read the Bible with sore eyes. Then he pummeled me till I was black and blue in the soul. Then we made peace, fastened up the house, set the watch-dog, and parted for the night as usual, I cursing philanthropy and he probably cursing me."[50]

In 1857 Chev apparently requested a divorce once more, this time on the grounds that since there was "no unkindness" between them, "therefore the present is the time for such a division."[51] Again Julia refused. She was still unwilling to part with Julia Romana and Harry, as Chev required, and she also knew that she could not survive as a divorcée. Her funds were not sufficient for this, and the society whose attention she enjoyed would never accept her presence or her publications if she were touched by scandal. Moreover, she had come to see the promises made in a marriage ceremony as absolute obligations. To break the bonds of marriage was as unacceptable to her as to renege on a contract.

Despite his failing health, Chev continued to try to control Julia. He forbade her to visit her brother Sam in Washington, where she had been invited to attend Lincoln's inauguration.[52] He continued to change houses and servants as he had in the past. He moved his family three times during the Civil War years, and Chev dismissed the staff at least twice. In the first of these changes, he fired Sammy's beloved nurse; in the second, he left Julia without a housekeeper.[53]

Julia was able to endure Chev's unkindnesses better than she had in the past, but she could not establish their marriage on a footing that would allow them both some freedom. Chev, on the other hand, even though he could no longer mangle Julia's emotional health, refused to stop criticizing, undermining, and interfering with her life. They were at a stalemate. Julia confessed to Annie that her "trouble-giving" husband, along with her six children, was "something of a burden."[54]

Compounding Julia's marital troubles in 1862 was a flagging sense of personal direction. Her studies went well enough, but she was at a loss to know what to do with them. Despite the success of the "Battle Hymn," Julia began to doubt that poetry was the best means of communicating her ideas.[55] She hungered for "personal contact with her audience; she felt that she must *speak* her message."[56] She wanted to have contact with people; she needed to see if her ideas matched at all the "normal direction of human experience."[57] Publishing poetry did not fill this bill. Even the pieces she wrote for *The Atlantic* and the *Tribune* did not help, for they did not offer the larger, more intoxicating, more powerful pleasure of an audience.[58]

In addition, Julia's relationships with her publishers were not easy. She wrote pieces for *The Atlantic* that got "lost" on the editor's desk. Money was a sore point, too. James Russell Lowell did not pay her very well; for "The Battle Hymn of the Republic," for example, Julia received five dollars.[59] Garrison paid her irregularly, and *A Trip to Cuba* brought in one-quarter of the sum she had been promised.[60] Chev permitted her to hold occasional reading parties at which she recited her poetry, but he would not allow Julia to receive any payment for these.[61] Her sense of frustration with her literary life was also affected by the failure of her second—and last—theatrical effort, *Hippolytus*.

After the failure of *The World's Own*, Charlotte Cushman had urged Julia to "do battle with the asses who have pronounced their dictum with regard to *The World's Own* . . . destroy their power with a new weapon whose force they cannot comprehend and they are worse beaten than they w (sic) be if we tried to convince them against their will."[62] Julia was trying to do exactly that when she began working on her new play in the summer of 1857. Since she and Edwin Booth had become friends, Julia decided that she would write the leading role for him. They conferred, the play was written, and Charlotte Cushman agreed to take the female lead. After the delays caused by her trip to Cuba and Sammy's birth, Julia finally secured the Howard Athenaeum, where the manager agreed to produce the play. Just before the play was to begin rehearsal, however, he backed out. An adequate role could not be found in the play for his wife, he claimed, and so the production was called off. Bitterly disappointed, Julia never again wrote anything for the theater.[63]

The play, written in blank verse, took up the Greek myth of Hippolytus, the son of Theseus, Athenian king, and the stepson of Theseus's second wife, Phaedra. The action takes place when Hippolytus is a young man. His father is away at war, and Phaedra is yearning for his attention. Hippolytus, however, has been dedicated to the chaste Artemis since birth, and other women are of no interest to him. Slighted by this lack of interest in love, Aphrodite determines to punish Hippolytus. She sends a special soothsayer to help Phaedra win the young man's heart. Their first plot, a seductive feast where Phaedra plans to give Hippolytus a love philter, fails when Hippolytus glimpses the moon, Artemis's emblem. He dashes off, leaving Phaedra desperate. The second plan works no better: Phaedra sends out a messenger with the false news that Theseus has been lost in the underworld, never to return. She meets Hippolytus and pretends to be grief stricken. She asks him for comfort; he refuses. As a last resort, Phaedra casts off all pretense and confesses her love for him. Hippolytus cruelly spurns her, and Phaedra's passionate love turns to passionate hate. When Theseus returns unexpectedly, Phaedra gets her opportunity for revenge. She tells the king that Hippolytus has not only usurped his throne, but also attempted to rape her. Theseus, in a rage, banishes his son, calling on Neptune to drown him. Phaedra, horrified at this turn of events, strangles herself. Realizing his mistake too late, Theseus rushes to the sea, only to find Artemis carrying his son out of the water. In his dying gasps, the son forgives his father. Then the goddess bears away the body of her cherished Hippolytus.[64]

Charlotte Cushman had urged Julia to write something using strophes and choruses in the manner of *Antigone*. In *Hippolytus*, Julia did turn to a classical theme, and she did in the last act use a chorus. In no other way, however, was the play built on classical lines. There is no unity of time and place, and the tension based on fate and individual character that typifies the great Greek dramas is also lacking. Instead, Julia built the play on the twin themes of Hippolytus's great virtue and Phaedra's sickened soul. Unlike Leonora in *The World's Own*, Phaedra is not an innocent woman cheated by corrupt men. She is herself the root of evil. Her passions rule her absolutely; she has no self-control. Her death, like Leonora's, is self-inflicted, but unlike the former heroine, she feels remorseful. It is the power of shame that leads her to "strangle herself with her scarf."

In this ending, the reader feels Julia returning to somewhat more conventional treatment of women, for both the role of woman as the corrupter of men and the image of the repentant siren were common depictions of women's nature. Yet there is something unconventional in the assertive passion of the heroines of both plays. Both are violent and both deal with lust. When she tells Hippolytus of her feelings, Phaedra is fervent:

> Here, love consumed, I sink before your feet,
> And clasp your knees for mercy . . .
> . . . let me first pour out
> The death song of my passion—hark! I love
> Not as a girl, with fond and blushful shame,
> Nor yet like Argive Helen, free as fair,
> Passing from lip to lip like hireling's wine,
> And wooing tamely back the lord she wronged
> I love thee with the power of earth and heaven,
> And for thy love will pledge myself to hell.

It is the women's responses to their inner natures that propel these plays, not "womanly" responsibility to fathers or families. The heroines command events, for better or for worse, by their moral (or immoral) power. In Julia's scripts, a woman was as powerful as a man to kill and to heal, to defend or to deceive. No moral impulse belonged solely to one sex or the other. It was a strong departure from conventional moral and literary thinking to suppose that the

143

inner voice of women could be composed of passions that subverted domesticity, ignored piety, and dismissed purity.

Julia would never dare such experiments in real life. Protected by her ancient and imaginary settings, however, she tested some of the implications of her theory of the "still, small voice." In exploring such shadowy territory, Julia laid further groundwork for her theories of individual moral autonomy.

As Julia looked at the failure of the Howard Athenaeum to produce her play, she had to recognize that of all the things she had written in the late 1850s and the early 1860s, only one had been successful, her "Battle Hymn." Yet the popular success of this one poem strengthened Julia's belief that she could communicate with the public. She had not yet hit on the right approach, but she was encouraged to keep looking. The pleasure of writing so easily and of having her own sense of competence confirmed by public opinion sustained her. Several new developments signaled her transformation into a more confident, determined, independent woman.

First, in the winter of 1863 Julia began to write an essay that she hoped would synthesize some of the ideas she had picked up in her philosophical readings. Her aim was to relate private belief to public questions of ethical behavior. She was not exactly sure what she would do with the essay. If she could not get a publisher, perhaps she could, like her early mentor, Margaret Fuller, read the essay aloud to interested groups of women. Julia consulted with Elizabeth Peabody, whose readings to men and women in her rooms on West Street had brought her a little income. Her friend was encouraging, so Julia began a series of public readings. Her success with these led her to a whole new sphere of activity.

Second, Julia began on February 9, 1863 to keep a journal. This was more than the copybooks of the 1850s that held, between their narrow margins, the seething emotional life of a struggling woman. This journal would become a lifelong habit, a repository for her household accounts, observations about her studies, records of social events, comments on her family, and analyses of her feelings. Although the journal entries were far more orderly than the outpourings of the fifties, they still provided a vent for her anguished feelings on occasion. More than that, they gave Julia a way to keep track of her emotional, spiritual, and intellectual growth. They testified to her solid, if sometimes small, achievements. They made concrete the progress of her struggle to create for herself something in life that was entirely her work, independent of Chev.

Julia's third signal was a new style of head covering. In January 1864, as she prepared for her first public address, Julia debated about what to wear on her head. To go bare headed was too bold, too masculine. To wear her usual thick bonnet was too cumbersome; she felt hidden under it. She finally chose a white lace cap. It allowed her to be both ladylike and assertive at once. Because it combined these characteristics so perfectly, Julia adopted it permanently. For the rest of her life, whenever she appeared on the public platform, Julia wore a white lace cap.

All these changes indicated that Julia had taken significant additional steps toward the independence, recognition, and sense of accomplishment that she craved. Unfortunately, Julia's search for the right calling came to an abrupt halt in May 1863.

NINE

Sammy, 1863-1864

In painful admiration of the skill
of God, who speaks his sweetest sentence short.

On Wednesday, May 13, Julia's journal entry contained an ominous note: "Walked out with dearest Sammy—his gaiters and scarf forgotten." The next day Julia wrote briefly: "Sammy isn't well—heavy in the morning. Slept on my bed."[1]

For the next two days Julia was too busy to sit down with her journal. The doctor had diagnosed "the kind of diphtheria that runs into membraenous croup."[2] Julia moved about "as in a dream, paralyzed by grief and terror," dispensing first sulphur and aconite and then hydriodide of mercury.[3] These doses, typical of homeopathic remedies, severely weakened the little boy. Not until his father returned on Saturday night, the 16th, did helpful treatment begin. Steam, fresh air, and oxygenated water considerably eased Sammy's sufferings. They could not, however, clear the thick membranes that coated his throat and that he unavoidably aspirated. Nor could these remedies prevent the deadly diphtheria toxoid from reaching his heart.[4] At 5:00 Sunday morning, three-and-a-half-year-old Sammy died.[5]

The stricken parents were "crushed . . . to the earth."[6] Grief nearly paralyzed them. Chev could not bear to attend the burial. To make matters worse for Julia, he followed his usual pattern during family crises, becoming confined to bed with a serious illness.[7] Julia could manage nothing, overcome by loss. Her journal has only two entries in the three weeks after Sammy's death: "Almost strangled with grief" and "I choke back my tears and try to work."[8] In the afternoons, she visited Sammy's nursery, turned over his toys in her hand, and opened the drawers containing his little clothes to touch and smell them once more. "I often sit on your bed," she wrote. "Sometimes I think you speak to me—sometimes all is silent. . . . The light shines in as it used to do, and I hear the hand organ, and children's voices in the street. It seems to bring you a little nearer to me, my dear lost one, but not near enough for comfort."[9]

On June 16 Julia began her "Last Letter to Sammy," from which the above quote was taken. This was a lengthy account of his brief life. Julia poured out every detail she could recall about her child's life and mortal illness. It was agonizingly painful for her to write it, but she did so not "to make myself miserable, but in order that I may have some lasting record of how you lived and died." She also wrote in order to begin the long process of accepting the most terrible loss of her life. In the letter, she recalled the trip to Mt. Auburn Cemetery.

> We drove along at a quiet pace, talking cheerfully enough, until we came near the gate of Mount Auburn, when I began to realize that the parting was very near. I now opened the casket, took your dear little cold hand in mine, and began to take silent farewell of you. And here, dearest child, I must stop—the remembrance of these last moments so cuts me to the heart, that I cannot say one word more about them, and not much about the life of loneliness and desolation which now began for me, and of which I do not see the end. God knows why I lost you and how I suffer for you, and He knows how and when I shall see you again, as I hope to do, my dearest, because Christ says we are to live again after this life, and I know that if I am immortal, God will not inflict upon me the pain of an eternal separation from you. No, we shall meet again. Sweet Angel Sammy—God grant that the rest of my life may be worthy of this hope, more dear than life itself.[10]

"The Last Letter to Sammy" was only one of a great number of pieces addressed to or written about Sammy. As was her habit, Julia turned to poetry to relieve her unhappiness. The full range of emotions associated with death—disbelief, anger, desolation, loneliness—exploded in verses.

> I stretch my arms to thee, stretch wide my arms to thee
> Tossed on this couch of affliction and pain
> Death will not come to me, never will come to me
> Death who my darling, my dearest has slain.

> My children dear, with joy and pride
> I've watched your progress great and small
> But on the night that Sammy died
> I knew no creature of you all,
> I only knew the tie that broke,
> The silent voice that loudest spoke.

> Shut in this solitary room
> 'Tis no offense to leave me

Since silent memory alone
Has precious things to give me

My baby's birth, my baby's death
The mysteries that screen them
My black dress and my little grave
And heaven all shut between them.[11]

Julia's writing, intended for herself alone, was not designed to tug artificial sentiment from the hearts and eyes of her readers. The outpourings of grief are innocent and original; the images are little darts of grief with quick, perfect aim. The force of her emotion transcends the sentimentality; a century later, the reader feels the power of an exposed and aching soul wrestling with grief hand-to-hand.

Julia longed for a religious resolution to her agony. Many times over she told herself that God knew best which lives to take, and that in heaven she and Sammy would unite once again.[12] Reconciliation did not come easily, however.

In dreams, she relived her moments with Sammy. In one he came back and asked his mother to join him at Christmas. At that stage in her grief, she would gladly have done so. She dreamed, too, that Sammy came to life again. In one particularly sad dream, she saw him in her bed and tried "to nurse him in the dark, as I have so often done. I thought that when his little lips had found my breast, something said in my ears 'My life's life—the glory of the world' quoting from my lines on Mary Booth. This woke me with a sudden impression. *Thus Nature Remembers*." In other dreams, she saw him alive, held him, and kissed him.[13] Every dream replayed the tragedy, for no matter how tenderly she held him in her fantasies, Julia always lost her Sammy upon awakening.

The freshet of poetry, writing, and dreaming slowed somewhat during the early summer. By late July it had quieted to a trickle, though Julia would continue to write poems to and about Sammy and to dream of him sporadically for another year.

In spite of this bitter tragedy, Julia did not succumb to the long, paralyzing depression that had enveloped her when her father and brother died. Instead she plunged into her studies, managing her grief very well. She had faced the worst thing life could offer her, and she had not crumbled. Nothing—not poverty, not divorce, not illness—could have tortured her more. Yet Julia had survived. She now had the calm strength of knowing that she could endure.

Chev's threats were serious, but Julia was no longer afraid. She knew she could count on herself to withstand any obstacles he might throw in her path. The loss of her dearest child had left Julia tougher, surer, and more self-reliant.

For Julia, mental effort was more healing than physical work. She threw herself into her reading and writing. Julia had begun, before Sammy's death, an essay that combined her own observations with ethical ideas she had collected in her studies of Swedenborg, Comte, Hegel, and Spinoza. After Sammy's death, she quickly finished that essay, entitling it "Proteus."[14] Working rapidly, Julia produced five more essays in two months.

The fast pace of writing did not escape family comment. "My Ethics are now the joke of my family, and Flossy, or any child, wishing a second helping, will say: 'Is it ethical, Mamma?' " wrote Julia to Louisa.[15] Julia polished a seventh essay, "The Dynamic Idea of God," before another month went by, declaring "I believe I have in this [essay on religion] built up a greater coherence between things natural and things divine than I have seen or heard made out by anyone else."[16]

A few days later, after reading the essay aloud to Mrs. Paddock, general factotum at the Institute, she began to rework the essay. By November 16 she had six essays in perfect shape. On that day she opened her lecture series in her own parlor. From then until December 18, with a break on December 14, Julia read one essay every Monday evening to a small circle of friends.[17] Although Chev had refused to allow her to receive compensation for her efforts, Julia found the course successful and satisfying. The audiences got better each time. She noted with pleasure the "excellent audience" and then the "large and attentive audience" that filled her parlors.[18] Among her listeners were "society friends," as well as Louis Agassiz, Edwin Percy Whipple, James Freeman Clarke, and William Rounseville Alger. Moreover, Julia believed she had instructed herself as well as others. "I learned somewhat to avoid anti-climax and to seek directness and simplicity of statement," she recalled. She taught herself to confine herself to a few points per lecture and to suit her language and examples to her listeners.[19] Julia no longer had to speak through "strange creatures" in dramatic scripts. She had found her true voice.

The pleasure was all the greater since, when the course began, Julia was in the midst of a minor scandal. In order to celebrate the opening of Boston's remodeled Music Hall, its board of directors had called for a commemorative ode. Julia, in her new position as public poet, fully expected the honor to fall to her. Instead, Annie Fields, wife of James Fields, won the coveted task.[20] More self-effacing than Julia, Mrs. Fields refused to read her poem at the festivities; indeed, she did not even sign her name to it. Julia was cross. She disliked being passed over, especially since she suspected her publisher of trying to push his wife's reputation at the expense of hers.[21] She disliked the poem; furthermore, she disliked the author's anonymity. She published a scathing review in the *Commonwealth*, intemperate in tone for someone who expected polite consideration of all her verses. Beacon Hill buzzed. Mrs. Fields wrote in her journal, "Julia Ward Howe has said and sung her last as far as Boston goes."[22] Julia wrote in hers that she had written the review only to stand up for herself, lest someone mistake the unhappy verses for her own.[23] Fortunately for Julia, the course of lectures took everyone's mind off her peevishness. Once again she was in the limelight, surrounded by friends and praise.

More work awaited her. In December 1863 Boston held its first Sanitary Fair. Organized entirely by women, this week-long fair was designed to raise money for the Sanitary Commission to spend on behalf of the Union Army. The *Commonwealth*, for which Julia was once again writing, was the only paper to cover the fair from beginning to end. Julia enjoyed her contact with the women who served on the organizing committee and those who worked at various tables and exhibits. She translated her enthusiasm into vigorous support for their efforts, puffing all the various articles available for sale and raffle.[24] Displays and events such as these drew unexpectedly large crowds. In a week, the women had raised over $140,000 for the Sanitary Commission.

As the new year rolled in, Julia busied herself with several new plans. On January 11 she met with some women friends at 4 Park Street to inaugurate The Ladies Social, a new club dedicated to literature, criticism, and wit. This group evolved within a year into The Brain Club, for which Julia wrote many charades and humorous pieces.[25]

Later that month Julia read her sixth lecture, "Duality of Character," to the Wednesday evening meeting at the Church of the Disciples.[26] This was her first public reading, and it was a decided success. Pleased, Julia determined to take her lectures farther afield. During the first months of 1864, she wrote and rewrote her essays.[27] She also scribbled dozens of letters: she would if she could travel from New York to Washington, lecturing as she went.

The big obstacle to her plan was Chev. He was entirely opposed to her reading in public and had made his position unpleasantly clear to her. "Some illusions left me today," she wrote, "giving way to unwholesome facts." His vigorous opposition and hostility left her undecided and anxious. Should she obey him, or should she follow her own impulse to travel, to speak, and to bring herself directly into contact with her audience? So nervous and fretful did Chev's unbending displeasure make her that leaving home seemed necessary, if only to avoid an "utter breaking down of body and of mind."[28] Finally she hit on what she hoped would be a solution. She would read her lectures in public to mixed audiences, and people would pay to hear her read. The profits from these fees, however, she would turn over to the Sanitary Commission. By supporting his organization in this manner, Julia hoped to win Chev's approval.

Julia hoped in vain. Chev continued to criticize her or ignore her. "Did he not suppose himself exempt from human errors, he could never berate me as he does," she wrote.[29] Nevertheless, Julia determined to go to Washington to deliver her lectures.

James Freeman Clarke had delivered a sermon earlier in the year that had comforted Julia. Based on her favorite text, "And after the fire, a still, small voice," Clarke's sermon encouraged Julia to heed her own inclinations. She decided to say her "word as well as I can, and as often as circumstances call for it." Her inner voice grew stronger. On the eve of her departure, Julia confided to her journal: "I leave . . . with a resolute, not a sanguine heart. I have no one to stand for me there, Sumner against me, Channing about unknown to me, everyone else indifferent. I do in obedience to a deep and strong impulse which I do not understand nor explain, but whose bidding I cannot neglect."[30]

All of Julia's appeals to Washington's important men had gone astray. Charles Sumner, for example, not only refused to help, but he also actively prevented some of Julia's Washington friends from assisting her.[31] Fortunately, Mrs. Charles Eames, wife of a prominent lawyer, put her parlors at Julia's disposal. After lectures in Bordentown and Philadelphia, Julia arrived in Washington to find an impressive list of guests whom Mrs. Eames was ready to invite. Julia fired off invitations. On the appointed day, distinguished members of Washington society poured in to hear her. Gideon Welles, William Henry Channing, the Eameses, Stephen Foster, and Salmon P. Chase all sat in Mrs. Eames's parlors for at least some of Julia's three lectures. Julia was immensely relieved.[32]

The lectures Julia read on this trip were the same ones she had read in Boston. None of them addressed the issues of grief or death; these essays were an alternative to mourning. By tackling questions of moral responsibility, individual faith, and the ideal social order, these essays affirmed life. Moreover, they reflected Julia's own life—her own time, place, and concerns.

Nowhere was the intersection of domestic life, personal philosophical reflection, and external events more prominent than in "Proteus: or Success in Life." Julia launched the first essay by examining Proteus, noted in classical literature for his ability to change his shape. Julia stressed the changing nature not of man's shape, but of his fortunes. Just as Proteus could not hold the shape of a powerful lion forever, so temporal power would evaporate with the passage of time. Riches, like the mighty tree, might grow, but one day they too would crumble, fall, and disappear. Political power, like the river, flows quickly past. Even domestic power fades. "The wife becomes familiar as ourselves and, like ourselves, ceases to give us conscious pleasure. The children crowd us from the table, and almost supersede us."[33] Change is inevitable.

From this ethical "fact" Julia went on to analyze the question of success. What, in an ever-changing society, were the true, enduring, and useful values that would enable people to hold fast and even triumph over loss and misfortune? To learn this, Julia took up what she believed to be the three main conditions in human life: wealth, power, and affection.

Julia's comments on wealth sound the first notes of a theme that would recur with increasing frequency. Unlike the Social Darwinists of the period, Julia believed that wealth did not necessarily accrue to those who worked hardest or who were smartest. Her life with Chev had taught her that. Instead, wealth seemed to come and go independently of exertion or virtue. Furthermore, she contended, manipulations of the stock market by selfish entrepreneurs and the graft of corrupt officials snatched the fruits of honest labor from many families. Julia's critical view of the distribution of wealth was matched by her contempt for the American obsession with money. She wrote sarcastically, " 'have money' is the motto of American life. Make it or marry it is the alternative. If you succeed in either enterprise, you need do no more—you are respectable."

Julia's criticism of the power of money reflected her belief that her heritage and her upbringing entitled her to a choice place among society's first families. Her connections with reform activity gave her an additional moral claim to leadership. When status and acclaim were not forthcoming, Julia blamed it on her lack of money and the popular worship of wealth. If society had clung to the proper standards, surely people like herself would claim the prize of high social status. She also worried that the unbounded pursuit of wealth would fundamentally damage society. In this, as in all things, Julia urged restraint and moderation. The pursuit of gain was noble so long as it did not become the ruling passion in life.

Power, too, had to be controlled. True power, in Julia's eyes, lay with those who were humble and forgiving, reasonable and thoughtful. Those who were grasping and greedy, who squandered money or natural gifts for an appearance of power, were only deceiving themselves. Such power would dissipate, yielding ultimately to those like the youth "who sets down the cup at the banquet, who leaves the revel early for the pleasures of thought and the pains of study; who is distant and modest in his loves, reserved and resolved in his friendships, who finds the nearest task and fulfills it to his best ability." Extravagance and pretension must go. In example after example of restraint, Julia stressed her theme that "the lost secret of power is measure [moderation]."

In her examination of affection, Julia returns to this theme. Simplicity, moderation, and unselfishness characterize true affection. Between spouses, this is especially important. To be happy, both partners must practice restraint. They should limit their demands, focusing instead on service for and charity toward each other. Moderation was required of both sexes in their physical and emotional relations.

These observations followed directly from personal experience and observation. In particular, her own marriage, ripped apart by selfishness and excessive demands, informed her views. Julia had broadened her grasp in this essay, however. She criticized tyrants, drunkards, gamblers, and adulterers for distorting family life with their excess. Similarly, nations that passed tyrannical laws such as the Fugitive Slave Act, or that condoned an immoral system like slavery, could not expect to escape chastisement. Success would return only when those nations resumed the paths of moderation and restraint.

The attempt by the South to split off from the United States suggested to Julia the idea she considered the most important of her whole series. In "Moral Trigonometry" (also known as "Moral Triangulation") her thesis "treated of a third element in all twofold relations,—between married people, the bond to which both alike owed allegiance; between States, the compact which originally bound them together. . . . Then the sacredness of the bond possessed my mind. 'Was an agreement, so solemnly entered into, as vital in its obligations, to be so lightly canceled?' I labored with all my might to prove that this could not be done."[34] Julia saw this sacred bond as a sort of "third party." The compact, bond, or agreement set up mutual obligations that had an independent life of their own. As a separate, or third entity, these obligations required as much respect as did the two individuals who entered into an agreement in the first place. Because of this, marriages could not break up; nations could not dissolve themselves. As Julia took up one example after the other, the message repeated itself: "it [the bond] was devised in solemnity, it cannot be broken in temper. It was signed in good faith, it cannot be annulled by ill faith."[35]

Built into her essay was the distress many northerners felt at the massive disorder that war symbolized. Julia was concerned about the fragile tissue of social obligation. "Your bond is given to society. . . . And, the bond once given, society is also bound to inspect and aid its' fulfillment. For society itself is build up of a network of such bonds, grandly coherent, and with the closest intersolidarity of obligation." Since bonds make up society, survival depends on strict adherence to them. Julia compared the bond, or "third party," to the keystone of the arch. When the keystone was removed, the arch collapsed. When obligations were tossed aside, society was in danger of collapse. War, chaos, and destruction threatened on all sides. Even laws, as important as they were, could not prevent this. Had not laws, after all, hanged John Brown and returned fugitive slaves? The only thing that could prevent this collapse was inner restraint.

The theme of restraint and moderation not only connected "Moral Trigonometry" to "Proteus," but it also linked Julia to a major intellectual trend in New England. The whole question of controlling a society disordered by expansion, urbanization, industrialization, and war preoccupied many northerners. They wished to infuse the population with ideals of mass discipline and order.[36] To Julia, the obligation to the "third party" provided an organizing, disciplining principle. "Passing into the region of individual morality, the third party comes in between ourselves and the objects of action and desire with supreme power of permission and denial. In ambition, its' cold 'thou shalt not' thrills like a tone struck from crystal. . . . It checks us in the leap of Pleasure—it spurs us in the spring of Duty." A tender individual and social conscience would spring from the recognition that all bonds—contracts, compacts, or any sort of mutual obligation—were sacred. It was an individual's duty to respect them and fulfill them, not only in matters of personal morality but also in matters of public significance.

The more abstruse essay "Doubt and Belief" (also known as "Philosophy and Religion") also built on Julia's personal experience. She began the piece on a strictly abstract plane. Philosophy equaled doubt. It questioned and criticized, challenged and condemned. It was also the lever that pushed thought onward, for as it questioned, it weeded out false and outdated ideas. Religion was belief. No act of will could produce belief. Belief came of itself.

155

"Belief . . . is not a creative act, but the becoming aware of that which already exists." The two tendencies battled each other, with one in ascendancy in one generation; the other, in the next. Julia had no doubt which one would win. "Doubt ministers to belief, not disbelief," she asserted. "Doubt is the process of thought, and belief the result. To be at all, we must believe, not that we seem to be, but that we are. Our whole human career is founded upon acts of faith which are monstrous, considering the limitations of our experience."[38] To live, individuals simply had to believe. In this Julia crossed swords with those radical Transcendentalists who were moving toward a denial of anything immaterial.

Some of the Transcendentalists sought a new religion that would go beyond their previous rejection of the divinity of Christ. They sought "freedom from bondage of sect and creed, from the provincialism even of Christianity itself." This new creed stressed faith in man, not in God. Men like Octavius Frothingham, Franklin Sanborn, George William Curtis, Thomas Wentworth Higginson, William Lloyd Garrison, and Ralph Waldo Emerson sought a new "religion of humanity" that "abandoned conventional Christian theism with its affirmation that God is working in the world."[39] To these religious radicals, God was no longer the center of belief; men and women were to have faith in themselves without reference to any divine presence. Her hard-won religious convictions were too precious for Julia to watch erode under this attack. She decided to rebut the radical arguments. She wanted to convey, clearly and simply, her own process of religious growth.

> The grammar of thinking frightens us. We doubt whether we know how to think, and this is the supreme doubt of all. Lay down the book, for God's sake—there is nothing in this room but an empty brain. All that is vital has vanished. Open the window—let the air rush in with a shock. Let in the young daybeams. . . . Light and heat are positive. Your little child runs to kiss you. He wants something of you, very positively. The household asks your help to place a shelf—the council will confer with you about a road. . . . A sonorous voice recites "I am the resurrection and the life." You are weary of question—that "I am" lifts you upon its' strong, solemn wings. Duty, love, self-sacrifice—these are resurrection, these are life. Belief now comes—it is his turn to help you.[40]

Duty and restraint were becoming familiar notes. Now Julia linked them to the power to believe. Duty and sacrifice, obligations and restraint were part of the ordinary struggles each individual encountered, just as did the weary parent in Julia's essay. The honorable performance of all these little tasks opened the window for the winds of religious conviction to blow in. Those who honored their obligations and chose a life of moderation and restraint would eventually know the comfort of belief in themselves and the comfort of divine help. Belief would conquer doubt. This had been her experience a decade ago; now in an age of doubt and strife, Julia held up part of her private experience in public to affirm the vitality of religious belief.

After years of doubt and disapproval, both from within and from others, Julia felt increasingly clear that she had a public role to play. Nowhere is this better illustrated than in her transition from plays to lectures. Both plays had been outlets for her inner tensions, but while they expressed her concerns, they did not solve the problems. The lectures, in a more tightly controlled, somewhat more indirect way, dealt with many of the same issues—eroticism, loyalty, and gender role. They also were intended to suggest solutions to these problems through the application of general philosophical principles. Furthermore, the lectures were written not for other people to act out, as were the plays, but for Julia to act on. From the passive role of scribe she moved to the more active role of lecturer-instructor.

The enthusiasm of her audiences strengthened Julia. To declare her belief in God was to declare that there was order and purpose on earth as in heaven. The death of a child, then, was no mere random torment, but part of a divine plan. In casting off doubt, Julia was beginning to heal herself. A year after Sammy died, Julia had a dream in which she saw "dearest Sammy was playing in my closet, and looked radiant and lovely. Presently he was gone. I knew he was dead and yet saw him and kissed and held him."[41] Her reconciliation was only partial, but it was beginning.

On her forty-fifth birthday, Julia Ward Howe wrote in her journal, "This year, begun in intolerable distress, has been I think the most valuable of my life. Paralyzed at first by Sammy's death, I soon found my only refuge from grief in increased activity, after my kind."[42]

The war had been helpful to Julia in suggesting those avenues of activity. The war stimulated her to write a popular poem, for which her reputation was growing daily. Outer change had stimulated inner change in Julia, and she had decided to pursue an independent vocation. Moreover, war had stimulated concern about disorder and discipline, thereby creating an audience for Julia's theories about restraint, obligation, duty, and belief.

Her activities for the six months following this May entry were equally as valuable. Nothing she did could make peace with Chev or compensate for the death of Sammy. Nevertheless, each new task strengthened Julia's sense of well-being. Her lectures gave her confidence in her inclinations to speak before audiences and to make some aspects of her studies public. She basked in the news that her talks had helped others; she relished the praise of friends and colleagues. Her work reassured her that she had a good instinct where her audiences were concerned. She was becoming convinced that her "inner voice" was sound and not misleading. That guiding light of her childhood, the hope of producing a work of enduring value to society, once again rose in her firmament. This time the star seemed within reach.

TEN

Philosophy, 1864-1867

Naked and poor thou goest, Philosophy!
Thy robe of serge hath lain beneath the stars;
Thy weight of tresses, ponderously free,
Of iron hue, no golden circlet bars.

. . . .

Thy hollow cheek, and eye of distant light,
Won from the chief of men their noblest love;
Olympian feasts thy temperance requite,
And thy worn weeds a priceless dowry prove.

I know not if I've caught the matchless mood
In which impassioned Petrarch sang of thee;
But this I know,—the world its plenitude
May keep, so I may share thy beggary.

During the months that followed her lecture tours, Julia was unable to transform her sense of purpose into concrete plans. Domestic and emotional problems kept her turned inward, away from the public whom Julia wanted so much to affect. She did, however, continue to study and to write. Her later essays brought her to a breakthrough in her convictions about woman's role.

When Julia returned from her Washington trip in May 1864, she learned that the Russian fleet had tied up in Boston as part of its goodwill mission. Julia gave several small parties in honor of the Russian officers, and she attended various social functions on board ship. All of these events were successful. Inexplicably even Chev caught the spirit on one occasion, allowing Julia to serve wine with dinner.[1]

No one could doubt that the "Battle Hymn" had contributed to Julia's social stature. Julia, however, wearied of being introduced everywhere as the author of those verses.[2] She felt "full of days' works," and she expected to do much more with her life than write one famous poem.[3] Nevertheless, the honor and fame were useful and bracing to Julia. She no longer felt herself sinking in an ocean of indifference. In the following months, she picked up the pace of her party giving, delighted that once again Chev "unbent his iron brow" and had a good time.[4] Sometimes the house was so full that Harry slept on a mattress on the grand piano.[5] Julia was delighted to attend the Barnstable Ball at the invitation of Governor and Mrs. Andrews. To this was added the pleasure of invitations to artists' receptions in Boston and New York.[6] According to the custom of the time, Julia also received callers at home every afternoon and evening.[7] Best of all, these professors, ministers, lecturers, and authors were, by the end of the war, her friends. Henry James, Sr., came often to her house, as did Louis and Elizabeth Agassiz. Moncure Conway, noted preacher and reformer, stayed with her when visiting Boston.[8] All these people were feathers in Julia's social cap.

Julia cemented her friendship with Oliver Wendell Holmes on a trip to New York in mid-November 1864. Both were headed for a celebration of William Cullen Bryant's seventieth birthday at the Century Club. The autocrat of the breakfast table soon engaged the author of the "Battle Hymn" in such strenuous conversation that they both forgot to eat lunch. After the celebration, the two rode home together, talking into the wee hours. Holmes honored Julia with the nickname "*Madame Comment*," and they remained lifelong friends.[9]

The Bryant celebration marked the first time Julia had been invited to speak publicly. Her verses were applauded and published with the other tributes written for the occasion. Julia knew she had received the invitation because she had written "the most stirring lyric of the war," as her introduction proclaimed.[10] Nonetheless, she was thrilled by the whole affair. "This was, I suppose, the greatest public honor of my life. I record it here for my grandchildren."[11] Her invitation meant not only that doors would be opened, but also that the writers and thinkers whom she had always admired would be holding these doors for her.

Other "days' works" awaited. The Civil War had brought to public attention the needs of the navy and merchant marine not only for armaments but various other forms of public support. Bostonians decided to hold a National Sailors Fair for twelve days in mid-November. Its sponsors hoped to raise sufficient funds to build a home for aged and disabled sailors, especially those who had fought in naval engagements on behalf of the North. The managers agreed to publish a paper during the course of the fair in order to publicize exhibits and to make announcements. Oliver Wendell Holmes, Edward

Everett, John Greenleaf Whittier, James Russell Lowell, Andrew Preston Peabody, and Edwin Percy Whipple formed the editorial council for this journal.[12] They chose *Boatswain's Whistle* as the title for the paper, and they chose Julia Ward Howe as editor.

Julia set up a table of her own where objects of particular interest were on display, including two valuable albums of photographs. Here she accepted brief essays, poetry, and short stories for publication. In addition, Julia solicited advertising and kept track of the latest changes in and additions to the fair. She prepared a daily editor's page consisting of major announcements, descriptions of the fair and of articles for sale, jokes and riddles, a list of raffle winners, letters to the editor, amusing clippings from other newspapers, and serious editorials praising the sailors and advancing the cause of the Seaman's Home. Her reporting covered everything from a 3,900-pound white ox named General Grant to the mock battle of the *Monitor* and the *Merrimac* staged on Frog Pond on the Boston Common. The descriptions of the articles to be raffled off were especially important since the raffles brought in the largest sums; on one night alone, the raffles raised $24,038.[13] To all this, Julia added a serialized story of 7,000 words that ran for seven days. A letter of thanks from the editorial council complimented her on her efforts, noting the extensive circulation of the paper and the general favor with which it was received by the general public.[14]

To Julia, who had felt the collapse of her hopes just three years before, the approval of her stint as editor of the *Boatswain's Whistle* was delightful confirmation of her worth and ability. She felt her powers bloom and expand, for now journalism held itself out as a possible career in addition to public speaking.

On April 10, 1865, Julia learned of the surrender at Appomattox. The end of the Civil War was now in sight. Julia was as excited as anyone. "Ribbons for victory, .40¢," she noted in her journal. "All flags out—shop windows decorated—processions in the street. All friends meet and shake hands. On the newspaper bulletins such placards as 'Gloria in excelsis Deo,' 'Thanks be to God!'"[15]

To Julia and her friends, this victory did indeed seem to be God's work.[16] The purgation of war was over; the rebuilding of the new and nobler society could begin. The old abolitionists gathered in the Republican Party, elated with the chance to reform the nation's institutions. "These are no times for ordinary politics; these are formative hours," declared Wendell Phillips. "The national purpose and thought grows and ripens in thirty days as much as ordinary years bring it forward. We *radicals* have all the elements of national education in our hands."[17] Chev supported most of the proposals of the Republicans. Although he disagreed with their treatment of the South, he did believe in special assistance to the freedmen and in granting their political rights.[18] Francis Bird, a friend of both Julia and Chev and head of the Republican Party in Massachusetts, looked forward to an extensive program of reform as well.[19] To Julia, whose eyes had "seen the glory," the hope of social progress was an infectious one. She, too, wished to participate.

The vision of a renewed society had a subtle effect on Julia's long-standing desire to contribute something of lasting value. Instead of leaving to posterity only artistic creations, she now wished to produce something more generally useful, a work that would touch "the sympathies of the average community," a platform "from which I might speak for their own good and mine."[20]

Although Julia was not entirely sure what her calling would be, she began to look at her lectures in this light: "All things point one way, viz: towards the adoption of a profession of ethical exposition, after my sort. . . . If I am sent for, and have a word to say, I should say it."[21]

Julia expressed such sentiments in her journal. She hoped her essays would "open such a vista of usefulness to me, and of good to others." She was determined "to hold on with both hands to the largeness of philosophical pursuit and study, and to do my utmost to be useful in this connection and path of life."[22]

The impulse to guide others' moral direction had seized her even before the end of the war. In defending her Washington lectures to Sumner, Julia had asserted: "It was honestly the atrocious tone of society on the occasion of your almost murder that first filled me with the desire to find this deep word of reproof. . . . My whole study has been to find that deeper vein of consideration which should shew the reasons for the mistakes that men make, and the sins they commit."[23]

In "Moral Trigonometry" Julia had linked her theory of strict adherence to duty to the general uplift of society. "It [the bond] was constructed to aid the principles which give human progress and development. . . . Most of all, its' spirit is in harmony with the cardinal tendencies and highest interests of human society." This sense of mission persisted. In the introduction to another series of lectures, Julia elaborated on her words to Sumner. She wrote her essays, she said, to fill a gap in the current discussion of the general drift of society. By exploring the ethical and moral component of human life, and by teaching the "intimate application of religion to the labor of life," she hoped to link abstract principles with action. She hoped her philosophy would provide a foundation for social uplift. "The student of philosophy has a higher task to fulfill towards his contemporaries than that of amusing their minds or of wringing their hearts. To him the commands of Holy writ especially applies: 'Freely have ye received, freely give.' "[24] Julia decided to give freely by lecturing as much as possible.

Julia's determination to continue a career of public readings of her essays had as much to do with her financial status as with her sense of mission. Julia needed to earn more money.[25] The *Commonwealth*, under new ownership, paid her for regular columns.[26] So did the *Tribune* from July through October, when she wrote her letters from Newport.[27] This was not enough, however. For example, when the owner of 13 Chestnut Street wanted to sell his house, Julia and Chev could not afford to buy it. They settled instead on a house in Boylston Place, a dark street in a much less fashionable district than Beacon Hill.[28] Harry was planning to enter Harvard College in the fall. The prospect of his tuition worried Julia as much as the loss of her favorite house. Pressed for funds, she thought about publishing a book of her *Tribune* letters.[29] When this proved fruitless, she took on a year's work as a writer for the *Home Weekly*.[30] More important, she set to work on a new volume of poetry.[31]

Later Lyrics, published in 1866, was written for money. The chilly welcome that reviewers extended to Julia's book was well deserved since the poems were generally undistinguished. The first section, devoted to poems of the Civil War, included the "Battle Hymn." This was the hook. The buyer then had to slog through poetry ranging from the moderately good to pure magazine sentiment. Even the poetry she selected from her Sammy poems was less than powerful. The book sold poorly. Julia, recognizing that she had lost her market, gave up. Not until she was an old woman would she publish poetry again.[32]

Since *Later Lyrics* was a failure, money worries still pressed Julia. Theoretically Chev was to keep up the household, but often he could not meet the bills. Julia then lent him money. Sometimes he repaid her, sometimes he did not.[33] To avoid constant battling over this, Julia placed twenty-year-old Flossy, Chev's favorite after Julia Romana, at the head of the household. Like a trusted housekeeper, Flossy managed the servants and the finances.[34] With her mother she settled accounts monthly; then to her father's office she went to discuss expenses.[35]

Until 1867, the sums at Julia's disposal were not large. She received quarterly cheques from Ward and Company, the inheritor of her father's business. Her once large estate was so ravaged by the mid-1860s that her investments yielded no more than eighty to one hundred dollars each quarter. Apparently Chev had given up his old practice of having Julia turn the money over to him; perhaps Julia's tenacity and determination to control some aspects of her own life had worn him down.

In early 1866 Julia received a small bequest of $111.81, the remains of the estate of her brother, Francis Marion.[36] Another bequest followed in April 1866, when Uncle John died. Julia expected a large inheritance, but she was disappointed. Although her brother Sam received a substantial inheritance, Julia and her sisters received modest shares.[37] This fact left her

> dull, sad, and perplexed. My uncle not having made me a rich woman, I feel more than ever impelled to make some great effort to realize the value of my mental capacities and acquisitions. I am as well entitled to an efficient literary position as any woman in this country—perhaps better than any other. Still, I hang by the way, picking up ten dollars here and there with great difficulty. I pray God to help me to an occasion or sphere in which I may do my utmost. I had as lief die as live unless I can be satisfied that I have delivered that whole value of my literary cargo—all at least that was invoiced for this world. Hear me, great Heaven—guide and assist me! No mortal can.[38]

Julia quickly resolved her disappointment. To Annie she wrote at length about her pleasures in Boston—books, brains, a lively and liberal church. As she settled back at home with her philosophy, she remarked, "Now you see sister, that I am rich without money. If I have ever greatly wanted the latter, it was to do for the girls and satisfy the Doctor."[39]

Another interesting measure of the inner balance Julia was finding in her midforties was the acceptance of the death of Uncle John without accompanying frights or depression. To Annie she wrote that their uncle seemed "far nearer to us now than before. I grouped the newcomer in the land of the spirits with those familiar to us as already there. . . . In church, one seems to face the spiritual world, and to see those who are no longer here as belonging there."[40] The "spirits" she saw were no longer threatening or sinister, but friendly. Julia envisioned her family—Mother, Father, Henry, Francis Marion, Sammy, and now Uncle John—as content, unified, and close. She transformed the mystery and danger of death into a re-creation of the Victorian family and was comforted.

In the late fall of that year came what Julia hoped would be an answer to her prayers. James Roberts Gilmore, businessman and magazine editor, asked her to edit a new journal, *Northern Lights*.[41] This was to be a weekly magazine dedicated to literature and short opinion pieces. It appeared beginning in January 1867.

Julia's position as editor was peculiar since she had power only to contribute her own manuscripts and to solicit other contributions. She could not make contracts with other writers, nor had she any say in the direction of the magazine. Nevertheless, at thirty dollars per week, the position was welcome.[42] Most of her energies were given over to writing to fill the pages. She wrote an editorial for each issue. In addition, Julia contributed to the first issues four poems, two humorous pieces, a short story, an analysis of Beethoven's Seventh Symphony, and a review of George Sand's "Dernier Amour."[43] In addition to all this, Julia wrote regularly to people who she thought might contribute stories or essays.[44] Unfortunately for Julia, the magazine lasted for only ten issues. In February 1867, Julia wrote, "All is up, as I feared, with *Northern Lights*, in its present form. Gilmore proposes to go to New York and to change its' form and character to that of a weekly newspaper." Although she was forced to retire as editor, Julia regarded this turn of events as something of a blessing. She would miss the money, but she would not miss her inconclusive position as editor.[45]

Moreover, money, for the first time since her girlhood, was suddenly no longer a problem. In January Julia learned, contrary to what she had been led to believe, that she had inherited a great deal of money from Uncle John. Although her portion of his estate was not great, the income from it was hefty: she received, twice a year, between $1,400 and $2,500. She was stunned. "The larger of these sums makes me a rich woman and I am frightened to think how I might waste this money, and relax my exertions to make the most of time and gifts. I pray God that I may not do so."[46]

This income nearly doubled Chev's, especially because Julia turned most of it over to him. Legally, the money was his, and morally, Julia felt obligated to help Chev meet family expenses.[47] Julia had "great misgivings" over the transaction. "His tyrannical instincts, more than any direct purpose, have made him illiberal with me in money matters, and if he can possibly place this so I cannot easily use it, he will, only because money is power, and a man never wishes a woman to have any which she does not derive from him." Julia's prediction was perfect. Of the $1,428.57 that she received as a first installment, Chev invested $1,100 and gave her the remainder.[48]

Julia's cool analysis of the situation suggests again that she was moving steadily toward inner balance and emotional self-sufficiency during this period. Her remarks lack the high level of emotion that previously accompanied her reactions to Chev's handling of her money. Though tinged with bitterness, her tone is basically matter-of-fact. She could be realistic without burning up with indignation. Furthermore, by acknowledging the fullness of Chev's tyranny, Julia had put herself in a different relationship with him, one less defensive and reactive. She no longer let herself be drawn into agonizing power struggles that she could only lose. As Julia moved away from intense identification of herself with her inheritance, Chev lost a weapon with which to hammer home her submission to him. Although he would irritate her in the future with his financial dealing, Chev would never again have the power to wound Julia over money.

The Howes, thanks to Julia, were now an upper-middle-class family. Chev held in trust for Julia the house and land at Lawton's Valley, worth $7,500, as well as one-half of their house at 19 Boylston Place. In addition, Chev controlled $10,000 in "money at interest" and other notes due, $10,000 in Union Pacific Railroad bonds, and 213 shares in other railroads, utilities, and manufacturing concerns.[49]

Not until Chev died, six and one-half years later, did Julia control one penny of this fortune. Furthermore, Julia could do nothing when Chev, restless as ever, talked of selling their houses to save money. First he threatened Lawton's Valley; later he rented out 19 Boylston Place.[50] That Julia owned these places in whole or in part meant nothing. No wonder she was exasperated when Chev consented to the sale of some valuable family real estate to Adolphe Mailliard, Annie's husband, for less than its actual worth.[51]

Julia's predicament was typical of the sort of situation that had long interested the women's rights movement. Control over property had been a major plank in their platform since 1848.[52] Julia, however, felt no sense of kinship with the women who advocated political and legal changes in women's status. The meeting at Seneca Falls seems not to have caught her attention. Ever since the late 1840s her reaction to women's rights had been inconsistent and waffling. Nonetheless, she did have some ideas of her own on the topic. As early as 1847 she wrote to Louisa that she considered too much childbearing "as materializing and degrading to a woman whose spiritual nature has any strength. . . . But I will not trouble your dear little well-ordered head with any suggestions upon the natural inalienable rights of women—it is to me a subject of painful interest."[53]

Later she defended women's education in *Eva and Raphael* and *The World's Own*. In *A Trip to Cuba*, Julia quoted a long discussion held on a sultry Havana night. She assented to the idea that women needed an education in order to instruct their sons, but added, "educate her for herself, that she may give good counsel, and discern the noble and the beautiful . . . for their own sakes, they [women] have a right to know all that elevates and dignifies life."[54] In this, Julia aligned herself with the traditional elements in the woman's movement.

A series of poems addressed to Florence Nightingale took up the theme somewhat differently. Julia admired Nightingale's work, but censured the system whereby men allowed only a few women to pursue the course of work to which they felt called.

> If you debase the sex to elevate
> One of like soul and temper with the rest,
> You do but wrong a thousand fervent hearts,
> To pay full tribute to one generous breast.
>
> . . . .
>
> But she had freedom—hearts akin to hers
> Are held as springs shut up, as fountains sealed
> The weighty masonry of life must part
> Before their hidden virtue be revealed.
>
> Women who weave in hope the daily web,
> Who leave the deadly depths of passion pure,
> Who hold the stormy powers of will attent,
> As Heaven directs, to act, or to endure;
>
> No multitude strews branches in their way,
> Not in their praise the loud arena strives,
> Still as a flameless incense rises up
> The costly patience of their offered lives.[55]

Some of her distaste for the cause she had inherited from her family. "I first heard of 'women's rights' when Fanny Wright came to America and lectured. The subject was always spoken of with te-heeing, as if women's right involved man's wrong."[56] The burgeoning woman's rights movement of the 1850s did not interest Julia either. New property rights statutes could not return to her control over her lost inheritance. Access to the colleges would not help her now; a professional career would not tone down Chev's demands. Julia's thoughts were on an inward course, and as she studied religion and philosophy, she sought answers in terms of personal change of heart. Protection for women would come only when men recognized their moral responsibility to be moderate and restrained. Laws could not arrange this, and the bold demands of women for new positions of public power could not effect it either. Only individual moral regeneration would suffice. "I hold that the greatest modifications of society come from within, not without, except where outward repression renders inward development impossible."[57]

Julia had, in fact, a basically uncharitable view of other women. In part this was because she had no close woman friends except for her two sisters. Not until her midforties did Julia acquire a circle of female acquaintances who supported her aspirations and comforted her in adversity. Her Brain Club, established in 1864, was Julia's first venture into building networks among women. The lack of an older woman to guide her may explain why Julia entered this aspect of sisterhood relatively late in life. Even among her acquaintances Julia knew of only a handful of women who, like Fanny Appleton Longfellow, were interested in study, or who, like Annie Fields, were dedicated to literature. Most women struck Julia as shallow, artificial, and consumed by the passion for luxury in dress.

In an essay of the midfifties entitled "The Woman's Rights Question," Julia condemned women for their ostentation in their drive for social status and for their ignorance of political questions. Furthermore, she claimed, women were guilty of supporting ignorant and corrupt ministers, of supporting slavery, of opposing politicians with noble principles, and of wasting their money and health on late hours, rich food, and fashionable dress. Putting it simply, Julia decided that women were unworthy of political rights. If they wished to gain them, she argued, then they must abandon their pursuit of selfish pleasure in favor of an interest in the public good. A plan of self-education in natural science, history, logic, literature, art, and mathematics would be essential. This could be accomplished without tampering with current legal conditions.[58]

Julia was hostile to other women who stepped outside of their "spheres." They merely degraded themselves, she asserted. More important, they undermined their traditional influence in the home. Julia mounted a passionate defense of conventional womanhood, idolizing Elizabeth Barrett Browning for her "womanly qualities" and disparaging Margaret Fuller as arrogant. She defended the idea of separate spheres for men and women as parallel and equal in value. Women were to pursue the moral, spiritual, and social aspects of life and to devote themselves to the critical task of motherhood. "I am inclined to hold the passion of Maternity above the passion of Love," she declared.[59] These, not public life, were the proper concerns of women.

In a later essay, another vein of criticism emerges that reflects back on Julia herself. Impressionable women, Julia argued, might not have the power to resist immoral forces, particularly the "power of insistance which a man derives from his extended activity." Law and social sanctions must exist to convince women to live pure and ethical lives.[60] What seemed to worry Julia was the disruptive force of sexual attraction, about which she knew from experience. The essay suggests that she feared her own sexual impulses as much as she did those of men. If so, the bonds of law and custom provided her with protection from herself. Apparently some of Julia's dislike of the women's rights movement stemmed from her fear and dislike of certain aspects of herself.

Overcoming this required a good many changes. Of significant help was her conversion to abolitionism in 1859. After that she could clearly identify herself with the side of right in political questions. The "Battle Hymn of the Republic" helped, too, in providing her with automatic status in the eyes of the public. Her acceptance by the literati of the Northeast, exemplified by her participation in the Bryant Festival, helped improve Julia's estimation of herself. Her success on the lecture circuit and her recognition as a journalist were further boosts to her self-esteem. Finally, the social success she enjoyed at the end of the war made it unnecessary for her to chase after recognition. She was now free to dress unfashionably if she liked, to entertain whom she pleased, and to place study above all other pastimes if she chose. She now had enough social power to be eccentric. She no longer spent great sums on food, dress, or entertainments. She could take high ground, condemning this behavior in others without feeling guilty herself.[61]

Julia still lacked an intellectual foundation for a switch to feminism. According to her separate spheres theory, women should stay away from male pursuits, and that was that. Obviously she did not fully believe this since she also believed that individuals must abide by the dictates of their own consciences. She had not, however, in the mid-1860s put together a cohesive theory that could square her two opposing ideas.

Nevertheless, the ingredients for such a theory were simmering in Julia's mind. Theodore Parker had long been an advocate of a widened sphere of action for women. As early as 1853 he declared that all but the most brutal fields of work should be open to women; for society to do less was "a monstrous waste of the most precious material God ever made." Although this provided Julia with specific encouragement to pursue her plan of writing and publishing, it did not replace her separate spheres theory. Indeed, a major part of Parker's sermon on the "Public Functions of Woman" stressed woman's moral superiority over man, thereby leaning, in part, on one major prop of the whole separate spheres argument.[62]

In 1866, as the nation debated the definition of protections required for freedmen's rights, Julia began to draw parallels between the position of the newly freed slaves and that of women. "The laws and duties of society rest upon a supposed compact. But this compact cannot deprive any set of men of rights and limit them to duties, for if you refuse them all rights, you deprive them even of the power to become a party to this compact, which rests upon their right to do so. Our slaves had no rights. Women have few."[63] Blacks had been unfairly oppressed, denied their rights, and prevented from developing their individual potentials. In order to correct this, reformers sought remedies in legislation, elections, and constitutional amendments. Political action, in other words, would remedy the freedmen's plight. When Julia was ready, nearly three years later, to pursue the analogy, she would select political action as a remedy for women, too. The slave analogy remained a model on which Julia could hinge her feminist theory.

The history of the slaves did not supply Julia yet with the theory she needed. Neither did her experience with Chev. Although his treatment of her might have led Julia to formulate at least an antimale, if not necessarily a profemale position, his autocratic behavior did not have this effect.

Yet Julia did suffer from Chev's demands. In particular, his unremitting hostility to her cherished projects of writing and speaking troubled her. He had criticized her trip to Washington, declaring that the whole family had been "much pained" by the expedition. He disapproved of her reading at the Century Club, where she was the only woman on the podium. He forbade her lecturing in Concord, and he prevented her from reading at Tufts University. When she defied him and read a lecture in Lexington for the Battle Monument Association, Chev berated her. He also told her not to preach to the prisoners in Charlestown Jail, as she wished to do. He repeatedly pinned her between the pressure of duty to her family and the power of her own inclinations. If she allowed the "internal necessity to conquer the external," then she paid a price.

. . . with the utmost vehemence and temper, [Chev] called my undertaking a mere display, a mere courting of publicity, would not argue, would not hear me at all. Threatened to shape the whole government of the family according to his wishes which he has always done so far as he could. I said little and suffered much. . . . I feel utterly paralyzed and brought to a standstill—know not how to live and work any further. I have been married twenty-two years today. In the course of this time, I have never known my husband to approve any act of mine which I myself valued. Books, poems, essays, everything has been contemptible or contraband in his eyes, because it was not *his* way of doing things.[64]

In Chev's opinion, a married woman had one responsibility and that was to her household. Any other notions of duty to society or oneself were delusions. While Julia had agreed with Chev's point of view in the mid-1850s, she no longer believed that women should be so confined. By 1865, Chev and Julia had had such separate lives for so long that neither understood the other's point of view, and neither wanted to.

Chev continued to be unreasonable in other ways, long familiar to Julia. In the fall of 1865, owing to his sale of 13 Chestnut Street, the Howes needed to find a new house. Chev refused to let Julia wait in Newport while he decided, instead requiring her to stay at the Institue, which she found detestable.[65] During the following month he tormented Julia by purchasing 19 Boylston Street and then threatening to sell it. Later that fall he put in a new hearth and grate in the parlor, causing extensive inconvenience and discomfort. When Julia complained

He retorted furiously, saying that it was all my fault, the result of my want of system. I told him these repeated chills would shorten my life, to which he replied that the confusion and dirt of the house were shortening his life. I said, "it does not seem to." He left and Maud cried and Flossy attacked me most severely. What was the truth? I had complained, not improperly, of a dangerous discomfort, from which I still suffer, and the only result was to excite Chev's passions and through these, those of the children against me.[66]

In December 1866 another disturbing element presented itself. Chev refused to allow Julia to accompany him to the Institute. "This caused me bitter pain," she confessed to her journal, "and suspicion as to the possible reason for such an exclusion."[67] It was not the first time Julia had suspected her husband of infidelity.

In spite of these difficulties, Julia was still loyal to Chev.[68] They usually managed to patch up their quarrels.[69] In the spring of 1866 Julia spent two weeks trying to secure for Chev an appointment to Greece.[70] When this failed, she wrote a poem to comfort him.

Another reason that Julia did not react with hatred was that, despite their stormy moments, Julia was beginning to learn how to live with Chev. Laura recalled that, for the most part, her mother learned to stay away from Chev when he was under stress, thereby avoiding the "northwest wind" of his temper. Julia had learned that argument was useless, so she saved her breath and confronted Chev with implacable silence. Chev once said of her that she met his views with the opposition of a sandbank, "which soaks up the force of the stream." To this quiet stubbornness, Julia added the advice of a Quaker gentleman. When Julia asked him how he had managed to make his house a safe haven for the Underground Railroad when everyone around him was hostile, he replied, "It was borne in upon me at an early period that if I told no one what I intended to do, I should be enabled to do it."[71] Julia began to keep her own counsel and to go quietly about her business.[72]

Moreover, Julia now felt confident in using the doctrines to which Parker had introduced her. She justified her behavior to herself by referring to the dictates of conscience. In her journal she wrote, "I have too often set down the moral weight I have to carry. . . . But the voice now tells me that I must bear it to the end, or lose it forever." Another entry declares, "Independently of ambition, vanity, pride, all of which prompt all of us, I feel that I must do what my hands find to do, taking my dictation and my reward from sources quite above human will and approbation."[73] Chev's direction mattered less and less to her. "I earnestly desire to live in Christian love and charity with him," Julia wrote, "but not so that my conscience shall be subject to his will."[74] [Chev's] "displeasure does not absolve me from the duty of exercising my talents. A husband's authority is relative and contingent—that of conscience is absolute. Does a woman abdicate this when she marries? Is marriage moral as well as civil death? Neither. It is a relation of sex and sympathy, not of soul and substance. Our moral attitude, our divine promptings and inspirations mark the latter—woe to him who would put the lower above the higher."[75]

Learning to deal with Chev brought Julia a step closer to advocating women's rights. The conflict in her marriage had not taught Julia to hate men. Instead it taught her to operate independently, to resist opposition by ignoring it, and to find alternative sources of support and justification for her plans.

In spite of her growing independence, Julia did feel discouraged periodically. Of course Chev's opposition to her "profession of ethical exposition" left her unhappy. She could think of no other path she might take that would allow her to contribute to the general progress and improvement of society. During 1865 and 1866 she complained to her journal of "spleen," her word for "a want of interest in life and of positive hope."[76] This feeling also had physical manifestations in addition to eye trouble and headaches. "Throughout my whole body I feel a mingled restlessness and feebleness, as if the nerves were irritated, and the muscles powerless." In other words, Chev's behavior once again brought on the familiar symptoms of depression. Occasionally she felt lonely, as if no one understood or cared about what she was doing.[77] At other times her sense of direction failed her temporarily. Her dream of helping society by expounding her ethical ideas seemed hopeless. "I see no outlook before me—so many fields for activity, but for passivity, which seems incumbent upon me, only uselessness, obscurity, deterioration. Some effort I must make."[78]

She did. Julia went on lecturing. During 1865 and 1866 she read her poetry and her essays at every opportunity. She read in Newport, Boston, New York, Bordentown, and, once again, Washington.[79] In August 1866 Julia attended the meetings in Northampton, Massachusetts, of the American Academy of Science. Even there, Julia read an essay, admittedly to a "fatigued and cold" audience.[80] Her determination never flagged for long.

One reason that Julia continued to lecture was because she was continuing to write new essays. Her titles for them shifted about, but it is clear that she wrote a series of essays under the general title "Limitations."[81] One of these, "Moving Forces," concerned aesthetics; another, the "Three Degrees of Law," concerned the legal and political limits of any state or nation. "The Fact Accomplished" also fell into this series. All of these essays, along with another entitled "Polarity," were finished in 1864, although Julia continued to polish them and rearrange them for several years.[82]

Julia based some of her theory on a combination of Comtian progressivism and the Hegelian idea of dialectics. She derived other of her theories from Spinoza. She describes him as setting up a theoretical continuum that stretched from the "Passive" to the "Active." As Julia saw it, the static pole consisted of governing principles; the active pole comprised phenomena. Both poles, however, were part of one and the same power. For example, on the continuum of friendship, there were people who were actively friendly toward one, others who were only potentially so, and, ultimately, the ideal of friendship.[83] Yet all of this was part of the power of friendship.

The best expression of this theory is "Polarity," in which Julia attempted to describe the nature of the two ends of the continuum and their interactions. Here Julia asserted her view that the passive or static pole was in fact an idea in the mind of God or, in her usage, the Ideal. The Ideal was a necessitating condition, "divine and absolute." All phenomena flowed directly from this Ideal. In other words, everything that existed or happened was simply a material manifestation of this Ideal.[84] Julia's Ideal was more than a passive idea. It had within it the potential for action, just as a nonfriend possessed the potential for friendship. The Ideal was, therefore, an active or "efficient" moral force that caused everything to progress to a higher state or to a condition closer to the Ideal itself.[85]

Within these arcane discussions, Julia found meat for the building of a better society. For example, she assured her listeners that the only country in the world in which the moral force of the Ideal could be made to work was the United States. Here thought flourished unencumbered by superstition or archaic formulas. People could more readily see the next steps necessary for social advancement. They had at their disposal the means to achieve these steps, too.[86] Perhaps Julia had in mind Chev's work with the blind. Although he had learned the rudiments in Europe, he was able to put the theories into practice much more efficiently in New England.

In "Polarity," Julia tackled an issue of utmost concern to her, the relationships between the sexes. The question of sex was widely misunderstood, Julia asserted. She intended to shed some light on this thorny dilemma, resolving the debate about the proper role for men and women in a manner "at once simple and satisfactory." (In her essay of 15,000 words, she succeeded at neither.)

Julia began this part of her essay by once again propounding the separate spheres argument. Men and women are fundamentally different, and each has important separate moral, as well as physical, functions. "The very existence of society depends upon the maintained integrity of these two types," Julia declared. To work her way out of this, Julia turned to her idea of poles, or opposites. Male and female were really only the two poles of one divine idea. Neither one was better or worse than the other. "In such a division, no inequality can be supposedly possible, since one part of what is divine cannot be more or less divine than the other."

This line of argument carried Julia a major step farther. In each sex lay the same moral, intellectual, and spiritual capacities, some in an "active" state and some in a "passive" state. "A soulful sympathetic man has the woman in him, a reasoning, energetic woman has the man in her." Ideally, all these qualities would be fully awakened in men and women. "The *vir* must be in both in order that both [sexes] should be fully human." Julia's view of Spinoza's continuum was surely at the root of this idea.

Julia readily admitted that this androgynous view of personhood was not apparent in society. But if one sex were assigned more prestige than the other, or if men monopolized the field of public action, this was not because men were better than women. It was because historically social progress had required an active and outward role for men and an inward and passive one for women. Foreshadowing the kind of argument that would seize the popular mind three decades later, Julia suggested that the time had come to abandon this false inequality. The polarization of the sexes belonged to a more primitive generation; the new society required the full expression of all powers of the individual. For women, "freer openings to the avenues of intellectual culture, of aesthetic delight, and of social cooperation" would permit them to overcome any deficiencies in judgment and experience that might hinder their participation in social progress.

For Julia, this was a significant breakthrough. She had succeeded publicly in discarding the theory of dual spheres. The ideas she had explored in her plays and private writings now took a new and intellectually acceptable form. She still believed that society had molded women to be more pious, intuitive, and domestic than were men. But this did not have to be the case forever. There were "male" qualities in women and "female" qualities in men, Julia noted. This view strengthened her respect for womanhood and set up a good argument for expanding woman's sphere. Soon Julia found even greater reason to pursue her plan of study and writing. She discovered confirmation of her latest ideas in the works of Immanuel Kant.

In January 1865 Julia took up, at the suggestion of George Bancroft, her first volume of Kant. She found the *Critique of Pure Reason* tough going at first. It challenged many of her preset ideas, and Julia discovered that, "My own cherished inventions and constructions had no basis of sound knowledge to stand upon."[87] Despite this, she persisted. She had found a philosopher whose general trend of thought was substantially like her own.

Julia pulled two theories from her study of Kant, which served as the backbone of her thinking for the rest of her life. The first was that of the power of the human will. The idea of will gave Julia a new way to understand salvation. It was the "leap of faith," the decision to believe, that mattered. Once this act of will was made, religious growth and ultimate redemption would follow. In an undated sermon, Julia expanded on the importance of this.

> The perseverance of the will is the only foundation of true morality. The most beautiful prophetic vision passes, the most satisfactory assignment wearies, and compells the mind to journey out of it. Good works show something better, and lose something of their charm in our eyes by losing their supposed completeness. But the persistent will that keeps on, thro encouragement and discouragement, that makes every failure a valuable lesson, and seeks in the future the care of the past. This is a central power in man or woman around which all that is most noble in thought and purpose will group and build itself surely and steadily. . . . You cannot command enthusiasm. You cannot have enthusiasm at will. But you can exert in your own bosom the moral power of willing to seek the right and to do it. And when your own will gives way, and lies prone under the burden of the natural impulses . . . then he [God] will send a deliverance before which the gates of triple steel shall open.[88]

Her studies of Kant taught Julia that individual will—not her father's Calvinism, not her first emotional conversion experience, not Transcendentalist intellectualism, not Chev's view of propriety—held the key to deliverance. Moreover, this theory made clear the value of decisive persistent activity. If Julia were going to free herself from Chev's domination and society's expectations, she could do so only by determination—the will "to seek the right and to do it." Will was a powerful agent of accomplishment; it meant determination and persistence to Julia.

Julia's changing view of the will matched her changed view of Jesus. From Swedenborg she had derived the idea of divine inspiration as the source of all moral action, and she believed that Jesus's choices in life were the result of God's direction. Now Julia saw the role of will in Jesus's life, for it had taken a strong will to carry out the divine instructions. Julia saw Jesus as a role model, as one who chose a difficult path on purpose. He had elected to face danger and death in order to accomplish his divinely inspired mission. Julia saw Jesus's life as an example of the power of will and of will as a force for good in the world. By extension, she could regard her own will as a beneficent and not a selfish force. For a daughter of orthodoxy and the wife of a domineering man like Chev, this was an important intellectual breakthrough.

The second major idea Julia pulled from Kant was an expansion of her theories concerning the Real and Ideal. Although she did nothing with these theories until later in 1865, her readings provided material for later contemplation. Julia began to believe that there was one permanent, everlasting pattern in all life and thought. This pattern was a creation of the divine mind; indeed, it was identical to it. All things, no matter how material or transient, derived their structure in time and space from that pattern.

Essentially Julia plucked from Kant the words and ideas she wanted to hear and transformed them to suit herself. Her studies of Kant strengthened her resolve to find her vocation and to act in accordance with it. If the course of life were to bring the individual ever more in accordance with the divine pattern or plan, and if will were the tool to bring this about, then Julia, as an individual, could justify selecting a public activity and pursuing it in determined fashion. For this reason, Kant became Julia's intellectual resting place: "If we have found our master, and are satisfied with him, what need have we of starting again, to make the same journey with a new guide. Once we have got there, it seems better to abide."[89] Her pursuit of Kant's idealist philosophy, combined with her study of Fichte, occupied Julia for the next year and a half.[90]

Several essays emerged as a result of these studies. The new essays were "The Ideal State," written in the fall of 1865; "The Two Necessities," written in May and June of 1866; "Representation," written in the winter of 1866-67; and "Opposition," written in January, 1867.[91]

Taken as a whole, the essays written from 1863 to 1867 reveal an interesting common trait. All tried to reduce the complexity of a changing society to neat, almost mathematical, formulas. The most common theme involved dividing the world into two parts. "Duality of Character," "Polarity," "Opposition," and "The Two Necessities" fit this pattern, as did "Doubt and Belief." "Limitations" and "Moral Triangulation" also used mathematical models, although in these Julia expanded her idea of the essential parts to three. The impulse to reduce everything to a simple pattern was understandable, but it was not, ultimately, a fruitful line of thought in strictly philosophical terms. Julia sought in this ordering of the moral universe guideposts for assessing contemporary issues.

In the introduction to this series of essays, Julia wrote that philosophy existed to promote "activity of mind and repose of heart." She offered her essays with that in mind, hoping especially to suggest to reformers profitable lines of thought. Her general tone was conservative. She argued that reformers tended to "spiritual tyranny," attacking the morality of others too freely and robbing them of the freedom to decide for themselves on the right course of action. Freedom to choose was, to her, the "indispensable condition of moral action." Any action forced by reformers could not, therefore, be moral.[92]

The essays closely reflected the times in her own experiences as she took up once again the issue of woman's rights. In particular, she addressed the question of woman suffrage. Julia did believe that people affected by any given law ought to be fairly represented in the debate on that legislation. Furthermore, she thought that the elected representatives of any community were honor bound to represent the best interests of their constituents. Nevertheless, once the "details of Government [are] confided by common consent to the state, . . . no portion of the community has thereafter the right to insist upon the exercise of functions other than those contemplated in the compact of coming together." This was the case for women, she argued, even though they had been excluded from making the compact. In other words, her view tended "to put the career of public ambition at a certain distance from the legitimate sphere of woman."[93]

On the other hand, a scrap of an essay from the same year took a different view. "What for instance [is] more unreasonable than that man should place woman in the position of a phenomenon, devoid of human rights and features, deprived of efficient will, of property and of representation? Will he degrade her to mere animality by making her personal centrality secondary and contingent upon his own? Will he confirm her in slavery by subjecting her to laws in whose adoption she has not been consulted, and by depriving her of the rights of property, plundering under the gilded *mancipium* of the nuptial ring?"[94] Julia was advocating woman suffrage, at least to herself.

Her last essay summed up her public position. In "Opposition," Julia returned to themes somewhat like those in "Moving Forces" and "Polarity." Men and women were certainly different, or opposite. Yet they represented the two poles of the same idea, humanity. The interplay between their different natures resulted in constant improvement for both sexes. Both poles were being pulled, through their dialectic contention, closer and closer to the ideal human being. The separate spheres were necessary for progress, but through progress, they would dissolve.

The study of philosophy and the practice of "ethical exposition" had brought her a long way from the hostility of the 1850s. "The new domain now made clear to me was that of true womanhood,—woman no longer in her ancillary relation to her opposite, man, but in her direct relation to the divine plan and purpose, as a free agent, fully sharing with man every human right and every human responsibility."[95]

Another manuscript fragment of the period argued strongly that women, however essential their domestic role, must be allowed a career outside of married life. Every woman possessed gifts, and she should strive to make the most of them. Her achievements ought not only to gratify the individual, but to uplift society as a whole as well.[96] Julia was convinced that justice, duty, and social progress required an expanded sphere for women. In 1867 she was poised on the edge of making a public commitment to woman suffrage, but she was not ready to take the plunge. Philosophy still held her imagination. Thought and study still appealed to her more than political action.

ELEVEN

Conviction, 1867-1868

The wheel is turned, the cards are laid;
The circle's drawn, the bets are made:
I stake my gold upon the red.

. . . .

I see the chasm, yawning dread;
I see the flaming arch o'erhead:
I stake my life upon the red.

In the summer of 1866, the Greek patriots on Crete had attacked their Turkish rulers. The leaders of the revolt called on Chev for assistance. Because he had fought in the Greek Revolution of 1825, Chev regarded any Greek cause as his own. Julia, too, found the cause important. She detested the Turks' Islamic faith, and her heart went out to the Greeks as fellow Christians. Bostonians also caught Chev's enthusiasm. At meetings to advance the Cretan cause, Chev raised considerable sums. Under Abby W. May, the Boston Sewing Circle met to make clothes for the relief of the Cretan refugees.[1]

Chev determined to go to Crete to distribute supplies to the refugees and to examine the situation for himself. In February 1867, Julia decided that she would go with him. The Howes left for Europe on March 13. Harry, a sophomore at Harvard, would stay home, as would Flossy and Maud. Flossy had just become engaged to David Hall, a young lawyer, so she had no desire to leave town.[2] She would provide continuity in the household and company for Maud. Maud was desolate. At thirteen, she could not imagine life without her doting mother and father. After a few weeks, however, she began to enjoy herself. "Gradually there came a dawning sense of individuality," she recalled. Her parents had left her a "half-grown girl"; they would return in six months' time to a confident young woman.[3]

The passage to Liverpool was smooth; the trip through London and France hasty. Bustling across the continent, the Howes reunited with Louisa in

Rome.[4] Although neither Julia nor Louisa found the other much changed, Louisa's household had a new aspect. Thomas Crawford had died, nearly a decade before, of eye cancer. In 1861 Louisa had married Luther Terry, an American painter. The Terrys set up housekeeping in the huge Palazzo Odescalchi. "The whole of my modest house in B. Place would easily, as to solid contents, lodge in the loftiest of those lofty rooms," observed Julia. "The Place itself would easily lodge in the palace."[6] The space was a good thing, for in addition to the three Crawford children, there were two new Terrys: Louisa Margaret (Daisy) was born in 1862, and Arthur Noel in 1864.

Julia had approached Rome with mixed feelings. This was her third visit; the two previous visits had been tinged with melancholy and marred by struggles with Chev. Here she had last seen Horace Binney Wallace. Here she had savored independence and had thrived in a small apartment of her own. When she had left Rome sixteen years before, she had departed "with entire determination, but with infinite reluctance. America seemed the place of exile, Rome the home of sympathy and comfort." Would she once again find Rome too seductive to leave easily? How would all her latest projects stack up against a Roman backdrop of luxury and refinement? Julia was infinitely relieved to find that Rome no longer played a siren song. "Rome, once a theme of fervent and solemn desire, becomes a mere page of embellishment in a serious and instructive volume."[7] After attending an Anglican service in Rome, she reflected on her new reactions. "I remembered the confusion of my mind when I was here sixteen years ago, and recognized how far more than equivalent for the vivacity of youth, now gone, is the gain of a stedfast standard of good and happiness. To desire supremely ends which are incompatible with no one's happiness and which promote the good of all—this, even as an ideal, is a great gain from the small and eager covetousness of personal desires—religion gives this stedfast standard, whose pursuit is happiness."[8] Julia could laugh at her old habits. When she had Rome to herself in 1851 she had ransacked the city for antiquities. "My rooms were the refuge of all broken down vases and halting candelabra. I lived on the third floor of a modest lodging, and all the wrecks of art that neither first, second, nor fourth would buy found their way into my parlor. . . . Those days are not now. . . . Today, in heathen Rome, I can find better amusements than those shards and rags were ever able to represent."[9]

Her new sense of purpose made Julia feel a little superior. Regarding Rome art and sculpture she remarked that "we want a world peopled with faithful and intelligent men and women. The Prometheus of the present day is needed to animate statues rather than to make them." Her scornful views of Catholicism, her confidence in American institutions, and her praise for the virtues of liberal Protestantism filled her journals and, ultimately, her book of travel notes, *From the Oak to the Olive: A Plain Record of a Pleasant Journey.*[10]

On May 1, Chev and Julia Romana set out for Greece, leaving Laura and her mother in Italy. This was not Julia's wish, but Chev was adamant. He "objects to the expense, but probably more to an indefinable fear of my predominance where he would wish to be the sole figure, which of course he would and ought to be."[11] These words show once more that Julia could analyze, and thus begin to deal with, Chev. She handled his rudeness to her by planning some adventures of her own.

Once Chev was gone, Julia decided to read one of her essays. Laura advised against this, but she forged ahead with plans.[12] An invitation from Chev to join him in Crete put a temporary halt to this scheme, however. Julia and Laura spent the first half of June making their way from Rome to Pireo, where they met Chev.[13]

From Pireo they went on to Athens, where Chev had retained an office and a secretary, a young Greek patriot named Michael Anagnostopoulos. Here Chev was at his best. Defying the order that had set a price on his head should he set foot on Crete, Chev dashed to the island for a brief inspection tour.[14] His Athens office hummed with visitors and messages as Chev stretched his limited relief funds to their limit. At the age of sixty-five, he continued to be arrestingly handsome, with his startling blue eyes, large brow, and still-thick, wavy hair.[15] His bushy, collar-length beard and his mustache were both white, but his figure was as trim as ever. Indeed, he still fit into his wedding jacket. Her freedom to analyze Chev and to admit his role in her misery also allowed Julia the objectivity to admire him. Julia dedicated *From the Oak to the Olive* to him, "the strenuous champion of Greek liberty and human rights."

After a few days in Athens, the Howes took a steamer to Nauplia and continued on to Argos, where groups of Cretan refugees awaited them. There Julia and her daughters distributed the cotton underwear, skirts, and sacques the various sewing circles at home had made.[16] The supply was insufficient and Chev, spurred by what he had seen of the refugees and of Crete, determined to speed back to raise more money and support.

Administrative business concerning the refugees detained the Howes in Athens, however. Julia very soon developed a lively social life, attracting invitations and entertaining callers. She gave two successful readings of her essays to the English-speaking colony, occasioning praise and pride. The first reading "was delightful to me," she wrote, "and is quite an epoch in my later life." Chev's worry that Julia would somehow get into the limelight had proved true. He managed to hold center stage alone for a week, however, when, after taking his family to Venice, he returned to Athens on emergency business.[17]

After that, the return trip to Boston was rapid. Julia managed to fit in another visit with her sister, a poetry reading, and several spending sprees as she steered her girls through Bavaria, Switzerland, France, Belgium, and London.[18] They arrived home in October to find their Boylston Place house let for a year, according to Chev's orders. Julia was in despair.[19] A trying period of melancholy and discouragement threatened to upset Julia's newfound balance of confidence for the next fourteen months.

Since Sammy's death, Julia had been relatively free of the long, debilitating periods of depression that had characterized the 1840s and 1850s. Even after Sammy's death, Julia shook off, in a relatively short time, the bitter grief that had enveloped her. She had suffered somewhat with her old nervous symptom of headaches and eye trouble in the spring of 1865 when Chev attacked her for speaking in public. Nevertheless, these spells of discouragement and perplexity had been relatively short-lived. In each case, study had helped Julia recover her spirits. The routine of reading Kant had soothed her, and the material she had read inspired her to begin writing her third series of lectures. The residual feelings of well-being that attended her status as author of the "Battle Hymn" had also sustained her in the mid-1860s.

After her return from Crete, however, Julia suffered miserably.[20] In the first place, she had to spend the winter in isolated South Boston. Not long after her return, Julia learned of the death of Governor Andrew, her "staunch friend." When Julia wrote some verses to read at his commemoration, Chev forbade her to go.[21] This pattern repeated itself throughout the fall and winter, with Julia yearning to tackle new projects and Chev opposing her wishes. In exasperation, Julia wrote in her journal, "Great God! what did I not suffer, standing between the new order and the old, and wishing to reconcile the courage required by one [public speaking] with the tenderness due the other [Chev]. Never can I suffer more as to a question of what I shall or shall not do."[22] More poor reviews of *Later Lyrics* depressed her, as did the loss of an election to office in her pet Brain Club in November. This was the month when she learned of the sale of the "Ranch," a piece of family property, to Adolph Mailliard. The ensuing disagreement with Annie further saddened

Julia.[23] From October through March, Julia was seized with "savage and tearful melancholy," "profound friendlessness," "mournful discouragement," "mental troubles," "dissatisfaction," and "malignant melancholy."[24] She suffered "torment of mind" not only over the obstacles to her public readings, but also concerning her children.

In 1865 the Howe children had numbered five. Without Sammy the family had realigned itself somewhat, and the old equilibrium of family life in the 1850s evaporated. Julia Romana and Flossy were allied with their father, with whom they worked closely. Julia often found herself at odds with Flossy and deeply concerned about Julia Romana.

Flossy felt free to upbraid her mother, especially when she thought Julia's readings were disturbing the peace and continuity of the household. In fact, both Julia Romana and Flossy had now joined Chev in attacking her for speaking in public.[25] Both insisted that she abandon her plans. Neither could accept the fact that Julia cherished her goal of public service. All they could see was the pain with which Chev regarded Julia's behavior. Flossy was not one to hold her tongue. When Julia reprimanded her "for some small act of neglect," Flossy told her "very harshly, that I was perfectly hateful about it, a very hard word, from daughter to Mother."[26] Flossy's irritability may have sprung from the frustration she felt at enduring a four-year engagement. David Hall, a childhood friend, had secured Flossy's and her parents' consent in February of 1867, but they could not be married until David built up his law practice. Flossy was caught in a bit of a bind. On the one hand, her engagement acknowledged her maturity; on the other hand, her residence with her parents assured her dependence. She was not quite wife but more than daughter. Furthermore, as a daughter, she was expected to give both of her feuding parents full support. Since Chev expected unflinching loyalty and obedience from his children, Flossy's tension landed on Julia.

But Flossy did not cause Julia the anxiety that her oldest daughter did. In 1867, when Flossy's engagement was announced, Julia Romana was nearly twenty-four years old, with no suitors. She was painfully shy and disliked social affairs. Marriage, which Julia regarded as the best situation in life for her girls, seemed an unlikely possibility in Romana's case. Undeniably talented, she might have begun to make her place as a poet or essayist. Unfortunately, whatever career she selected would have to take into account her unpredictable and unbalanced personality.

The full extent of Julia Romana's emotional problems is not known. Her sisters covered them up in their recollections of her, and Romana herself died at forty-three, before she could even think of writing her memoirs. After her emotional breakdown in 1859, she seems to have lived a quiet, sheltered life, working closely with her father at the Institute. Periodically, however, bizarre behavior erupted. On Maud's thirteenth birthday, she turned on the little sister to whom she had been almost a second mother and initiated a series of quarrels. These took Maud by surprise, but she fought back until her mother was "almost crazed by their irritability and quarreling."[27] On another occasion, Romana threw her dinner out of the window, furious that her parents had saved no meat for her.[28] Other entries in her mother's journal indicate that Romana was a thorny personality.[29] Julia felt, at times, a total stranger to this difficult daughter.[30]

Laura, though five years younger than Flossy, was no longer paired with Harry, but with the older girls. They all went to dances at Papanti Hall, to receptions, to teas, and even to Harvard Class Day.[31] This left Maud as the odd one out. With Sammy, she had had someone else to bring up the end of the family. Now she was the baby, "solid, heavy, elastic, indefatigable." "She promises," wrote Chev, "to be the brightest, handsomest, and wildest of all."[32] Thirteen years old in 1867, Maud was a "stormy petrel" whose passionate nature gave Julia great anxiety, especially when it led to quarrels with her older sisters.[33] And true to her father's prediction, she was handsome. But brightest she was not. Her mother had to console her that the "oak was a tree of slow growth."[34]

Harry was the "hobble-de-hoy . . . neither man nor boy."[35] His preparation for college and career took him out of the domestic circle and out of Julia's sphere of direct concern. She did worry about him from time to time, however. He was fond of mischievous tricks such as dropping, from his seat in the topmost balcony, raw oysters onto the pates of baldheaded gentlemen below.[36] On the verge of manhood, he should have been thinking about his studies and a profession. Instead he was arrested for throwing fire buckets out of Tremont House.[37] While Julia was sure that his behavior was like that of Chev's at a similar age—mischievous, but not malicious—she worried that he might "turn out ill for want of forethought."[38] One night, on a wild drive home from Newport, when Julia cautioned him to slow down, Harry told her to "hold her tongue" and "dry up."[39] Some nights, Julia confessed to her journal, she lay awake "worried, and wondered what to do about everybody."[40]

To make matters more complicated, Michael Anagnostopoulos (shortened to Anagnos) had arrived in Boston to be groomed as Chev's successor at the

Institute. Beginning in Greece and continuing back in Boston, Michael Anagnos tutored Julia regularly in Greek. This was a language Julia had longed to learn all her life, and she threw herself into her studies.[41] Exactly what Michael's relationship was to Julia was not entirely clear. It certainly seemed, for the winter and spring of 1868 at least, to be more than that of a tutor.

Since Michael was substantially younger than Julia, he was hardly a likely or appropriate intimate companion. Nevertheless, he accompanied Julia virtually everywhere. He was not her lover, but Julia referred to him in her journal as "my darling." Michael was, of course, much too old to replace Sammy, yet Julia called him "a dear son to me."[42]

Julia suffered "great private pain" as she tried to sort out her feelings.[43] Chev's coldness and indifference, contrasted with Michael's warmer nature, smote Julia once again with the fact that her marriage was crippled. Yet to entertain any feelings disloyal to Chev caused Julia pangs of guilt. Michael's presence, then, however attractive in some ways, carried with it a sense of inadequacy, frustration, and guilt. That Julia fantasized about Michael as her lost son only made matters worse. His very presence made Sammy's absence all the clearer. Julia had to admit that Michael was not Sammy and that the reunification she so badly wanted would not take place on earth.

To make matters still worse, Julia Romana was in love with Michael. Julia seems not to have been aware of this at the time. None of the comments written about Julia Romana in her journal suggest any knowledge of the situation. Her mother's lack of perception about her daughters contributed to the anxiety and tension in the household which, in turn, bothered Julia.

Julia's depression continued into March and April 1868. She had little social life. She worked hard on a fair for Crete, with substantial success, raising over $20,000.[44] Even this achievement did not comfort her. Her journal mentions her mental unrest, her dissatisfaction with life, a pervasive sense of dullness, and "extreme depression." Again eye trouble plagued her.[45] During the summer she was distressed by a sense of her own shortcomings and prayed for a renewed life. "My divine Master—receive I pray thee, the thoughts and intentions of this day as a fresh starting towards a career of renewed zeal and effort. The period just past has left few records on these pages. Afflicted by its faults, I yet leave its' sum and settlement in thy hands. I only ask that from this moment, I may seek with greater directness and pray with greater power, and that nothing may withhold me from truly endeavoring after an energetic and useful life, wronging no man, and leaving the fulfillment of no duty unattempted."[46] When Julia had been sad in the past, she had turned to writing—letters to her sisters, poetry, plays, her scrawled-out snippets of essays, her journal—to relieve this. In 1868 she did little, if any, writing. No major works date from this time. She did read before the Free Religious Association, but she used old manuscripts. She reread her essays, put her 1867 travel diary in shape for publication, and wrote a handful of short poems, but this was a low output for a woman who had poured her soul onto paper for nearly thirty years. Letters to her family are almost nonexistent. Her journal, usually crammed with philosophy, household accounts, and reports of her social and literary life, is virtually empty from May through December. Only one page is cut out; the rest did not get written. Possibly other works were attempted and burned—Julia was a great destroyer of unhappy correspondence—but if so, the record is silent about them. One senses an emotional life so confused, so fragile, so dried out by unhappiness that even the creative juices that turmoil often set loose in Julia were no longer flowing.

As her prayer suggests, Julia turned increasingly to the comfort of her Unitarian faith in these difficult days. Her journal made repeated references to her reliance on religion: "To church today, where my mental condition speedily improved. . . . Hymns and prayers all congenial and consoling." "Church was blessed." "Prayer and sermon equally dear."[47] On another occasion Julia entered the following resolution: "Some mental troubles have ended in a determination to hold fast till death the liberty wherewith Christ has made me free."[48] Julia was making a major effort to recall the lessons of Kant in order to steady her sense of vocation. Jesus had demonstrated the power of moral action; by effort of will she could achieve those things her inner voice commanded of her; the effort of will would release the brightness of belief, harmony, and reintegration that accompanied her peak experiences. In addition, more frequently than in the past Julia framed her frustrations and hopes in the form of prayers. "May I this year have energy, patience, goodwill, and good faith: May I be guilty of no treasons against duty and my best self!" "On! Master, in this new month forsake me not!" "I begin to take heart a little. Almighty God, help me!"[49]

The tremendous surge of religious feeling did indeed help Julia relieve her persistent depression. In an Easter sermon Julia analyzed the crucifixion of Christ, and in doing so restated the connection between doubt and the resolution of doubt through the sensation of belief: "this second birth of Christ exemplifies the agony from which the soul issues, divorced from the slavery of self. . . . and emancipated into the general joy and freedom of the world." Of what did this emancipation consist? "The consciousness of spiritual things, the real, great value which outward things only symbolize. . . . The new birth brings out the novelty of the soul, winged towards the infinite. . . . And the soul shakes off its miserable distresses. And in so doing, it becomes aware of a great relationship, a nearness of kin to the divine father—soul of the Universe. . . . [It] has been born, not only once, but twice, once into the natural world, and once into the spiritual world, where despair cannot pursue him.[50]

Julia did not expect prayer and religious thoughts to solve her financial crises, to cure Julia Romana, to straighten out Harry, or to convert Chev into a tolerant and supportive husband. What she knew it could do was focus her thoughts on the problems that bothered her most and summon her inner reserves to keep on dealing with those difficulties. Julia used religion to keep herself from being swallowed by depression. By stretching always for nearness to the "divine father-soul," Julia avoided bogging down in a morass of intractable problems. By keeping her sights on "the real, great value" of life rather than on its material conditions, Julia asserted her determination not to be hemmed in by despair or to be overcome with wretchedness. In writing "Almighty God, help me!" Julia was expressing a kind of hope, and this hope separated her current melancholy from the miserable depressions of the 1840s and 1850s. For the first time in her life, Julia could be sad without being afraid that "that Giant Despair" would pursue her to insanity.

In addition, Julia turned to religion because she was becoming increasingly involved with it intellectually. In November 1867 Julia joined the Free Religious Association. Made up of men and women from Boston, Cambridge, and Concord, the club included many of the old Transcendentalists and some of Boston's leading reformers. Ralph Waldo Emerson, Octavius B. Frothingham, James Freeman Clarke, William Henry Channing, Frederick Henry Hedge, Thomas Wentworth Higginson, Benjamin Peirce, John Weiss, Carl Shurtz, Henry Wadsworth Longfellow, Bronson Alcott, David Wasson, and John Sargent read and discussed papers there. Women, too, including Ednah Dow Cheney, Mary Livermore, and Louise Chandler Moulton, contributed.[51] To this assemblage Julia read "Doubt and Belief," "Limitations," and "Representation." So gratifying was this participation that Julia devoted twenty-three pages to it in her *Reminiscences*.[52]

The club had its roots in the earlier Parker Fraternity, and it maintained close ties with the New York Free Religious Association. Later Julia called it simply the Radical Club. Julia recalled the meetings, usually held at the home of the Reverend John T. Sargent. After listening to a fairly lengthy paper, both the radicals and the conservatives of the day debated its points.

> I did indeed hear at these meetings much that pained and even irritated me. The disposition to seek outside the limits of Christianity for all that is noble and inspiring in religious culture, and to recognize especially within these limits the superstition and intolerance which have been the bane of all religions—this disposition, which was frequently manifested both in the essays presented and in their discussion, offended not only my affections, but also my sense of justice. I had indeed been led to transcend the limits of the old tradition; I had also devoted much time to studies of philosophy, and had become conversant with the works of Auguste Comte, Hegel, Spinoza, Kant, and Swedenborg. Nothing of what I had heard or read had shaken my faith in the leadership of Christ in the religion which makes each man the brother of all, and God the beneficent father of each and all,—the religion of humanity. Neither did this my conviction suffer any disturbance through the views presented by speakers at the Radical Club.[53]

The club was indeed full of radicals, many of whom, Julia thought, had given over Christianity entirely. The Reverend John Weiss she once described as having "deformed" powers of reason. "He seeks something better than Christianity without having half penetrated the inner significance of that religion."[54] Christianity, Julia claimed, laid out the best path for discovering and pursuing that Ideal. Here Julia would have parted company with some members of the Radical Club, for they were far from sure that Christianity provided the best way to achieve reconciliation with God and with other men and women. They, for example, looked with interest to the religions of the East. Julia criticized some of her colleagues for their absorption in the Vedas. "It would be difficult to preach any practical reform upon their text," she observed.[55]

Julia also disagreed with the radicals' tendency to criticize religion from "an extra-Christian standpoint." She took them to task for condemning the Christianity of others, reminding them that such intolerance infringed on others' moral liberty. Even if others were mistaken, Julia reminded them, all religious practices were necessary steps in religious progress. "It is easy to dogmatize," she acknowledged, "to rest in formulae ourselves and to impose them as a condition of true belief on others."[56]

In spite of all this, Julia could claim some ground in common with her colleagues in the Free Religious Association. Like them, she firmly believed that religion should not be defined by form. Ritual observances, formal prayers, and the like could be cast off when they no longer fit.[57] She shared the radicals' attitude toward miracles. They were merely phenomena. They held no significance in proving Christ's divinity. Instead their merit lay in what they represented, the power of the Ideal, or God, to love or to forgive or to heal.[58]

She also shared their interest in practical Christianity, believing that religious ideas showed their true value in their practical applications.[59] Were they useful? Could they advance society along the paths of improvement? The message she had received from Parker and Swedenborg she was now ready to proclaim herself. Religion would lift all people from petty personal concerns to a broader sympathy for society as a whole. A religious person would not, therefore, focus on questions of death, heaven, and hell as much as on issues having to do with life, with existence on earth.[60] Practical Christianity was her emphasis; she looked not so much for the purest idea as for the most useful one.[61] "He [the true Christian] must in his measure aid to uphold the social order, and to ennoble the aims of the community in which he lives."[62]

Just as the country best suited to the "efficient moral force" of the Ideal was the United States, it was the U.S. that was best suited to the exercise of practical Christianity. Here Christian precepts "not only may but must be carried out in their fullest application." What did this mean, precisely, to Julia? She believed these precepts would lead to a clearer understanding of the mutuality of obligations and to the brotherhood of man. They would extend to the ex-slaves their rights.[63] These precepts would end the degradation of women, extend to workers their full dignity, and make employers aware of their full responsibilities to their employees. They would lay the basis for world peace.[64] "The true progress of the age is entirely in the direction of the Christian idea. In the conception and ministration of Christ the abstract doctrines of right [have] become fused with a power of comprehensive benevolence . . . which still leads our philanthropies."[65]

Moreover, they all shared a common belief in the primacy of conscience, a direct inheritance from their forerunner, Theodore Parker. Julia's private use of it has been mentioned; now she brought her thesis out to encourage others. Christianity embodied "a higher form of individuality." God would inspire each individual to choose the path most suitable to him or herself. No other person could direct an individual's choice. This was a matter subject to divine will and not to external compulsion.[66] " 'In Jesus Christ there is neither male nor female,' is a good sentence. . . . I feel that a woman's whole moral responsibility is lowered by the fact that she must never [according to social usage] obey a transcendant command of conscience. Man can give her nothing to take the place of this. It is the *divine* right of the human soul."[67] Julia wrote further, "Every human soul if religiously inspired, will feel that it has a single and special work to do in and for the world. Morals are individual. The doctrines of duty are universal . . . so let us relate ourselves directly to God, who is able and willing to guide and inspire us."[68]

In asserting the importance of individual moral autonomy, Julia had arrived at a full articulation of the idea that had stimulated her since the late 1840s. She was now easy and comfortable writing and speaking about it. Because she had not yet made connections with moderate feminists, Julia's philosophy had little impact on the woman's movement in the mid-1860s. Yet hers was a significant contribution to the rhetoric of that movement. By holding up a vision of women as independent moral agents alongside her reassuring credentials as a conventional middle-class matron, Julia would help make feminism accessible to the white middle-class Protestant woman. "Men and women, dear friends, I am here to say that the kingdom of heaven is at hand, & to say that it is within you. Great changes are working themselves in your society. . . . But with uplifted hearts, we may attack the questions of the day. . . . If we have the kingdom within us, we may hope to aid in bringing it about us."[69]

TWELVE

Conversion, 1868

In late 1868, those Republican reformers who hoped that at least a temporal version of the kingdom of heaven might be within reach surveyed the political scene with some dismay. Elizabeth Cady Stanton and Susan B. Anthony had bolted the party, carrying the issue of woman suffrage down what looked like a dangerous stream of feminist issues. These included topics like divorce and unionization of working women. Not only did this suggest to the party that they might not remain the engine powering reform in postwar America, but it also suggested that woman suffrage, a valuable reform in itself, might run aground. The moderate and conservative Republicans of Massachusetts decided that a new organization was needed. They set out to form a woman suffrage association.[1]

The association they envisioned would be regional in scope, broad in appeal, and Republican in its politics. It would have to put the Republican program of Reconstruction first on its agenda, making woman suffrage a secondary concern.[2] They knew that the combination might be tricky, so to strengthen their hand the organizers sent out invitations to a meeting to be held in Boston on November 18 and 19, 1868. Thomas Wentworth Higginson, Stephen Foster, and Henry Wilson carefully omitted the names of Stanton, Anthony, and their allies. (When Stanton got an invitation by mistake, Foster wrote requesting her not to accept.)[3] Instead, they drew on a list of old abolitionist friends who might be willing to support woman suffrage if it did not interfere with freedmen's rights.

Julia had joined dozens of other New Englanders in issuing the call to the meeting. Her name was third from the top in a list of signers, which included James Freeman Clarke, Thomas Wentworth Higginson, Bronson Alcott, Samuel May, Francis Bird, Samuel Sewall, Stephen Foster, Lidian Emerson, Angelina Grimké Weld, Caroline Severance, Elizabeth Peabody, Mary Mann, Louisa May Alcott, and Lydia Maria Child.[4] These were moderate and conservative Republicans, some of whom had never before been involved in suffrage work.[5] So conservative was it, in fact, that the call avoided the term "woman suffrage" altogether.

> We, the undersigned, recognizing the so-called "woman question" as fundamental in its relation to society . . . unite in calling a convention for the discussion of the principles involved in it, and for the formation of a society to secure their application.
>
> We propose, as the basis of our discussion and subsequent action, the equality of the sexes before God . . . and the rights of the individual as set forth in the ever-memorable words of the Declaration of Independence. . . .
>
> We hold it a self-evident truth also that these principles, applied to women as to the men of any nation or race, must produce the best results; and that such application is necessary to the normal development of society.[6]

Woman suffrage was very much on the minds of everyone, however. The assembled men and women lost no time in forming a "permanent association for the wise, sympathetic, and efficient advocacy of woman suffrage and its kindred political and civil rights."[7] The New England Woman Suffrage Association, the first organization of its type, was thereby launched. Julia Ward Howe was its first president.

The *National Anti-Slavery Standard*, which had published nothing by or from the radical suffragists since 1866, gave several columns to this event. The editor, Aaron Powell, was startled to see a woman catapulted into leadership who had done none of the "most difficult pioneer work," but he approved the choice.[8] Julia, with her large family, her carefully cultivated social status, and her widely respected philanthropist husband, gave the organization a sheen of propriety and substance that a more radical person could not have provided.

On the second day of the convention, after her selection as president, Julia delivered a speech. She spoke briefly and effectively, according to the *National Anti-Slavery Standard*. "We are to discuss the present question not on the basis of division [from men]," she proclaimed, "but on the basis of a larger and more perfect unity." She went on to reject all her old arguments against woman suffrage, admitting that times had changed and that she had changed with them. She closed her address with an explanation of why she had altered her position. "I first became converted to the right of woman suffrage on finding that the negro was inevitably to receive the franchise. Voting thus became a fundamental human right and function, from which women could no longer be excluded. And I am glad that we shall come in after the negro whose wrongs and sufferings . . . have made him in our eyes an august, a heroic personage. I hope and believe that we shall make as good a use of our newly acquired powers as he will make of his."[9]

Julia's own recollections of the meeting in Horticultural Hall were not nearly as prosaic as the *Standard*'s account. As Julia recalled, the first day of the convention was a major turning point in her life. "The morning was inclement; and as I strayed into Horticultural Hall in my rainy-day suit, nothing was further from my mind than the thought that I should take part in any of the day's proceedings." Julia remembered also a sense of confusion. Since she did not wish to be noticed or to speak at the meeting, she was disconcerted when a message reached her "requesting me to come up and take a seat on the platform. This I did very reluctantly. I was now face to face with a new order of things. Here indeed were some whom I had long known and honored. . . . But here was Lucy Stone, who had long been one of my imaginary dislikes."[10]

As she listened to what Stone had to say, however, Julia found herself strongly affected. "The arguments to which I now listened were simple, strong, and convincing. These champions, who had fought so long and so valiantly for the slave, now turned the searchlight of their intelligence upon the condition of woman, and demanded for the mothers of the community the civil rights which had recently been accorded the negro." When at length the organizers of the meeting called upon her to speak, Julia answered simply, "I am with you."[11]

The facts of the meeting and Julia's recollections are at odds. She stresses her hesitation and inadequacy; the *Standard* describes her as eager and competent. Julia could recall only a minor role in the proceedings; the *Standard* reported her selection as president of the New England Woman Suffrage Association. Julia's private writings call her account into even further question. She had already advocated woman suffrage nearly a year before the convention met.

It is tempting, then, to throw out Julia's account as too subjective. Her contention that the speeches at the meeting effected her conversion to woman suffrage is not entirely believable. Yet it is dangerous to ignore someone's claim to a conversion. Julia remained insistent on this definition of her experience for the rest of her life. In a speech given when she was nearly ninety, Julia still recalled the convention as a conversion experience. "Soon after the war . . . a woman suffrage convention was held in Boston. I . . . sat on the platform. There for the first time I met the monster woman suffrage face-to-face. My conversion was instant. . . . I embarked then on the good ship, woman suffrage."[12]

Something had changed for Julia on that rainy day in November. It was not, as she claimed, that she was converted from hesitant onlooker to enthusiastic supporter of woman suffrage. Instead, the change was from private support to public advocacy. This was an enormous leap for Julia.

Six months earlier Julia had had an opportunity to make public her views on woman suffrage. Caroline Severance had invited men and women reformers and intellectuals to a mass meeting in the hope of founding a club for women. This club would not only provide a "quiet and central resting place where friends might meet informally" in Boston.[13] It would also, she hoped, serve as a useful tool of social change. The participants agreed. They established the New England Woman's Club, planning a program that would get underway in November. In her address to the meeting, Julia insisted that women had the right to contribute their talents and energy to the community if they so desired. She did not, however, say a word in favor of suffrage.[14]

What held her back? Though she was nearing the end of this path, Julia was still on an inward trek. She had been depressed. The topics that interested her were of mind and spirit, of philosophy and faith. Political action seemed remote. Julia also stayed outside the discussion of freedmen's rights because this was Chev's field. She did not till it with him since, as demonstrated in Greece in 1867, they could not work together without stepping on each other's toes. She was peripheral to the debate about impartial suffrage, and that debate was peripheral to her.

Furthermore, the whole idea of women's associations was one to which Julia came late. She had had virtually no experiences that would have suggested the advantages of an association for women. The New England Woman's Club had not yet commenced its program. Julia had little experience with female benevolent societies, none with antislavery societies, and only a bit with the Sanitary Commission. She believed that her interests alienated her from other women. Not until 1864 did she know the pleasures of friendship with other women in the Brain Club, and even then she had no perception of a club's possibilities as a tool of social reform. A society organized to fight for woman suffrage, then, would not have struck Julia as an obvious step.

Other things restrained Julia. Like most Republican reformers, she believed that the rights of freedmen had to take precedence over those of women. Women had men to defend them, the reasoning went. Blacks had no one, and thus needed the strong arm of constitutional amendment to protect them. Julia concurred in this theory. She refused to join the Women's Loyal League or the Equal Rights Association because both these organizations originated with feminists who wanted to keep woman suffrage on an equal footing with freedman's rights. In fact, Julia had tried to counter the Loyal League by engineering, along with other moderate men and women reformers in Boston, a movement to shun luxury. The New England Women's League for Diminishing the Use of Luxuries During the War resolved "to retrench expenditure in dress, in the household, in social entertainments and in all luxuries."[15] This organization was set up in deliberate contrast to the Loyal League, where Stanton and Anthony held sway. These feminists put their own demands on a par with the abolitionists. Julia would show that women, in a traditionally feminine way, could aid the union cause without interfering in the plan for freedmen's rights. Julia also aligned herself with the American Anti-Slavery Society, agreeing that the nation should "Let every man have the suffrage. It were well if every woman also could have it, but we must not risk the loss of so great a step as the former by complication. One thing at a time. And the gaining of the first will immediately facilitate the second."[16] Not until Julia believed that the rights of the freedmen were protected could she assent to the demand for woman suffrage.

Given these difficulties, what impelled Julia to embrace woman suffrage publicly? The ratification of the Fourteenth Amendment in July 1868 removed one stumbling block. Julia no longer needed to worry that her support of woman suffrage would detract from Reconstruction efforts. The participation of Republican reformers reassured her that this new organization would not impede the drive for freedmen's rights. Woman suffrage was the next logical step. Indeed, it was an essential one, since women were effectively precluded from voting by that very amendment.

Second, Julia was beginning to realize that her "profession of ethical exposition" was not reaching as many hearts and minds as she had hoped. After reading "Ideal Causation" one Sunday, she found to her dismay "that it did not greatly interest my hearers, and that one was reported to have wondered 'what Mrs. Howe was driving at!'"[17] Later she recalled "I made no real progress, but went round and round in a sort of circle of metaphysical and mystical reasoning which rather separated me from the minds of others."[18] Julia recognized too that her theories were difficult to apply in practical situations. She prayed once again for a more positive, active way to make her contribution.[19]

The meeting was the third factor influencing Julia's decision publicly to embrace woman suffrage. The whole structure of the event had all the elements of a conversion experience.

Julia had wrestled with the issue of whether or not woman suffrage was an appropriate remedy for the wrongs done to women. For the most part she thought it might be a good thing, but individual change of heart was more important. It was to that end that all her ethical lectures had aimed. More important, Julia was struggling, and had been for years, with the question of vocation. To take up the call for woman suffrage would be to abandon all previous methods of work and to undertake something sure to "inflame Chev's passions" against her. This was not only public work, involving publishing and speaking; it was reform work, something that had been, up to now, primarily Chev's turf. No wonder, then, that Julia recalled entering Horticultural Hall in a state of uncertainty and doubt. This disequilibrium only increased as the organizers drew Julia to the platform. Public attention focused on her, and the pressure to align herself with the suffragists was great. Julia Ward Howe was indeed on the "anxious bench."

In those difficult hours, Julia did experience some sort of overwhelming inspiration. In her account, she moved from literal and figurative darkness into literal and figurative light. "The light of the good life shining in every feature of her [Lucy Stone's] face" combined with the "searchlight of intelligence" in Julia's own mind. Julia refers again to this sense of light. "During the first two-thirds of my life, I looked to the masculine ideal of character as the only true one. . . . In an unexpected hour a new light came to me, showing me a world of thought and of character quite beyond the limits within which I had hitherto been content to abide. The new domain now made clear to me was that of the true womanhood."[20] Melancholy gave way to relief. Julia recalled a sense of resolution both immediate and profound. As she expressed it later, "For years past, I had felt strongly impelled to lend my voice to the convictions of my heart. . . . I now found a sphere of action in which this mode of expression no longer appeared singular or eccentric, but simple, natural, and under the circumstances, inevitable."[21] Thomas Wentworth Higginson later recalled this change. "From the moment she came forward in the woman suffrage movement. . . . there was a visible change [in Julia Ward Howe]; it gave a new brightness to her face, a new cordiality in her manner, made her calmer, firmer; she found herself among new friends, and could disregard old critics."[22]

The mechanism that permitted Julia to resolve her conflict was Lucy Stone's speech.[23] When Julia sat on the platform, she was anxious; her old equilibrium was gone. As she listened to Stone's argument, the words she had heard before became unavoidably clear: What was right for the ex-slaves was right for women. The only way to bring about the necessary improvements for women was to take action. And the only way Julia could do that was to make her private convictions public. The speech allowed Julia to restore the balance among her conflicting impulses and to make a clear decision for woman suffrage.

The speech also handed Julia a perfect justification to offer others. By blending together the cause of the freedmen and the woman, Stone's arguments transformed woman suffrage from a foreign and dangerous idea to a familiar and reasonable proposal. All reform was of one piece. Armed with this argument, Julia had a defense of her position that spoke to Chev on his own terms. Not only that, but it was palatable to her reformer friends. The theory was easily propounded and politically safe. Woman suffrage was as important as black suffrage and for the same reasons: it offered protection and conferred a badge of equality.

Lucy Stone had provided Julia with a jolt she needed to resolve her confusion about woman suffrage. With a public commitment to the cause, Julia was ready for the most significant change in her life. She would no longer deal exclusively with the narrow spheres of domestic concerns or private philosophies. She would be an active advocate of women's rights.

Julia chose to launch her career as a suffragist by taking the speaker's platform. At the first convention of the American Woman Suffrage Association in Cleveland, which she helped organize, she spoke as the "prophet" of the convention.

In this speech, she enumerated the many complaints of women: "the partial laws, the unequal judgments, the inferiority of education, the inequality in the distribution of labor, and the greater inequality in the distribution of wages. [We] know that one half the human race has hitherto been negatived by the other half." To this familiar litany she added an explanation of the virtues of suffrage. "It would at once place woman on the footing of a noble and conceded equality with man. It would open to her at once the avenues of thought and action, of art, of culture, of educational and political efficiency. It would do this in justice to individuals, and to the society which they compose." Julia sought both justice for women and improvement for society in the same stroke. Woman suffrage would accomplish this, for in lifting the "value of individuals," the "value of society" was uplifted as well.[24]

Most important, Julia believed suffrage would grant to women the freedom of action and decision that would allow them to be fully moral beings.

And we, the representatives of women, rise up, and appeal back to the bond of Christian brotherhood, which allows no human being to oppress another. We say, Christian men and women, the present way of the world has been hitherto held to be the right way, but it is the wrong way. In debarring conscience from her final action, you debar her from her final exercise. If I, a woman, may not do what I think most virtuous, useful, and honorable, without deference to usage and prescription, neither may I think it. Others must think it for me, and I must be content to adopt their errors for my intuitions, and to take their abuses in place of my uses.[25]

Her audience might have been perplexed to hear that if they could not act, then they could not think, but this was the heart of Julia's convictions: there is no freedom without action. Without a free field of action, a woman might never imagine the various choices available. If she could not see the choices, then she could not exercise her conscience to the fullest. Unless women could see, face, and grapple with moral choices by themselves, they were lesser human beings.[26] Suffrage thereby became not merely a question of justice or of improving woman's daily lot, but of recognizing her full moral capacity.

The still, small voice had emerged. Buoyant and energetic now, it had been developed in years of experimentation and practice. Poetry, although it ultimately turned out to be a dead end, gave Julia early confidence that she had something to say. The "Battle Hymn of the Republic" assured Julia's status as a woman of letters, opening up opportunities for public expression. Her travel books, however slight their interest now, gave Julia experience in developing her powers of observation, anecdote, and reflection. All during the prewar period her huge corpus of letters provided an unfettered opportunity for Julia to give voice to feelings and ideas in courageous, vivid, and often humorous ways. In her plays Julia allowed herself to probe her dark side, to experiment with relationships between men and women, to push the boundaries of experience, and to explore her own ideas about gender. In these private and public works Julia's thought showed no single line of development but grappled in a variety of ways with the question of individual moral responsibility.

After the war Julia's philosophical writings allowed her to refine her thought, to expand her mental vocabulary of images and paradigms, and to fold in the religious feeling that had always been a part of her interior life. The biggest step for Julia was the series of public readings that she commenced in 1864, for she faced not only the challenge of developing a cogent line of thought satisfactory to herself, but also the discipline of presenting it so that her audience could follow and appreciate it. She was forced to clarify, to prune, and to focus her prose. As she found her writing style Julia also discovered a comfortable style for public speaking, both feminine and forthright. In private homes, wearing her simple white lace cap, she articulated with growing confidence her increasingly solid conviction that the right to and responsibility for moral choice was the center of human dignity. Philosophy and Christianity all pointed to it and supported it. Drawing on all these experiences, Julia Ward Howe had at last found the thing she most needed to say and the forum in which she could say it.

Julia went on to develop a wide range of prosuffrage arguments. In a sermon given a year after the Cleveland Convention, Julia advanced the sort of arguments that historians now describe as "domestic feminism." The "whole world is a home," Julia claimed, and women were the ones who would make it a fit place in which to live. Women's special role as mothers qualified them to serve their communities in a unique way. "So I wish to say that I see in the new womanhood only an extended and glorified motherhood. . . . Every woman is not, in God's Providence, a wife, and every wife is not actually a mother. But every true woman has the mother in her and this grand, spiritual motherhood, exerting its influence and watchfulness in all the walks of life will give every woman a noble part to perform in the great drama of the world."[27]

Using the separate spheres argument to advantage, Julia turned her old argument against suffrage on its head. The very things that made women different from men now qualified them for public life. "A great part of what I should call applied Christianity is waiting for women to carry it out, and to embody it in practical and social life. The very simplicity and literalness with which women are apt to take a precept and work after it is a power which men seem to lose thro' sophistications of reason, and the passions of their social warfare."[28]

Julia Ward Howe was using two kinds of arguments as she confronted the opposition to woman suffrage. She combined arguments based on philosophy and Protestantism, which recognized the moral similarity of men and women, with expedient arguments rooted in the sphere of conventional womanhood. In "Opposition" she contended that men and women were ordained to use their complementary powers as fully as possible to advance humanity. As they did so, each sex would come a little closer to the position of the other, uplifting the whole society as they went. "In the new manhood, the strong are to be the champions of the weak. In the new womanhood, the mother's heart is to embrace, with tender vigilance, the interests of the race."[29] Here was the androgyny she had grappled with in the mid-1850s in new and useful form.

Julia traveled the country, and even England, stumping for suffrage. Her spirits improved drastically. After two years of silence, Julia Ward Howe's 1871 journal has the relieved tone of a patient who has passed the crisis in some prolonged disease. Although terse, the entries are full of projects, speeches, parties, and visits. The pages convey a sense of life and vigor renewed.[30]

One factor that contributed to Julia's increasing public activity was the simple passage of time. She never became a good housekeeper, for example, but she finally could count on her daughters to handle that responsibility. And her children no longer troubled her. Harry, reformed and serious, had begun a brilliant career as a metallurgist by enrolling at the Massachusetts Institute of Technology. The three older girls married in quick succession in 1870 and 1871: Julia Romana to Michael Anagnos, Flossy to David Hall, and Laura to the shy but determined Henry Richards. Her daughters all agreed that this emptying of the nest gave Julia free time to study and work. "This woman, lifting her eyes from the empty spaces, saw Opportunity beckoning from new heights, and moved gladly to meet her."[31]

Twenty years earlier, such large chunks of flexible time had been unimaginable and unattainable. Few of her family before her had lived to see all their children grown and in new families of their own. Julia, however, was typical of the late-nineteenth-century demographic trend in which women who survived childbirth frequently survived past the maturity of their last child. Julia lived forty years after Maud turned sixteen, long enough for a full career. Ultimately the solution to the overwhelming burden of child care and the depressions that went with them was at least partly physiological—she outlived them.

The solution to her conflicts with Chev, likewise, had much to do with the passage of time. After a difficult five years when his temper was increasingly erratic, Chev died of a brain tumor in 1876.[32] Released from the burdens of caring for an invalid, Julia mourned briefly and then increased the pace of her club and suffrage work.

The suffrage campaign was Julia's primary interest in the 1870s, but her list of involvements in public causes grew rapidly. In part her energy was fueled by an expanded network of women friends, whom Julia met almost daily. When suffrage work slackened, the New England Women's Club provided satisfying opportunities to propound and defend the woman's rights cause. In

1873 Julia snatched a fledgling organization, the Association for the Advancement of Women, out of the hands of its New York organizers, thereby acquiring another platform from which to expound her views and extend her contacts. Julia made friends all over the country. These women encouraged, admired, and supported Julia in her undertakings, renewing with delightful frequency Julia's sense that she had chosen her life's work well.[33]

Her gift for inspiring other women and her facility in public speaking insured that Julia would live the rest of her life as a public figure. During the next forty years she helped establish dozens of local women's clubs. Through the Association for the Advancement of Women she encouraged the study of problems pertaining to women and the organizations of women to tackle those problems. She worked for world peace, inventing the first Mother's Day celebrations to advance the cause. She remained an officer of both the NEWC and the AWSA for the rest of her life. She contributed endless articles on woman suffrage and on social reform to periodicals ranging from *The Woman's Journal* to *Cosmopolitan*. She testified annually before state legislatures, and she exhorted countless groups of women, all for the cause of woman's rights. Julia organized women ministers and encouraged women professionals. She publicized women's work through her role as head of the woman's departments of two large expositions.

Travel, writing, speaking, and organizing would fill Julia's life until her death in 1910. From her New York roots, where she felt, at times, submerged in the private world of the Wards; through the strictures of her marriage and the limitations of young motherhood; through the private agonies of depression; into publication, war work, studying, writing, and public speaking, Julia Ward Howe had emerged a notable and public person. Her change of heart at the Boston Convention compressed this lifetime of experience into a few hours, giving her inner revolution an outward form and expression. For the rest of her life it served as a symbol of her turning from a closed life to one open and outward. Her impromptu speech at that convention inaugurated a new era for Julia, one that built on her "still, small voice," capitalized on her experience, and called her forth to speak about social justice and women's rights. Julia had struggled to "clear her throat," so to speak—to define her message, to choose her vocabulary, to discover her style. By 1870 she had succeeded.

Notes

ABBREVIATIONS

AW	Anne Eliza Ward	JWH	Julia Ward Howe
AWM	Anne Ward Mailliard	LW	Louisa Ward
FMW	Francis Marion Ward	LWC	Louisa Ward Crawford
JRC	Julia Rush Cutler	LWCT	Louisa Ward Crawford Terry
JRCW	Julia Rush Cutler Ward	SGH	Samuel Gridley Howe
JW	Julia Ward	SW	Samuel Ward

EDITOR'S INTRODUCTION

1. Edward T. James, Janet Wilson James, and Paul S. Boyer. eds. *Notable American Women, 1607-1950: A Biographical Dictionary*, 3 vols. (Cambridge: Harvard University Press, 1971); Barbara Sicherman and Carol Hurd Green, eds., *Notable American Women, the Modern Period: A Biographical Dictionary* (Cambridge: Harvard University Press, 1980).
2. New York: R.R. Bowker, 1979.

INTRODUCTION

1. Julia Ward Howe, *Reminiscences* (Boston: Houghton Mifflin, 1899; reprint ed., New York: New American Library, 1969), p. 381.
2. This reconstruction is based on Julia Ward Howe's own description in ibid., pp. 380-81, and on Deborah P. Clifford, "An Invasion of Strong-Minded Women: The Newspapers and the Woman Suffrage Campaign in Vermont in 1870," *Vermont History* 43 (1975): 1-19.
3. Clifford, "Invasion of Strong-Minded Women," p. 16.

CHAPTER ONE

1. Laura Elizabeth Richards and Maud Howe Elliott, *Julia Ward Howe, 1819-1910*, 2 vols. (Boston: Houghton Mifflin, 1916), 1: 14 (hereafter cited as Richards and Elliott).
2. Ibid., 1:10, 1:8. The ascription of characteristics reflects nineteenth-century assumptions about men and women. From the grandmother came "feminine" qualities, such as gaiety and a quick temper; from the grandfather came the

more substantial "masculine" qualities: force, integrity, strength, and business instinct.

3. Howe, *Reminiscences*, p. 36.
4. Richards and Elliott, 1: 13.
5. Ibid., 1: 12.
6. Louise Hall Tharp, *Three Saints and a Sinner: Julia Ward Howe, Louisa, Annie, and Sam Ward* (Boston: Little, Brown, 1956), p. 21 (hereafter cited as Tharp).
7. Ibid., p. 21; Richards and Elliott, 1: 13.
8. Tharp, p. 22.
9. Ibid., p. 20.
10. Edward T. James, ed., *Notable American Women*, 3 vols. (Cambridge: Harvard University Press, 1971), 2: 71-72.
11. Despite nine years of tutelage, Julia Cutler never learned to write or spell particularly well, as her letters attest.
12. Tharp, p. 22; Richards and Elliott, 1: 17.
13. Deborah P. Clifford, *Mine Eyes Have Seen the Glory: A Biography of Julia Ward Howe* (Boston: Little, Brown, 1979), p. 10.
14. JRC to SW, September 1812, 9, 27 August 1813, Howe papers, Houghton Library, Cambridge, Massachusetts.
15. JRC to SW, 27 January 1812, Howe papers.
16. A portrait is included in Richards and Elliott, 1: 16.
17. Ibid., 1: 4; for information about this branch of the family, see pp. 4-14.
18. Ibid., 1: 4.
19. Ibid., 1: 6.
20. Ibid., 1: 16.
21. Ibid., 1: 6.
22. Howe, *Reminiscences*, p. 46.
23. Richards and Elliott, 1: 16.
24. SW to JRC, 18 May 1812, Howe papers.
25. SW to JRC, 19 March-20 September 1812, Howe papers.
26. SW to JRC, 7 June 1812, Howe papers.
27. SW to JRC, 7 September 1812, Howe papers.
28. SW to JRC, 28 May 1812, Howe papers.
29. SW to JRCW, 25 August 1813, Howe papers.
30. JRC to SW, September 1812, Howe papers.
31. Barbara Welter, "The Cult of True Womanhood: 1820-1860," *American Quarterly* 18 (Summer 1966): 151-74.
32. JRC to SW, 25 June 1812, Howe papers.
33. JRC to SW, 27 July 1813, Howe papers.
34. SW to JRCW, 3 June 1821, Howe papers.
35. JRCW to SW, 15 July, 9, 23 August, 21 March [1822], Howe papers.
36. JRCW to SW, 6 September 1813, Howe papers.
37. Illness gave women an escape from role demands of passivity, submissiveness, and self-denial. It also allowed women to command the attention and energy of whole households. See Carroll Smith-Rosenberg, "Hysterical Woman: Sex

Roles in Nineteenth-Century America," *Social Research* 39 (Winter 1972): 652-78.

38. Howe, *Reminiscences*, p. 5.
39. JRCW to SW, 6 September 1813, Howe papers.
40. Richards and Elliott, 1: 17.
41. SW to JRCW, 7 July 1814, Howe papers. I have taken the details of Julia Cutler Ward's conversion from Tharp, p. 27. Since Tharp provides no footnotes to substantiate this story, it may be apocryphal. Most likely the events were described to Tharp by one of Julia Ward Howe's granddaughters. Even if the story is not true, it has the ring of truth. Sensitized by the religious excitement around them and by frequent direct confrontations with death, women of the nineteenth century were quick converts to evangelical Christianity. Furthermore, in an early letter to her husband, dated 1813, Julia Cutler Ward revealed that even in pregnancy she suffered terrible fears at night, especially about death (JRCW to SW, 17 August 1813, Howe papers).
42. Whitney R. Cross, *The Burned-Over District: The Social and Intellectual History of Enthusiastic Religion in Western New York, 1800-1850* (Ithaca: Cornell University Press, 1950; reprint ed., New York: Harper, 1965), p. 13.
43. Ibid., p. 28.
44. For a good discussion of the theology of the Second Great Awakening, see Bernard A. Weisberger, *They Gathered at the River: The Story of the Great Revivalists and Their Impact Upon Religion in America* (Boston: Little, Brown, 1958), chaps. 3 and 4. Clifford S. Griffin, *Their Brothers' Keepers: Moral Stewardship in the United States, 1800-1865* (New Brunswick, N.J.: Rutgers University Press, 1960), chapters 1 and 2, explains the general impulse toward organized reform. The particular role of women in the Benevolent Empire was first examined in Keith Melder, "Ladies Bountiful: Organized Women's Benevolence in Early Nineteenth-Century America," *New York History* 47 (July 1967): 231-54.
45. Howe, *Reminiscences*, p. 18. Richards and Elliott, 1: 48. Clifford, *Mine Eyes Have Seen the Glory*, p. 19.
46. SW to JRCW, 10 February 1822, Howe papers. His resistance is documented in an early letter, dated 7 July 1814. Other letters reveal the same deference to her religious views (SW to JRCW, 11 September 1823).
47. Tharp. p. 10. This is most likely the understanding of Julia's grandchildren as conveyed to Tharp.
48. Howe, *Reminiscences*, p. 45.
49. Richards and Elliott, 1: 6.

CHAPTER TWO

1. Howe, *Reminiscences*, p. 10.
2. Ibid., p. 11.

3. Richards and Elliott, 1: 21.
4. Tharp, p. 37.
5. Ibid.
6. JRCW to Sarah Mitchell Cutler, 24 July [1823], Howe papers. It was in character for Julia to express her nervousness this way. Later in life, Julia described the effect of music on her, revealing a sensitive temperament. "The power and sweep of great orchestral performances, or even the suggestive charm of some beautiful voice, will sometimes so disturb the mental equilibrium of the hearer [herself] as to induce in him [her] a listless melancholy, or, worse, still, an unreasoning and unreasonable discontent" (Howe, *Reminiscences*, p. 19).
7. JRCW to SW, 17 August [1823], Howe papers. See also JRCW to SW, 31 August, 11 September 1823.
8. Florence Howe Hall, *Memories Grave and Gay* (New York: Harper, 1918), p. 8.
9. For this and the discussion of the world of women, I have drawn from Carroll Smith-Rosenberg, "The Female World of Love and Ritual: Relations Between Women in Nineteenth-Century America," *Signs* 1 (Autumn 1975): 1-29.
10. See Nancy Cott, *The Bonds of Womanhood: "Woman's Sphere" in New England, 1780-1835* (New Haven: Yale University Press, 1977), chap. 5.
11. Smith-Rosenberg, "Female World of Love and Ritual," p. 14.
12. Howe, *Reminiscences*, p. 31.
13. Ibid., p. 12. Julia's niece rememberd that her mother suffered from constant sore throats, which she blamed on inadequate winter clothing. Mary Crawford Fraser, *A Diplomat's Wife in Many Lands*, 2 vols. (New York: Dodd, Mead, 1910), 1: 8.
14. Richards and Elliott, 1: 37.
15. Howe, *Reminiscences*, p. 19.
16. Ibid., p. 18.
17. Robert V. P. Steele [Lately Thomas]. *Sam Ward, "King of the Lobby"* (Boston: Houghton Mifflin, 1965), p. 28.
18. Richards and Elliott, 1: 23.
19. This anecdote is contained in Julia Ward Howe, "The Ethical Office of the Drama," speech, 1902, Howe collection, box 1, Library of Congress, Washington, D.C.
20. JRCW to SW, 28 January 1822, Howe papers.
21. Richards and Elliott, 1: 30.
22. Ibid., 1: 30-31.
23. Ibid., 1: 35.
24. Ibid., 1: 31-32.
25. Ibid., 1: 33.
26. Richards and Elliott, 1: 33-35. Other titles include "All things shall pass away," "We return no more," "Mine is the Power to make thee whole," "Redeeming Love," and "My Heavenly Home." Some of these are found in the Howe papers, among her manuscript poems.

27. Howe, *Reminiscences*, pp. 15, 49; Richards and Elliott, 1: 61.
28. SW to JRCW, 18 July 1812, Howe papers.
29. Howe, *Reminiscences*, pp. 15, 50.
30. Richards and Elliott, 1: 16-17.
31. Griffin, *Their Brothers' Keepers*, p. xii. Griffin later makes clear, in a chapter entitled "God and Mammon," that rich men used Calvinist theology to defend their investments and their stake in society.
32. Ibid., chap. 5, p. 23.
33. Kathryn Kish Sklar, *Catharine Beecher: A Study in American Domesticity* (New Haven: Yale University Press, 1973), p. 82. Sklar presents this view in her discussion of Lyman Beecher, a contemporary of Samuel Ward's.
34. Howe, *Reminiscences*, pp. 46, 43.
35. Ibid., pp. 45-46.
36. Steele, *Sam Ward*, pp. 17-18.
37. Fraser, *A Diplomat's Wife*, 1: 19.
38. Julia Ward Howe, "Story of My Girlhood," manuscript article, n.d., Howe collection, box 4, Houghton Library.
39. Howe, *Reminiscences*, p. 53.
40. Richards and Elliott, 1: 36.
41. Howe, *Reminiscences*, p. 49.
42. Sklar, *Catharine Beecher*, p. 11.
43. Richards and Elliott, 1: 22.
44. Howe, *Reminiscences*, p. 13.
45. Ibid., p. 12.
46. Richards and Elliott, 1: 41.
47. Ibid.
48. Francis Marion Ward to Samuel Ward, Jr., 24 July 1838, Samuel Ward papers, New York Public Library. One of the sons, Ward McAllister, grew up to be as handsome and charming a snob as New York City ever entertained.
49. JRCW to SW, 3 July 1813, Howe collection, Houghton Library. In a letter describing her sister's exhaustion, Julia wrote, "She does all the chamber and parlor work, sews for the children, and puts them to bed. When mother is not around, she sits and cries."
50. Francis Marion Ward to Samuel Ward, Jr., 9 August 1838, Samuel Ward papers. In later life, family members lodged against Aunt Eliza the more serious complaint that she "never had much reason or judgment" (Julia Ward Howe, Journal, 30 August 1865, Howe papers).
51. Richards and Elliott, 1: 25.
52. Eliza Cutler to Samuel Ward, Jr., 14 February, 30 December 1825, Samuel Ward papers.
53. Eliza Cutler to Samuel Ward, Jr., 30 December 1825, Samuel Ward papers.
54. Eliza Cutler to Samuel Ward, Jr., 24 June 1826, Samuel Ward papers.
55. Julia Ward Howe, manuscript poems, Howe collection, box 3, Houghton Library.

56. Eliza Cutler to Samuel Ward, Jr., letters dated 1825-1826, Samuel Ward papers.
57. Richards and Elliott, 1: 28.
58. Ibid., 1: 27.
59. Benjamin Clarke Cutler to Samuel Ward, Jr., 25 May 1826, Samuel Ward papers.
60. Howe, *Reminiscences*, pp. 45-46, 53.
61. Richards and Elliott, 1: 19. A glimpse of the sisters' religious views is available in a barely literate letter written to the Ward girls while they were in their teens ("everything in this world is vanity and passeth away"). Anne Catherine Ward to Julia, Louisa, and Annie Ward, [1838], Howe papers. A long grim letter to her sister-in-law reveals the same Calvinist frame of reference ("the pleasures of this world I think of with pain"). Anne Catherine Ward to JRCW, 25 December 1821.
62. Fraser, 1: 88.
63. Richards and Elliott, 1: 242.
64. Ibid., 1: 60.
65. Ibid., 1: 64-65.
66. Laura Elizabeth Richards, *Stepping Westward* (New York: Harper, 1918), p. 106; Howe, *Reminiscences*, p. 19.
67. Richards, *Stepping Westward*, p. 104; Richards and Elliott, 1: 22.
68. Tharp, p. 43.

CHAPTER THREE

1. Joseph F. Kett, *Rites of Passage: Adolescence in America, 1790 to the Present* (New York: Basic Books, 1977), pp. 14, 29, 36.
2. Howe, *Reminiscences*, p. 44.
3. Young women of this period often suffered a stormy adolescence as they dangled between childhood and wifehood. As society modernized, they could no longer count on fitting into the adult idea they had been taught to expect as children, and until they married, they had no clear function to fulfill. See Nancy Cott, "Young Women in the Second Great Awakening in New England," *Feminist Studies* 3 (Fall 1975): 15-29.
4. Howe, *Reminiscences*, p. 17.
5. Julia Ward Howe, Untitled reminiscence, 1891, Howe collection, box 4, Houghton Library.
6. SW to LW, 5 April 1842, Howe papers.
7. Howe, Untitled reminiscence.
8. Howe, "Story of My Girlhood."
9. Howe, *Reminiscences*, pp. 49, 50.
10. Richards and Elliott, 1: 47.
11. Ibid.

12. Howe, *Reminiscences*, p. 15.
13. Ibid., p. 47.
14. Ibid., p. 46.
15. Francis Marion Ward to SW, 5 October 1838, Samuel Ward papers.
16. Richards and Elliott, 1: 49.
17. Ibid., 1: 51-52.
18. JW to LW and AW, 17 July 1838, Howe papers.
19. SW to Samuel Ward, Jr., 16 July 1838, Samuel Ward papers.
20. LW to SW, 6 October 1838, Samuel Ward papers.
21. JW to AW, 2 July 1838, Samuel Ward papers.
22. Howe, *Reminiscences*, p. 20.
23. Richards and Elliott, 1: 57-58.
24. Ibid., 1: 104. In an earlier letter Julia teased, "Annie's letter was very sweet, but I am afraid she knows I have what is vulgarly called a sweet tooth, or she would not put in so many little bits of that which I would denominate *flattery* were it not almost too strong an epithet. I am already sufficiently vain, and as I happen to have a taste for sugarplums of this kind, let me request that I may not be indulged in it." JW to LW and AW, 17 July 1838, Howe papers.
25. Maud Howe Elliott, *Uncle Sam Ward and His Circle* (New York: Macmillan, 1938), pp. 175-76.
26. Julia Ward [Howe], "Thou Alone," unpublished poem, 1834, Howe collection, box 2, Houghton Library.
27. Julia Ward Howe, "Matilda, Thou Hast Seen Me Start," unpublished short story, [1850s], Howe collection, box 4, Houghton Library.
28. Richards and Elliott, 1: 55.
29. Tharp. p. 56.
30. Richards and Elliott, 1: 58.
31. Henry Marion Ward to JW, 25 July 1840, Howe papers.
32. Tharp, pp. 57-58.
33. An inscription in Cogswell's diary reads, "Makes continual mention of a nameless Goddess with whom he is in love. Her name was Julia Ward!" Joseph Greene Cogswell, Diary, October 1836-February 1837, Howe papers. In a letter to his brother, Francis Marion Ward disapproves of Julia's attachment to a "professional man," elsewhere referred to as "Prof." FMW to SW, 20 March 1842, Samuel Ward papers, box 3. This may have been Henry Wadsworth Longfellow, with whom Julia flirted for several years. JW to LW and AW, 6 July 1838, Saturday [1842], Howe papers.
34. Howe, *Reminiscences*, p. 53.
35. Ibid., p. 44; Richards and Elliott, 1: 39.
36. Samuel Ward, Jr., to JW, n.d., Howe papers.
37. Howe, *Reminiscences*, pp. 43-59.
38. Richards and Elliott, 1: 43; Howe, Untitled reminiscence.
39. Linda Grant DePauw, *Four Traditions: Women of New York During the American Revolution* (Albany: New York State American Revolution Bicentennial Commission, 1974), pp. 5, 36.

40. Cott, *Bonds of Womanhood*, pp. 113-18.
41. Howe, *Reminiscences*, p. 43.
42. Richards and Elliott, 1: 45-46.
43. Howe, *Reminiscences*, p. 60.
44. JW to LW, 16 July 1838, Howe papers.
45. JRCW to Samuel Ward, Jr., 6 October 1821, Howe papers.
46. Howe, *Reminiscences*, p. 57.
47. Ibid., p. 60.
48. FMW to SW, 1 August 1838, Samuel Ward papers.
49. Steel, *Sam Ward*, chaps. 3 and 4.
50. Howe, Untitled reminiscence.
51. Tharp, pp. 59, 60; Howe, *Reminiscences*, pp. 44, 57.
52. David Allmendinger, *Paupers and Scholars: The Transformation of Student Life in Nineteenth-Century New England* (New York: St. Martin's Press, 1975), p. 2.
53. Howe, *Reminiscences*, p. 44.
54. Ibid., p. 60.
55. Ibid., p. 20.
56. Ibid., pp. 57, 58.
57. Ibid., p. 49.
58. Ibid., p. 20; Richards and Elliott, 1: 67.
59. Howe, *Reminiscences*, p. 68.
60. Examples include Susan B. Anthony (*Notable American Women*, 1: 51), Elizabeth and Emily Blackwell (*Notable American Women*, 1: 161-65), Olympia Brown (*Notable American Women*, 1: 256), and Abby W. May (*Notable American Women*, 2: 513). Susan Phinney Conrad has noted the same pattern among intellectual women of the early nineteenth century in *Perish the Thought: Intellectual Women in Romantic America, 1830-1860* (New York: Oxford University Press, 1976), p. 238.
61. SW to LW, 13 May 1842, Howe papers; FMW to SW, 8 April 1842, Samuel Ward papers; SW to Samuel Ward, Jr., 16 July 1838, Howe papers; Howe, *Reminiscences*, p. 47.
62. JW to LW and AW, 3 July 1838, Howe papers; JW to Mary Ward [Dorr], Tuesday 17 [n.d.], Tuesday 10 [n.d.], Howe papers; Howe, *Reminiscences*, p. 66.
63. JW to LW and AW, Saturday [1842?], Howe papers. See also Howe, *Reminiscences*, p. 78.
64. JW to SW, reprinted in Elliott, *Uncle Sam Ward*, p. 192.
65. Howe, *Reminiscences*, p. 57.
66. FMW to SW, 12 February 1842, Samuel Ward papers.
67. FMW to SW, 24 July 1838-9 December 1841, 22 February, 5 March 1842, Samuel Ward papers.
68. FMW to SW, 8 April 1843, Samuel Ward papers.
69. JW to LW and AW, Thursday 19th [1840], Howe papers.

70. The minister's name was penciled on the margin of the letter by Julia's daughter, Laura Elizabeth Richards.
71. Henry Marion Ward to JW, 25 July 1840, Howe papers.
72. FMW to SW, 1, 2, 9 August 1838, Samuel Ward papers.
73. JW to Eliza Cutler Francis, 2 October 1839, Howe papers; FMW to SW, 1 August 1838, Samuel Ward papers. Julia had actually begun to take over some of the household duties before Aunt Eliza left. This may have prompted the Ward children's decision to make a permanent change. SW to Samuel Ward, Jr., 16 July 1838, Samuel Ward papers; JW to LW, 16 July 1838; JW to LW and AW, 29 June, 6 July 1838, Howe papers.
74. JW to LW and AW, 6 July 1838, Howe papers.
75. AW to LW, n.d., Samuel Ward papers.
76. JW to AW, n.d., Howe papers.
77. JW to LW and AW, 25 January 1840, Howe papers.
78. JW to LW and AW, Wednesday 3rd, Howe papers.
79. Tharp. p. 94.
80. Richards and Elliott, 1: 52; JW to Samuel Ward, Jr., 4 August, 11 July 1837, Howe papers.
81. Richards and Elliott, 1: 37.
82. Mary Ward [Dorr] to JW, 23 October 1839, Howe papers.
83. Mary Ward [Dorr] to JW, 11 December 1841, Howe papers.
84. "In sharp contrast to their distant relations with boys, young women's relations with each other were close, often frolicsome, and surprisingly long-lasting and devoted. . . . Within such a world of female support, intimacy, and ritual, it was only to be expected that adult women would turn trustingly and lovingly to each other. It was a behavior they had observed and learned since childhood. A different type of emotional landscape existed in the nineteenth century." Smith-Rosenberg, "Female World of Love and Ritual," pp. 21, 28.
85. Mary Ward [Dorr] to JW, 3 October 1839, Howe papers. "Think how much you will require of one to whom *your whole life* and *yourself* are given, and be sure that he for whom you make this sacrifice . . . is worthy."
86. Mary Ward [Dorr] to JW, [1843], Howe papers. Perhaps Julia's wedding, mentioned later in the letter, preyed on Mary's mind. She may have worried (correctly, in fact) that Julia's husband would engage all of Julia's energy and attention and that their friendship would begin to dwindle.
87. Mary Ward [Dorr] to JW, 3 October 1839, Howe papers.
88. Mary Ward [Dorr] to JW, 26 February 1842, Howe papers. "They would not univerally interest," she wrote of the poems, "because they express but a very partial view of the truth of one religion, and that one of a stern, painful, ascetic character to which the whole spirit of the times is opposed."
89. Mary Ward [Dorr] to JW, 11 December 1841, Howe papers.
90. Mary Ward [Dorr] to JW, 3 October 1839, Howe papers.
91. Conrad, *Perish the Thought*, p. 41.
92. Annie Ward [Mailliard] to Samuel Ward, Jr., August 1841, Samuel Ward papers.

93. JW to LW and AW, n.d., Howe papers.
94. Conrad, *Perish the Thought*, p. 63.
95. Howe, *Reminiscences*, p. 53.
96. Ibid., p. 52.
97. Howe, *Reminiscences*, pp. 53-54. Mary Ward recorded the same observation in a letter to Julia. Mary Ward [Dorr] to JW, 26 February 1842, Howe papers.
98. JW to LW and AW, 20 January 1841, Howe papers.
99. JW to LW, 5 December 1840, Howe papers.
100. Quoted in Richards and Elliott, 1: 66.
101. Julia Ward Howe, "The world lost in darkness and sin," sermon, n.d., Howe collection, folder 58, Library of Congress.
102. JW to LW and AW, Monday [1842], Howe papers.
103. Richards and Elliott, 1: 66.
104. JW to Mary Ward [Dorr], 10th Tuesday, Howe papers.
105. Richards and Elliott, 1: 67; JW to LW and AW, Wednesday 3rd, 25 January 1840, Howe papers.
106. JW to AW, 8 December [1844], Howe papers.
107. Nearly all her letters to her sisters and to Mary Ward from 1838 to 1842 reflect her religious concerns. See for example JW to LW, 5 December 1840; JW to LW and AW, 25 January, February 1840; JW to Mary Ward [Dorr], Tuesday the 10th, Howe papers.
108. Kett, *Rites of Passage*, p. 68.
109. Mary Ward [Dorr] to JW, 11 December 1841, Howe papers.
110. Howe, *Reminiscences*, p. 61.
111. From a letter quoted in full in Richards and Elliott, 1: 69.
112. Howe, *Reminiscences*, p. 62.
113. Ibid.
114. Howe, Untitled reminiscence.
115. Mary Ward [Dorr] to JW, 11 December 1841, Howe papers.
116. William R. Hutchison, *The Transcendentalist Ministers: Church Reform in the New England Renaissance* (New Haven: Yale University Press, 1959), chap. 3.
117. Ibid., chaps. 1 and 2.
118. Howe, "Solitude and Religion," sermon, n.d., Howe collection, folder 57, Library of Congress.
119. When Louisa sent her son, future novelist Frank Marion Crawford, back to the U.S. from Italy to attend boarding school, she stipulated that he was not to spend his vacations with Julia. Her main objection was that Julia held nonconformist religious views.
120. "Religious identity allowed women to assert themselves, both in private and in public ways. It enabled them to rely on an authority beyond the world of men and provided a crucial support to those who stepped beyond accepted bounds—reformers, for example." Cott, *Bonds of Womanhood*, p. 140.
121. Tharp. p. 83.
122. JW to Mary Ward [Dorr], n.d., Howe papers.

CHAPTER FOUR

1. Howe, *Reminiscences*, p. 82,
2. Ibid., p. 230.
3. Laura Elizabeth Richards, *Samuel Gridley Howe* (New York: Appleton-Century, 1935), pp. 130, 181.
4. Richards, *Stepping Westward*, p. 3.
5. Tharp, p. 160.
6. Harold Schwartz, *Samuel Gridley Howe, Social Reformer, 1801-1876* (Cambridge: Harvard University Press, 1956), p. 39.
7. Howe, *Reminiscences*, p. 142.
8. Schwartz, *Samuel Gridley Howe*, pp. 1-5.
9. Ibid., pp. 14-38.
10. Ibid., pp. 41-48.
11. Ibid., pp. 49-51, 54-61.
12. SGH to Charles Sumner, 17 September 1844; SGH to SW, 3 February 1843, Howe papers. Chev explains that his investments yield an additional $1,000 per year.
13. Schwartz, *Samuel Gridley Howe*, pp. 69-70.
14. JW to LW and AW, Monday [1842], Howe papers.
15. Julia Ward Howe, "A Dream of Carnival," unpublished poem, 1844, Howe collection, box 3, Houghton Library.
16. JW to LW and AW, Wednesday morning [1843], Howe papers; Tharp, p. 85.
17. SGH to Charles Sumner, n.d. [1843], Howe papers.
18. SGH to Henry W. Longfellow, n.d. [1843], Howe papers.
19. Copy of indenture agreement, 26 April 1843, Howe collection, box 4, Houghton Library.
20. SW to SGH, 4 April 1843, Howe papers.
21. Richards, *Samuel Gridley Howe*, p. 3.
22. JWH to LW, n.d. [November 1845], 31 January 1847, Howe papers.
23. Howe, Journal, 24 April 1865, Howe papers.
24. SGH to Charles Sumner, 11 September 1844, Howe papers. Chev quotes Julia to this effect in this letter. Other evidence concerning Chev's extreme attachment to his men friends is found in his letters. See, for example, SGH to Charles Sumner, Thursday evening ("I sometimes fear that the fountains of affection are growing less abundant."); SGH to Charles Sumner, 28 October 1845 ("Secretly, I am defunct without you."); SGH to Horace Mann, n.d. ("You have never been out of my mind, never out of my heart. I have not written simply because I had little or nothing to say, except that I love you and that you know well enough.").
25. Richards and Elliott, 1: 78.
26. JWH to Eliza Cutler Francis, n.d. [27 April 1843], Howe papers.
27. Howe, *Reminiscences*, p. 117.
28. Ibid., pp. 91-117.

29. JWH to LW, 2 June 1843, Howe papers. Julia used her tongue in the company of her English hosts, too, at one time berating them for their rudeness in complaining about the failure of their American speculations. (JWH to SW, 29 July 1843, Howe papers.)
30. JWH to LW, 23 May 1843, Howe papers, Houghton Library.
31. Richards and Elliott, 1: 83.
32. For a later account of this visit, see Julia Ward Howe, "Ireland," lecture, 1910, Howe collection, box 4, Houghton Library.
33. Julia Ward Howe, Scrapbook, 1843, Howe papers.
34. Howe, *Reminiscences*, p. 117.
35. Julia Ward Howe, "The Present is Dead," unpublished poem, 4 June 1843, Howe collection, box 3, Houghton Library.
36. Julia Ward Howe, Untitled poem, 1843, Howe collection, box 3, Houghton Library.
37. Julia Ward Howe, "The Darkest Moment," unpublished poem, 1844, Howe collection, box 3, Houghton Library.
38. Julia Ward Howe, "The Dawning of Light," unpublished poem, 1844, Howe collection, box 3, Houghton Library.
39. JWH to John Ward, 4 October 1843, Howe papers; Tharp, pp. 106, 116.
40. Howe, *Reminiscences*, pp. 123-27.
41. Richards and Elliott, 1: 96.
42. Julia Ward Howe, "A Genius Came to the Ladye," unpublished poem, 8 March 1844, Howe collection, box 3, Houghton Library.
43. At the birth of their third child, Chev was forced to help Julia during the unexpectedly fast birth. Julia reported that Chev did not know how to assist her and that she suffered unnecessarily in delivering the baby's shoulders. JWH to LWC, 18 April 1848, Howe papers.
44. Howe, *Reminiscences*, p. 133.
45. JWH to SW, 8 July 1848, Howe papers.
46. JWH to LWC, Saturday 23 [August 1845], Howe papers.
47. JWH to SGH, Thursday [1846], Howe papers.
48. Richards and Elliott, 1: 77.
49. Richards, *Stepping Westward*, pp. 12, 18-19; Tharp, p. 161; JWH to LWC, 29 September 1846, Howe papers; Richards and Elliott, 1: 103.
50. Richards, *Samuel Gridley Howe*, pp. 9, 123.
51. Howe, *Reminiscences*, p. 214.
52. JWH to LW, Wednesday, April 1845, Howe papers.
53. Julia Ward Howe, "There was ever music in thy halls," unpublished poem, 1844, Howe papers.
54. Richards and Elliott, 1: 111.
55. JWH to LW, Wednesday 14 [May 1845], Howe papers.
56. Howe, *Reminiscences*, p. 215.
57. JWH to LW and AW, Tuesday [September 1844], Howe papers. Even in later years, Julia admitted to being intimidated by her cooks and chambermaids. JWH to LWC, 16 November [1846].

58. JWH to LWC, Tuesday 1 April [1845], Howe papers. Although this was a large number of servants for a middle-class family, Julia had reason to think they could afford it. Their combined incomes exceeded $6,000 per year, and they paid their cook and their housekeeper only $3 per week. JWH to LWC, [October 1945].

59. JWH to LW, Tuesday, 18th [April 1845], Howe papers. JWH to LWC, Saturday, 13th [1846], Howe papers. JWH to Anne Ward Mailliard (hereafter AWM), Saturday [1849?], Howe papers.

60. JWH to LWC, 15 May 1847, Howe papers.

61. Howe, *Reminiscences*, p. 133.

62. JWH to AWM, Saturday [1849?], Howe papers.

63. Richards, *Samuel Gridley Howe*, p. 177.

64. JWH to LWC, n.d.; JWH to AW, 17 August 1846, Howe papers.

65. JWH to AWM, Saturday [1849?], Howe papers.

66. JWH to AWM, [March 1850], Howe papers.

67. JWH to LWC, 29 September 1846, Howe papers.

68. SGH to Samuel Ward, Jr., Wednesday 23 [1844], Howe papers.

69. SGH to Charles Sumner, 11 September 1844, Howe papers.

70. Ibid.; SGH to Charles Sumner, 17 September 1844, Howe papers.

71. SGH to SW, 14 October 1844; JWH to SW, [December] 1844, Howe papers.

72. Trust documents, Howe collection, box 4, Houghton Library.

73. SGH to Charles Sumner, 17 September 1844, Howe papers.

74. SGH to John Ward, 5 July 1845, Howe papers.

75. SGH to JW, 9 July 1845, Howe papers.

76. SGH to JW, 12 July 1845, Howe papers.

77. JWH to SW, Saturday [July 1845], Howe papers.

78. SGH to JW, 24 July 1845; MSS request addressed to John Ward and Samuel Ward, 28 July 1845; receipt from SGH, 27 January 1846; SGH to JW, 4 May 1846, Howe papers.

79. SGH to JW, 24 July 1845, Howe papers.

80. Trust documents, Howe collection, box 4, Houghton Library.

81. JWH to LW, Wednesday [April 1845], Howe papers.

82. JWH to AW, n.d.; JWH to AW and LW, April 1845; JWH to AW, 8 December [1844]; JWH to LW, Wednesday April 1845, Howe papers.

83. JWH to AW, n.d., Howe papers. Julia spent $50 on a set of laces, velvet jacket, and velvet cloak. See also Howe, Scrapbook, p. 18, Howe papers.

84. JWH to SGH, n.d., Howe papers.

85. JWH to Eliza Francis, 11 July [1847], Howe papers.

86. JWH to AW and LW, April 1845, Howe papers. JWH to LWC, 29 September 1846, Howe papers.

87. SGH to LW, 2 November 1844, Howe papers.

88. Anne L. Kuhn, *The Mother's Role in Childhood Education: New England Concepts, 1830-1860* (New Haven: Yale University Press, 1947), pp. 71-171. See also Cott, *Bonds of Womanhood*, pp. 63-100.

89. Richards, *Samuel Gridley Howe*, pp. 184-86.

90. JWH to AW, n.d., Howe papers.
91. One cannot help but wonder if Chev sought the return of Julia's attention by this method. See SGH to Horace Mann, Saturday evening [April 1848]; JWH to LW, 1 October 1845; SGH to Theodore Parker, 5 November 1850, Howe papers.
92. JWH to AW, June 1846, Howe papers.
93. JWH to LWC, 31 January 1846, Howe papers.
94. JWH to LWC, 1 January 1847, Howe papers.
95. JWH to Francis Lieber, 31 July [1847], Howe collection, box 1, Library of Congress. The German phrases are little jokes. Julia tells Lieber he may discuss nothing about madness "except love"; nothing about prisons "except marriages"; and everything about literature "except Longfellow's poems."
96. Howe, Scrapbook, p. 31. Richards and Elliott described the problem: "She [was] the wife of a man who had neither leisure nor inclination for 'society'; a man . . . devoted to causes of which she knew only by hearsay; moreover, so absorbed in work for these causes, that he could only enjoy his home by snatches" (1: 103). See also JWH to LWC, 15 February 1846, Howe papers: "My nature is to sing, to pray, to feel. His is to fight, to teach, to reason."
97. See John Mack Faragher, *Women and Men on the Overland Trail* (New Haven: Yale University Press, 1979), pp. 2-15.
98. JWH to LWC, 15 February 1846, Howe papers.
99. JWH to SGH, Thursday, 1846, Howe papers.

CHAPTER FIVE

1. Richards and Elliott, 1: 104.
2. JWH to LWC, November 1845, Howe papers. See also JWH to LW, Wednesday 14 [May 1845]: "I wash and dress the baby, feed her, put her to sleep, and sleep with her myself, in all which I have some fatigue much pleasure."
3. JWH to LWC, [October 1845], Howe papers. See also JWH to SGH, Tuesday [May 1846], in which Julia complained of feeling "worn to death" by her children.
4. JWH to AWM, n.d. [1851?], Friday [1852], Howe papers.
5. JWH to LWC, 15 June 1847, Howe papers.
6. JWH to LWC, 1 December 1846, Howe papers.
7. JWH to AWM, 17 April [1853], Howe papers; Richards and Elliott, 1:103.
8. Julia Ward Howe, "Brook Farm," lecture, n.d., Howe collection, box 2, Library of Congress.
9. Julia Ward Howe, "What Life Means to Me," *Cosmopolitan*, July 1906. In a manuscript entitled "New Yorker in Boston," Julia recorded these other observations: "The streets appeared sombre, the shops few in number, the society reserved. . . . The society recognized as the best was more intimate than

extensive." Julia Ward Howe, "New Yorker in Boston," manuscript essay, 1906, Howe collection, box 3, Houghton Library.

10. Howe, *Reminiscences*, p. 150.
11. Richards and Elliott, 1: 129.
12. JWH to LWC, 18 February 1853, Howe papers.
13. JWH to AWM, 17 April [1853], Howe papers; Howe, *Reminiscences*, pp. 214-15.
14. JWH to LWC, Saturday 23 [August 1845], Howe papers.
15. JWH to LWC, [November 1845], Howe papers.
16. JWH to LWC, Saturday 23 [August 1845], Howe papers.
17. JWH to LWC, 30 May 1846, Howe papers.
18. JWH to LWC, 31 January 1846, Howe papers.
19. JWH to LWC, 15 February 1846, Howe papers.
20. JWH to AWM, [June] 1846, Howe papers.
21. JWH to LWC, 31 January 1846, Howe papers.
22. JWH to LWC, 30 May 1846, Howe papers.
23. Richards and Elliott, 1: 128; JWH to John Ward, Monday 9th [July] 1847, Samuel Ward papers.
24. JWH, excerpt from letter, n.d., Howe collection, box 4, Houghton Library.
25. JWH to AW, Friday [1846], Howe papers.
26. JWH to LWC, 29 September 1846, Howe papers.
27. JWH to Eliza Cutler Francis, Monday 10 March; JWH to LWC, 31 March 1847; JWH to AWM, 3, 19 October 1849, Howe papers.
28. JWH to AW, Saturday 13 [1846], Howe papers.
29. Howe, Scrapbook, p. 32.
30. JWH to AWM, Saturday 13; JWH to LWC, Tuesday 29 September 1846, 16 November [1846], Howe papers.
31. JWH to LWC, 31 January 1847, Howe papers. Isolation combined with the burdens of managing a young family were problems for many talented women of the period. Tillie Olson, in her foreword to Rebecca Harding Davis, *Life in the Iron Mills, or the Korl Woman* (Old Westbury, N.Y.: Feminist Press, 1972), pp. 117-27, points out that Davis suffered a nervous breakdown as she tried to balance her call to her work and her responsibility to her family. Her short story, "The Wife's Story," details the conflict women endured in their commitment to both serious work and the people in their family circle.
32. JWH to LWC, 31 January 1847, Howe papers.
33. Ibid.; JWH to Eliza Cutler Francis, Sunday [1847]; JWH to AWM, [March 1847], Howe papers. All contain news of her social successes.
34. JWH to AWM, Monday [March 1847], Howe papers.
35. JWH to LWC, 15 May 1847, Howe papers.
36. JWH to LWC, 1 December 1846, 31 January 1847; JWH to AWM, Monday [March 1847], Howe papers.
37. JWH to SGH, Monday [1847], Thursday [1847], [April 1847], Howe papers.
38. JWH to LWC [31 March 1847], Howe papers.

39. JWH to SGH, Thursday [1847], Monday [1847]; JWH to AWM, [1847], Howe papers.
40. JWH to LWC, [15 June 1847], Howe papers.
41. JWH to LWC, 15 May 1847, Howe papers.
42. JWH to LWC, 16 November 1847; Howe papers. See also JWH to AWM, Monday 20 [November 1847]; JWH to LWC, 23 January, 18 April 1848.
43. JWH to LWC, 15 May 1847, Howe papers.
44. Howe, Scrapbook, pp. 18, 17, Howe papers.
45. Ibid., p. 26.
46. JWH to LWC, 1 November 1844; JWH to AWM, Friday 13th [January 1854], Howe papers.
47. All the Ward sisters shared this affection and need for each other. "How strongly I can sympathize in Lou's longing for her sisters . . . this feeling lies deep at the bottom of my heart—Rome looks far more beautiful to me, since our Wevie is there, and I am sure New York could not look so bright if you were not in it," wrote Julia to Annie before her marriage. JWH to AWM, Saturday 13th [1846], Howe papers.
48. SW to JWH, 19 January 1847, Howe papers.
49. Tharp, p. 149; JWH to AWM, 15 December [1848], Howe papers.
50. JWH to AWM, 15 December [1848], Howe papers.
51. JWH to SW, Saturday 23; JWH to SW, enclosed in a letter from SGH, 5, 29 November 1847, Howe collection, Houghton Library.
52. Tharp, p. 149.
53. Trust documents, Howe collection, box 4, Houghton Library.
54. JWH to LWC, 31 January 1847, 13 June 1848, Howe papers.
55. JWH to LWC, 29 September 1846, Howe papers.
56. JWH to SGH, Thursday [1846]; see also JWH to AWM, 25 November [1851], Howe papers.
57. JWH to Eliza Cutler Frances, Sunday [1847], Howe papers.
58. JWH to AWM, 16 December 1849, Howe papers.
59. JWH to LWC, 31 January 1847, Howe papers.
60. JWH to AWM, Monday 20 [November 1847], Howe papers.
61. JWH to AWM, 15 December 1849, Howe papers.
62. JWH to LWC, 25 July 1854, Howe papers.
63. "I have lived in a state of somnambulism, only half conscious of the world around me, occupied primarily with digestions, sleep, and babies. Thank God, this mist has been lifted from my eyes, for a time at least." JWH to LWC, 13 January 1847, Howe papers. See also JWH to AWM, Monday [March 1847], 15 December 1849, Friday 8th [1850].
64. JWH to LWC, 13 January 1847, Howe papers.
65. JWH to AWM, 19 July [1854], Howe papers. At another time Julia confessed that she kept to the back streets when she went out. JWH to AWM, Monday 20 [November 1847].
66. JWH to AWM, Friday 8th [February 1850], [March 1850], Howe papers.
67. JWH to LWC, 18 April 1848, Howe papers.

68. SGH to LWC, 5 April 1848, Howe papers.
69. JWH to LWC, [October 1845], Howe papers.
70. JWH to LWC, 30 May 1846, Howe papers.
71. SGH to LWC, 5 April 1848, Howe papers.
72. JWH to LWC, 18 April 1848, Howe papers.
73. JWH to AWM, [March 1850], Howe papers.
74. JWH to LWC, 1 October 1845, 15 February 1846, Howe papers.
75. JWH to LWC, October 1845, Howe papers.
76. JWH to LWC, [October 1845], [15 February 1846], Monday 16 November [1846], 1, 31 January, 15 June 1847, Howe papers.
77. JWH to AWM, n.d., Howe papers.
78. JWH to LWC, 13 June 1848, Howe papers.
79. JWH to LWC, 13 January, 15 May 1847, 13 June 1848, Howe papers.
80. SGH to LWC, 5 April 1848, Howe papers.
81. Richards and Elliott, 1: 128.
82. JWH to LWC, November-December 1848, Howe papers.
83. Ibid.
84. JWH to AWM, [March 1847], Howe papers.
85. JWH to LWC, 15 May 1847, Howe papers.
86. JWH to LWC, 18 April 1848, Howe papers.
87. Scraps of these plays are in box 2 of the Howe collection, Houghton Library.
88. JWH to AWM, 3, 19 October [1849], Howe papers. In a later letter to Louisa, Julia describes her winter as "wretched" and "overcome with sorrow." JWH to LWC, [June 1850].
89. JWH to AWM, 16 December 1849, Howe papers.
90. JWH to AWM, 12 October [1849], Howe papers.
91. JWH to AWM, Friday, 8 [February 1850], Howe papers.
92. JWH to LWC, Tuesday 18 [March 1845], Howe papers.
93. JWH to LWC, 15 May 1847, Howe papers. Another indication of the distance between them appears in Julia's *Reminiscences*, pp. 82-89, 371. In introducing her husband to the reader she devotes eight pages to him, focusing almost exclusively on his accomplishments in public life. She includes very little about their family or married life, or even about Chev's personality. His strong will, his energy, and his tendency to dominate emerge from her description, but nowhere does Julia expand on the implications of his personality and interests. It is as if, in the long view of old age, she saw him as an admirable and noble public man who happened to accompany her partway through life. The same sort of distance occurs in her account of his death. It is strangely cold and impersonal; Julia describes the facts of his death, the eulogies accorded him, and her admiration for his "solid power of work, untiring industry, prophetic foresight and intuition, [and] grand trust in human nature." It is as if they shared no private life at all. This was a lonely situation for one who had dreamed of a "perfect union of minds."
94. JWH to AWM, 12 October [1849], Howe papers.
95. Ibid.

96. JWH to LWC, November-December 1848, Howe papers.
97. JWH to LWC, n.d., Howe papers.
98. JWH to LWC, [June 1850], Howe papers.
99. Ibid.
100. Ibid.
101. Tharp, p. 167.
102. JWH to LWC, November-December 1848, Howe papers.
103. JWH to LWC, 31 January 1847, Howe papers. In several letters Julia gives the impression that she does not know how to proceed. She invokes heavenly assistance frequently as she recounts her struggles to unsnarl her life: "life is the body; religion & imagination, etc., are the soul . . . now to put soul and body together requires the direct agency of God, to keep them together requires the daily gentle help of Providence, how can I do it? Courage! to do it will be God-like! So one had best try!" JWH to AWM, [spring 1849]. See also JWH to SW, Saturday 23 [June 1849].
104. JWH to AW and LW, Saturday 21st [1844], Howe papers. See also JWH to AWM, Saturday 13 [1846], [March 1847], 23 January 1848, 3, 19 October [1849], [February 1850], [March 1850]; JWH to LWC, [31 January 1846], [June 1850].
105. The letters of authors of major works (usually male) are frequently collected and edited for publication. The letters of lesser-known literary women are rarely collected, in part because these writers did not produce the large *oeuvre* of their male counterparts. In general, this low productivity reflected lack of time. Nevertheless, their informal writings deserve attention as literary works in themselves. Personal letters, diaries, and even business letters can reveal lines of great literary power. Sermons, addresses to meetings, and speeches likewise contain much of merit, but these, too, are never collected. In other words, some of the best writing of literary women never gets published. This was certainly the case for Julia Ward Howe, whose published, conventional literature is far inferior in descriptive power, evocation of mood or personality, and force of argument to her unpublished work.

CHAPTER SIX

1. Howe, *Reminiscences*, pp. 189, 190.
2. Richards and Elliott, 1: 133.
3. Howe, *Reminiscences*, p. 190.
4. Tharp, p. 169.
5. Howe, *Reminiscences*, p. 191.
6. Conrad, *Perish the Thought*, p. 168.
7. Howe, *Reminiscences*, pp. 162, 196.
8. Tharp, p. 169.

9. George Egon Hatvary, "Horace Binney Wallace: A Study in Self-Destruction," *Princeton University Library Chronicle* 25 (Winter 1964): 137-49.
10. Ibid., pp. 140-41, 146.
11. JWH to LWC, 18 February 1853, Howe papers.
12. Howe, *Reminiscences*, pp. 190-200.
13. Julia Ward Howe, Untitled poem, n.d., Howe collection, box 2, Houghton Library.
14. JWH to LWC, 28 October 1851, Howe papers.
15. JWH to AWM, November 1852, Howe papers.
16. JWH to Horace Binney Wallace, 7 January 1853, Howe papers.
17. JWH to LWC, 28 October 1851, Howe papers.
18. JWH to AWM, Wednesday 17 [December 1851], Howe papers.
19. JWH to LWC, 27 June 1852; JWH to AWM, April 1852, Howe papers.
20. Howe, Journal, 2 April 1880, Howe papers.
21. Julia mentions happy moments in JWH to LW, 13 March 1845; JWH to LWC, October [1845], November [1845], Howe papers.
22. JWH to LWC, 13 June 1848, Howe papers.
23. Julia Ward Howe, "From the Lattice," *Words for the Hour* (Boston: Ticknor & Fields, 1857), pp. 119-20.
24. JWH to AWM, Wednesday 17 [December 1851], Howe papers.
25. JWH to AWM, 25 November 1851, Wednesday 17 [December 1851], Howe papers.
26. JWH to AWM, 1 October [1852], Howe papers.
27. JWH to AWM, Thursday 9 [September 1851], Howe papers.
28. JWH to AWM, 8 November [1852], Howe papers.
29. Ibid.
30. JWH to AWM, 3 December [1852], Howe papers.
31. JWH to AWM, 25 November 1851, Howe papers. Julia reassured Annie on this point: "Don't misunderstand me—there is no reason for my feeling ill, and no possibility of any." JWH to AWM, Thursday 9 [September 1852].
32. Julia Ward Howe, Untitled poem, n.d., Howe collection, box 2, Houghton Library.
33. JWH to AWM, 18 February 1853, Howe papers.
34. JWH to AWM, 8 December 1853, Howe papers.
35. Julia Ward Howe, Untitled poem. Julia never indicated any guilt about the suicide. Her affection and subsequent withdrawal to return to South Boston may, however, have triggered a depression leading to his suicide. Wallace's biographer certainly hints as much. Hatvary, "Horace Binney Wallace," p. 147.
36. JWH to AWM, 3 December 1852, Howe papers; see also JWH to LWC, 18 February [1853]; JWH to AWM, Thursday [winter 1853], Saturday 12 [March 1853].
37. JWH to AWM, 13 July [1853], Howe papers.
38. JWH to Edward Twisleton, 20 April 1853, Howe collection, Houghton Library.
39. Receipt dated 26 February 1853, Howe papers.

40. JWH to AWM, Thursday [March 1853], Howe papers.
41. JWH to Edward Twisleton, 17 April 1854, Howe collection, Houghton Library; JWH to AWM, 1 April [1853], Howe papers.
42. JWH to AWM [March or April 1853], Thursday [March 1853], Saturday 12 [March 1853], 1 April [1853], Howe papers.
43. JWH to Samuel Gray Ward, 25 July 1853, Howe papers.
44. Howe, *Reminiscences*, pp. 150, 161; JWH to Theodore Parker, Tuesday 22nd, Howe papers.
45. JWH to Henry Wadsworth Longfellow, 30 November [1853], Longfellow papers, Houghton Library.
46. JWH to Henry Wadsworth Longfellow, June 1852, 8 March, 30 April 1853, Longfellow papers.
47. JWH to Henry Wadsworth Longfellow, 30 April 1853, Longfellow papers.
48. Tharp, p. 199.
49. JWH to AWM, Thursday [March 1853], Sunday 17 April [1853], 13 July [1853], Howe papers. Julia wrote "social and literary criticism," notices concerning Oliver Wendell Holmes's and James Russell Lowell's lectures, as well as a paper on Harriet Beecher Stowe and George Sand. Howe, *Reminiscences*, p. 253.
50. JWH to Edward Twisleton, 20 April 1853, Howe papers.
51. JWH to AWM, Sunday 17 April [1853], Howe papers.
52. JWH to AWM, 1 October [1852], Howe papers.
53. JWH to LWC, 30 September 1852, Howe papers.
54. Howe, *Reminiscences*, p. 221.
55. Tharp, p. 176.
56. JWH to Henry Wadsworth Longfellow, 30 November [1853], 10 December [1853], Longfellow papers.
57. JWH to AWM, 14 November [1853], Monday December [1853], Howe papers.
58. JWH to AWM, Monday December [1853], 8 December [1853], Howe papers.
59. JWH to AWM, 29 December [1853], Howe papers, HL.
60. The role of "woman of letters" was static at this point in American history, and no threat to the popular cult of true womanhood still prevailing in white middle-class circles. The romantic orientation common to most women writers was the very opposite of reason, which was always attributed to male, and denied to female, minds. As women called forth their "finer sensibilities" in a literary mode of wonder, awe, and romanticism, they separated themselves firmly from male traditions. (See Conrad, *Perish the Thought*, pp. 185-86.) Because Jula Ward Howe's poetry fits neatly into this category of writing, it is inappropriate to see it as a fundamental challenge to the conventional spheres of manhood and womanhood. Its importance lies in the personal victory it represented to Julia.
61. Julia Ward Howe, "Thoughts," *Passion Flowers* (Boston: Ticknor & Fields, 1853), pp. 95-98.
62. "Correspondence," ibid., pp. 88-90.

63. JWH to LWC, 23 July 1854; SGH to Charles Sumner, 16 June 1854, Howe papers.
64. JWH to LWC, 18 February 1853, Howe papers.
65. JWH to Edward Twisleton, 20 April 1853, Howe papers.
66. Julia Ward Howe, "The Shadow That Is Born With Us" and "The Nursery," *Words for the Hour*, pp. 128-31, 96-97.
67. JWH to Edward and Ellen Twisleton, 17 April 1854, Howe papers.
68. JWH to AWM, 27 May 1854; JWH to LWC, 23 July 1854, Howe papers.
69. JWH to AWM, 19 June [1854], Howe papers. In old age, Julia recalled having "tantrums" during her pregnancy with Maud. JWH to Laura Elizabeth Howe Richards, 24 February 1872.
70. SGH to Charles Sumner, 16 June 1854, Howe papers.
71. JWH to LWC, 23 July 1854, Howe papers.
72. JWH to AWM, 19 June 1854, Howe papers.
73. JWH to LWC, 23 July 1854, Howe papers. There is no evidence of the identity of the woman.
74. JWH to SGH, 22 April [1854], Howe papers.
75. Maud Howe Elliott, *Three Generations* (Boston: Little, Brown, 1923), pp. 11, 94.
76. Julie Ray Jeffrey, *Frontier Women: The Trans-Mississippi West, 1840-1880* (New York: Hill and Wang, 1979), p. 63, discusses this traditional consideration.
77. JWH to SGH, 22 April [1854], Howe papers.
78. JWH to AWM, 19 January, 1 June 1855, October 1854, Howe papers.
79. JWH to AWM, 19 June 1854, Howe papers.
80. When he was on his deathbed, Chev told Julia of his love affairs. See JWH, Journal, 23 November 1875, Howe papers.
81. Portraits are reproduced in Richards and Elliott, 1: 186; Richards, *Samuel Gridley Howe*, pp. 134, 252.
82. Maud Howe Elliott, *This Was My Newport* (Cambridge, Mass.: Mythology Co., 1944), pp. 95-96.
83. Elliott, *Three Generations*, p. 62.
84. Laura Elizabeth Richards, *When I Was Your Age* (Boston: Estes & Lauriat, 1894), pp. 14-39.
85. JWH to AWM, 25 November [1851], Howe papers.
86. JWH to LWC, 23 June 1854, Howe papers.
87. Richards, *Two Noble Lives: Samuel Gridley Howe and Julia Ward Howe* (Boston: Dana, Estes, 1906), pp. 56-57; Richards and Elliott, 1: 149.
88. JWH to AWM, Sunday May [1853], Howe papers.
89. Richards, *When I Was Your Age*, pp. 22, 129, 133; Richards and Elliott, 1: 147.
90. Richards, *When I Was Your Age*, pp. 87-93.
91. JWH to AWM, 8 November [1852], 14 November [1853], 8 December 1853; JWH to LWC, 23 July 1854; JWH to AWM, 13 August [1854], Howe papers.
92. JWH to AWM, 1 June 1855, Howe papers.
93. JWH to LWC, April 1852; JWH to AWM, Sunday 26 [1852], 13 July [1853], Howe papers.

94. Richards, *When I Was Your Age*, p. 179; Richards, *Stepping Westward*, pp. 62, 66; Hall, *Memories Grave and Gay*, pp. 77, 84; Elliott, *Three Generations*, p. 46.
95. JWH to AWM, Sunday 26 [1852], Howe papers.
96. Elliott, *Three Generations*, pp. 49-50.
97. Richards, *When I Was Your Age*, p. 154.

CHAPTER SEVEN

1. JWH to AWM, 8 November [1852], Howe papers. See also JWH to AWM, Wednesday 17 [December 1851], 3 December [1852], 13 August [1854]; JWH to LWC, April, 27 June 1852, 30 September 1852.
2. JWH to LWC, 30 September 1852, Howe papers.
3. Richards, *Two Noble Lives*, pp. 53-54.
4. Richards, *Stepping Westward*, p. 31. See also JWH to AWM, Good Friday [1852], Friday 3 December [1852], 13 August [1854], Howe papers.
5. Howe, *Reminiscences*, p. 239; JWH to AWM, 13 July 1857, Howe papers.
6. JWH to AWM, Monday 5 August [1856], Howe papers.
7. Howe, *Reminiscences*, pp. 267, 62; JWH to AWM, Sunday 8 December 1844, Howe papers.
8. JWH to AWM, Sunday 8 December 1844, Howe papers.
9. Howe, "New Yorker in Boston."
10. Theodore Parker to SGH, 6 December 1857, Howe papers.
11. John L. Thomas, "Romantic Reform in America, 1815-1865," *American Quarterly* 17 (Winter 1965): 656-81.
12. Howe, *Reminiscences*, p. 204; JWH to LWC, 15 June 1847, Howe papers.
13. Sydney E. Ahlstrom, *A Religious History of the American People* (New Haven: Yale University Press, 1972), p. 485.
14. Jean Strouse, *Alice Janes: A Biography* (Boston: Houghton Mifflin, 1980), pp. 12-17.
15. Julia Ward Howe, "After the fire, a still, small voice," sermon, n.d. [1890s], Howe collection, box 4, Library of Congress.
16. Julia Ward Howe, "The liberty wherewith Christ has made us free," sermon, n.d., Howe collection, box 4, Library of Congress.
17. JWH to Edward Twisleton, 7 July 1853, Howe collection, Houghton Library.
18. "It [Hegel's idea] justifies the instinct by which we involuntarily distrust the system, whether of religion, politics or morals, claims to be too perfect, too final, and sets barriers to the mind. . . . The relative nature of reality all we know and believe is to be much visited upon." Julia Ward Howe, Commonplace book, Howe papers.
19. Ibid., frontispiece.
20. Howe, *Reminiscences*, p. 210.
21. Howe, Commonplace book, last page.

22. Howe, *Reminiscences*, p. 211.
23. JWH to Edward Twisleton, 17 April 1854, Howe papers.
24. Howe, *Reminiscences*, p. 212.
25. Julia Ward Howe, "Fichte and Spinoza," lecture, n.d., Howe collection, box 10, Houghton Library.
26. See Julia Ward Howe, "Your head is wild with books, Sybil," essay, n.d., Howe collection, Houghton Library.
27. The paper, which Julia used only at midcentury, and the handwriting, which is neither so fine as that of the 1840s nor so scratchy as that of the 1870s, indicate that these papers were written in the late 1850s or early 1860s. For example, she uses the same paper and handwriting in a note to Longfellow dated 1856. (See JWH to Henry Wadsworth Longfellow, June 1856, Howe papers.) A piece of stationery, directed to Annie's father-in-law, Joseph Mailliard, is another piece of evidence. Slipped between two pages of a manuscript play, the paper is dated February, 1857. Occasional references to literary failure provide internal evidence in favor of dating these efforts in the mid- or late 1850s.
28. Julia Ward Howe, "Universal Truth Cures Special Sorrow," essay, n.d., Howe collection, Houghton Library.
29. Julia Ward Howe, "To write a book," and "Olympia's Letters," Howe collection, box 9, Houghton Library.
30. Julia may have derived the character of Laurence/Laurent in part from Horace Binney Wallace, whose appearance was somewhat effeminate and whose sexual preferences are unclear. His sensitivity and the suffering he endured because of his impressionable mind are mirrored in Laurence's life.
31. Julia Ward Howe, *Eva and Raphael*, unpublished novel, Howe collection, box 1, Houghton Library.
32. This manuscript comes as something of a shock. Not all biographers get their subject's fantasy life handed to them in such direct form. The possible interpretations seem both limitless and limited, for although numerous ideas spring to mind, this is still only one piece of evidence rescued from a lifetime of writing and dreaming. Any interpretation, too, must be balanced by the recognition that normal, happy people may have weird fantasies from time to time. Most people simply do not write them down. Julia's writing suggests not so much her neurosis as her ability to avoid it by using her talent for writing.
33. Howe, *Eva and Raphael*. Julia's idea of madness or insanity would correspond to our twentieth-century notion of psychosis.
34. Julia Ward Howe, Manuscript fragment, Howe collection, Houghton Library.
35. The principal women characters in the play bear a strong resemblance to Charlotte von Stein, lady-in-waiting to the Weimar court and Goethe's intimate. A cool, intelligent woman, von Stein taught Goethe good manners when he first appeared at Weimar. Their friendship lasted ten years, with von Stein maintaining the upper hand. See Richard Friedenthal, *Goethe: His Life and Times* (Cleveland: Ward, 1965), pp. 208-12.
36. Howe, *Reminiscences*, p. 230.

37. JWH to Samuel Ward, Jr., Monday [1857], Howe papers.
38. Julia Ward Howe, *Leonora, Or The World's Own*, Howe collection, Houghton Library.
39. Samuel Ward, Jr., to JWH, Saturday [1857], Howe papers.
40. Charlotte Cushman to JWH, n.d. [1857], Howe papers. This play was not finished until later and not produced at all. In both style and subject matter, it differs substantially from *Leonora*.
41. Howe, *Reminiscences*, p. 305.
42. Howe, *Words for the Hour*, pp. 16-17, 26.

CHAPTER EIGHT

1. JWH to AWM, 6 May 1857, Howe papers.
2. Laura Elizabeth Richards, *Letters and Journals of Samuel Gridley Howe*, 2 vols. (Boston: Dana, Estes, 1909), 1: 251-52.
3. Schwartz, *Samuel Gridley Howe*, pp. 195-216.
4. John Noyes to SGH, 1874-1875, Howe papers.
5. Tharp, p. 217.
6. Howe, "Recollections of the Anti-Slavery Struggle," manuscript essay, n.d., Howe collection, volume 5, Schlesinger Library, Cambridge, Massachusetts.
7. Howe, Scrapbook, Howe papers. In this Julia broke with her family, for they opposed the free soil agitation. SW to JWH, 1 February 1852, Howe papers. In 1848 she contributed a poem to Maria Norton Chapman's annual, the *Liberty Bell*, to help raise money for the antislavery cause. Florence Howe Hall, *The Story of the Battle Hymn of the Republic* (New York: Harper, 1916), p. 9.
8. Howe, *Reminiscences*, p. 259.
9. Julia's lack of interest in abolitionism, as opposed to her support of the limitation of slavery to existing slaveholding territories, lasted until 1859. She strongly opposed extension, convinced that slavery would "gradually ameliorate and slowly die out." Julia Ward Howe, *A Trip to Cuba* (Boston: Ticknor & Fields, 1860), pp. 214-15.
10. JWH to AWM and LWC, 4 April 1858, Howe papers.
11. Richards and Elliott, 1: 170.
12. Howe, *Reminiscences*, p. 231.
13. Howe, *Cuba*, pp. 85, 126-27.
14. Ibid., pp. 98-99.
15. Ibid., p. 214. This was written by the same woman who would, in thirty months' time, write "The Battle Hymn of the Republic."
16. Ibid., pp. 12-13.
17. Ibid., pp. 120, 166, 196, chap. 18.
18. Ibid., pp. 234, 236, 237. Julia was consistent in her dislike of abolitionists, even when she herself had come closer to their views. See her criticism of Wendell

Phillips in Julia Ward Howe, "Newport Correspondence," New York *Tribune*, 18 August 1859.
19. Howe, "Recollections."
20. Schwartz, *Samuel Gridley Howe*, pp. 217-36. The "Secret Six" were Theodore Parker, George Stearns, Thomas Wentworth Higginson, Gerrit Smith, Franklin Sanborn, and Samuel Gridley Howe. None of them knew of Brown's precise plans, and none was an accomplice.
21. JWH to AWM, 6 November 1859, Howe papers.
22. Schwartz, *Samuel Gridley Howe*, p. 242. The story of Chev's behavior after Harpers Ferry appears on pp. 237-46.
23. Ibid., p. 237.
24. Howe, *Reminiscences*, pp. 254, 256.
25. JWH to AWM, 6 November 1859, Howe papers.
26. For a similar argument, i.e., that periods of struggle and suffering can stimulate an even greater willingness to take risks and suffer for the cause, see Sylvan Tomkins, "The Psychology of Commitment: The Constructive Role of Violence and Suffering for the Individual and Society," in Martin Duberman, ed., *The Anti-Slavery Vanguard: New Essays on the Abolitionists* (Princeton: Princeton University Press, 1965), pp. 270-98.
27. Julia Ward Howe, "Last Letter to Sammy," ed. Deborah P. Clifford, *Harvard Library Bulletin* 25 (January 1977): 50-62. This is a faithful edition of the original, which is in the Howe collection, box 3, Houghton Library.
28. Ibid., pp. 52-57.
29. George Fredrickson, *The Inner Civil War: Northern Intellectuals and the Crisis of the Union* (New York: Harper, 1965), p. 99.
30. Howe, *Reminiscences*, pp. 269, 271.
31. Fredrickson, *Inner Civil War*, p. 99.
32. Howe, *Reminiscences*, pp. 270, 271, 274.
33. Ibid., pp. 274-75. An earlier account of this experience, though far less elaborate, contains the same elements, the same metaphors, and the same themes. Julia describes waking at night and lying still in her bed with "line after line shaping itself in my mind, and verse after verse." After writing these down in the "dim twilight," Julia fell asleep again, relieved and content. She stresses the feeling of effortlessness in the writing, the transformation of night (or dark) into day (or light), and the sense of peace on completing the poem, just as she did in her later account. Julia Ward Howe, "A Note on the 'Battle Hymn of the Republic,' " *The Century* 34 (December 1887): 629-30.
34. Edmund Wilson, *Patriotic Gore: Studies in the Literature of the American Civil War* (New York: Oxford University Press, 1962), pp. 92-93.
35. Fredrickson, *Inner Civil War*, pp. 61-82.
36. Howe, *Reminiscences*, between pp. 276-77. Julia made several changes in the text. The published version, and the one generally known today, is given below.

Mine eyes have seen the glory of the coming of the Lord

He is trampling out the vintage where the grapes of wrath are stored,
He hath loosed the fateful lightning of his terrible swift sword,
His truth is marching on.

I have seen him in the watchfires of an hundred circling camps
They have builded him an altar in the evening dews and damps,
I can read His righteous sentence by the dim and flaring lamps
His day is marching on.

I have read a burning Gospel writ in fiery rows of steel
As ye deal with my contemners, so with you my grace shall deal
Let the hero born of woman crush the serpent with his heel
Our God is marching on.

He has sounded out the trumpet that shall never call retreat,
He has waked the earth's dull sorrow with a high ecstatic beat,
Oh! be swift my soul to answer him, be jubilant my feet.
Our God is marching on.

In the beauty of the lilies he was born across the sea
With a glory in his bosom that shines out on you and me,
As he died to make men holy, let us live to make men free
Our God is marching on.

37. Howe, *Reminiscences*, p. 253.
38. Howe, "Letter," p. 55.
39. Howe, Journal, February 1864.
40. Ibid., 28 August 1865.
41. Howe, "Letter to Sammy," pp. 53-54.
42. Howe, Journal, 13 July 1864.
43. Ibid.; 16, 17 April 1866.
44. Richards and Elliott, 1: 195.
45. Howe, "Our Orders," *Later Lyrics* (Boston: J. E. Tilton, 1866), pp. 18-19.
46. Elliott, *Newport*, p. 59. In *Three Generations*, Elliott describes Henry James, Sr., Ralph Waldo Emerson, William Rounseville Alger, Edwin Percy Whipple, Frederick Henry Hedge, and Elizabeth Palmer Peabody, all of whom frequented Newport.
47. Howe, "Letter," p. 54.
48. Ibid., pp. 52, 56; JWH to [LWC], 31 January 1860, Howe papers.
49. Laura recalled that "The last decade of my father's life brought him much physical suffering. . . . Neuralgia, persistent and torturing, became almost his constant companion." Richards, *Samuel Gridley Howe*, p. 255.
50. JWH to AWM, n.d. [1857?], Howe papers.
51. Tharp, p. 235.
52. JWH to AWM, 11 March 1861, Howe papers.

53. Howe, "Letter," p. 56; JWH to AWM, 23 March 1862, Howe papers.
54. JWH to AWM, 23 March 1862.
55. Howe, *Reminiscences*, p. 305.
56. Richards and Elliott, 1: 195, my italics.
57. Howe, *Reminiscences*, p. 304.
58. Contact by printed word could have its dangers. Julia wrote unguardedly about people in her *Tribune* letters and found herself "much abused by them in return." JWH to LWC, 31 January 1860, Howe papers.
59. Clifford, *Glory*, pp. 128, 146, 147, 164.
60. JWH to [LWC], 31 January 1860, Howe papers. Ironically Elizabeth Cady Stanton, heretofore the *Tribune*'s major woman contributor, was at this time at odds with Greeley. Julia, by taking her place, was making money off Stanton's quarrel. This was not the last time the two of them would be at opposite poles.
61. Howe, Journal, 7 October 1863.
62. Charlotte Cushman to JWH, n.d. [1857], Howe papers.
63. Howe, *Reminiscences*, pp. 239-40.
64. Howe, *Hippolytus*, 1861, Howe collection, box 3, Library of Congress.

CHAPTER NINE

1. Howe, Journal, 13 and 14 May 1863.
2. Howe, "Letter," p. 58.
3. Until the advent of modern-day therapy, physicians sometimes relied in desperate cases on small doses of poisons to "burn out" serious disease. Mercury sets up a virulent reaction in the body, with fevers reaching 106-107° even in adults. This high heat kills the cells that carry the disease. Of course, high fevers can result in convulsions, brain damage, nerve damage, and death. That Sammy's physician ordered such an extreme remedy is an indication of the seriousness of the case.
4. Even those children who survived intubation (a treatment to prevent suffocation) did not neccesarily survive the toxoid. Any vigorous movement could stimulate the toxoid's action which, in essence, sent signals to the brain to stop the heartbeat. This is probably why Sammy died "without a struggle." I am indebted for this information to Harold T. Yates, M.D., of Alexandria, Virginia.
5. Howe, Journal, 17 May 1863; Howe, "Letter," pp. 58-60.
6. Richards and Elliott, 1: 178.
7. Howe, Journal, 5 June 1863.
8. Howe, Journal, 20 May, 5 June 1863.
9. Howe, "Letter," pp. 57, 62.
10. Ibid., pp. 60, 61.
11. Julia Ward Howe, Howe collection, boxes 2 and 3, Houghton Library.
12. Howe, "Letter," pp. 61, 62.

13. Howe, Journal, 16 August, 14 November 1863, 30 December 1865, 28 May, 3 June, 11 December 1864, 30 December 1865.
14. Ibid., 27 May 1864.
15. JWH to LWCT, September 1863, quoted in Richards and Elliott, 1: 196.
16. Howe, Journal, 24 September 1863.
17. Ibid., November and December 1863. The lectures, in order, were: "How Not To Teach Ethics," "Doubt and Belief," "Equality," "Moral Trigonometry," "Proteus," "Duality of Character."
18. Ibid., 16, 30 November 1863, 21 December 1863.
19. Howe, Reminiscences, pp. 306-7.
20. Tharp, pp. 256-57.
21. JWH to Samuel Ward, Jr., 17 December 1881, Howe papers.
22. Tharp, p. 257.
23. Howe, Journal, 16 November 1863.
24. Tharp, pp. 260-61.
25. Howe, Journal, 12 February 1864; Julia Romana Howe to AWM, 12 March 1865, Howe papers.
26. Howe, Journal, 20 January 1864.
27. Howe, Journal, 15, 28 January, 6 February, 10, 23 March 1864.
28. Howe, Journal, 16, 17, 25, 30 January 1864.
29. Ibid., 13 February, 18 April 1864.
30. Ibid., 30 April, 11 May 1864.
31. Ibid., 6 March 1864.
32. Ibid., 28, 30 April, 14-20 May 1864.
33. Julia Ward Howe, "Proteus," lecture, Howe collection, box 3, Library of Congress.
34. Howe, Reminiscences, p. 307.
35. Julia Ward Howe, "Moral Trigonometry," lecture, Howe collection, box 2, Library of Congress.
36. Fredrickson, The Inner Civil War, pp. 102-9; see also Robert H. Wiebe, Search for Order, 1877-1920 (New York: Hill and Wang, 1967), chaps. 2, 6.
37. Howe, "Trigonometry."
38. Julia Ward Howe, "Doubt and Belief," lecture, Howe collection, box 2, Library of Congress.
39. Ralph Henry Gabriel, The Course of American Democratic Thought (New York: Ronald Press, 1940), pp. 186-87.
40. Howe, "Doubt and Belief."
41. Howe, Journal, 3 June 1864.
42. Ibid., 27 May 1864.

CHAPTER TEN

1. Howe, Journal, 6-15 June 1864.
2. Ibid., 18 May 1864.
3. Howe, *Reminiscences*, p. 270.
4. Howe, Journal, 26 February 1865.
5. Richards, *When I Was Your Age*, p. 160.
6. Howe, Journal, 4 October 1865; 2, 7 January 1866.
7. Ibid., 7 March 1866.
8. Howe, *Reminiscences*, pp. 323-26.
9. Ibid., pp. 277-80.
10. Howe, Journal, 5 November 1864. See also George Bancroft to JWH, 22 October 1864, Howe papers. This is the invitation to the celebration. Bancroft mentions that Howe will be the only woman on the platform.
11. Howe, *Reminiscences*, p. 279; Howe, Journal, 5 November 1864.
12. A letter of thanks from all the members of the council to JWH, 25 November 1864, Howe papers, contains the full list of the members, as does the masthead of *Boatswain's Whistle*, Library of Congress.
13. Ibid., pp. 6, 36, 76.
14. Edward Everett, Andrew Preston Peabody, Oliver Wendell Holmes, James Russell Lowell, and Edwin Percy Whipple to JWH, 25 November 1864, Howe papers.
15. Howe, Journal, 10 April 1865.
16. "The millennium is on the way—three cheers for God!" Theodore Tilton to Susan B. Anthony, quoted in Ellen Carol DuBois, *Feminism and Suffrage: The Emergence of an Independent Woman's Movement in America, 1848-1869* (Ithaca: Cornell University Press, 1978), p. 53.
17. Wendell Phillips to Charles Sumner, 24 March 1866, quoted in Michael Les Benedict, *A Compromise of Principle: Congressional Republicans and Reconstruction, 1865-1869* (New York: Norton, 1974), p. 166.
18. Schwartz, *Samuel Gridley Howe*, pp. 266-67.
19. Benedict, *Compromise of Principle*, p. 64.
20. Howe, *Reminiscences*, p. 311.
21. Howe, Journal, 23 March 1865.
22. Ibid., 28 September, 19 November 1865.
23. JWH to Charles Sumner, 1 March 1864, Howe papers.
24. Howe, "Introduction to Ethical Lectures," 1867, Howe collection, box 8, Houghton Library.
25. Howe, Journal, 29 July 1865.
26. Ibid., 15-30 July 1866. Julia was also writing an occasional piece for *The Atlantic*; JWH to AWM, 11 March [1861], Howe papers.
27. Howe, Journal, 18, 30 July, 13 August, 19 September, 5 October 1866.
28. Ibid., 7-10 October 1865.
29. Ibid., 14 January 1865.

30. Ibid., 10 June 1865.
31. Ibid., 9, 10, 14 October 1865.
32. Julia Ward Howe, *From Sunset Ridge: Poems Old and New* (Boston: Houghton Mifflin, 1898).
33. Statements to this effect are scattered throughout the journal, e.g., 9 February 1863, 15 June 1864, 21 December 1865.
34. Among many references to this in Howe's journal are 6 May, 14 November 1865, 4 October 1868. Julia described this plan in JWH to AWM, 4 October 1868, Howe papers.
35. See Howe, Journal, January-March 1865, for frequent comments on this setup.
36. Ibid., 7 February 1866.
37. Ibid., 4 April 1866.
38. Ibid., 12 April 1866.
39. JWH to AWM, 15 April 1866, Howe papers.
40. Ibid.
41. Howe, Journal, 26 October 1866. For a brief history of Gilmore and an earlier magazine of his, *The Continental Monthly*, see Frank Luther Mott, *A History of American Magazines*, 2 vols. (Cambridge: Harvard University Press, 1930), 1: 540-42.
42. Howe, Journal, 26 October 1866.
43. This information was found in clippings contained in the Howe collection, vol. 2, Schlesinger Library.
44. Howe, Journal, 26 October-3 November 1865.
45. Ibid., 14, 19 February 1867.
46. Ibid., 25 January 1867.
47. JWH to AWM, 15 April 1866, Howe papers.
48. Howe, Journal, 1, 6 February 1867.
49. Printed forms filled out by the assessor's office, dated 1 May 1864, Howe papers.
50. Howe, Journal, 9 June 1865, 25 October 1867.
51. JWH to LWCT, 18 July 1867, Howe papers.
52. The Declaration of Sentiments that was passed in Seneca Falls made control over property a primary issue.
53. JWH to LWC, 31 January 1847, Howe papers.
54. Howe, *Cuba*, p. 204.
55. Howe, "Florence Nightingale and her Praisers," *Words for the Hour*, pp. 40-41. See also poems on a similar theme, pp. 38-39, 42-43.
56. Julia Ward Howe, "Debt to Pioneers," speech to Boston Equal Suffrage Association, 23 March 1904, Howe collection, vol. 4, Schlesinger Library.
57. Howe, "Proteus."
58. Julia Ward Howe, "The Woman's Rights Question," essay, n.d., Howe collection, box 9, Houghton Library.
59. Ibid.
60. Julia Ward Howe, "Polarity II," 1865, Howe collection, box 3, Library of Congress.

61. Howe, Journal, 1, 17 January 1867.
62. Theodore Parker, "The Public Functions of Woman," sermon preached at the Boston Music Hall, 27 March 1853, published in *Essays and Addresses on Woman Suffrage* (n.p., n.d.), pp. 2, 18-19.
63. Howe, Journal, 25 February 1866.
64. Ibid., 29 May, 5 November 1864, 8-9 January, 11-19, 23 March, 23 April, 7-8 December 1865.
65. Ibid., 7 September 1865.
66. Ibid., 13 November, 18 December 1865.
67. Ibid., 12 December 1866.
68. Shortly afterward, Julia found herself attracted to the Viscount de Chabrol. "Were I young, this person would occupy my thoughts some," she commented. She did not, however, follow up her inclinations, as Chev did. Ibid., 19 December 1866.
69. Chev would suddenly write Julia a kind note or speak sympathetically to her. See ibid., 22 April, 24 May 1866, 7 January 1867.
70. Ibid., 28 April-14 May 1866; JWH to Laura Elizabeth Howe Richards, 8 May 1866; SGH to Charles Sumner, 20 May 1866, Howe papers. The poem, "To S.G.H.," is quoted in Richards and Elliott, 1: 248.
71. Richards, *Samuel Gridley Howe*, pp. 178-80.
72. Howe, Journal, 8 December 1865.
73. Ibid., 6 October, 9 December 1865. For similar statements, see 5 June, 19 November, 9 December 1865, 27 May 1866.
74. Quoted in Tharp, p. 301.
75. Howe, Journal, 7 December 1866.
76. Ibid., 19 February 1865.
77. Ibid., 3 June 1865; see also 21 November 1867.
78. Ibid., 28 September 1865. Julia expressed similar sentiments on 6 February 1865.
79. Her journal records readings on 21 September, 24 November, 8 December 1865; 7, 12, 21, 24, 26, 27 February, 2 March, 27 April, 15 May, 10, 23 August, 8 September, 7 December 1866; 6 January, 7 March 1867. A trip to Crete brought her career to a temporary halt. After that point, the journal is incomplete.
80. Ibid., 10 August 1866.
81. Ibid., 10, 23 March, 13, 22 July 1864.
82. A somewhat amended version of her initial essay in the "Limitations" series is in the Howe collection, Library of Congress; another copy is in the Howe collection, Houghton Library. "Three Degrees of Law" does not appear by name in any collection, but it may be the same essay as "Limitations" in the Howe collection, Houghton Library. Copies of "Moving Forces" and "The Fact Accomplished" in manuscript form are in the Houghton Library. A copy of "Moving Forces" is also in the Library of Congress.
83. Julia Ward Howe, "Spinoza," n.d., Howe collection, box 10, Houghton Library.

84. Julia Ward Howe, "Polarity," [1864], Howe collection, box 3, Library of Congress.
85. Howe, Journal, 1 October 1865.
86. Howe, "Moving Forces," p. 51.
87. Howe, "Fichte and Spinoza."
88. Julia Ward Howe, "For the fashion of the world passeth away," sermon, n.d., Howe collection, box 4, Library of Congress.
89. Howe, *Reminiscences*, p. 213.
90. References to her study of Kant can be found, for example, in Howe, Journal, January, 7 May, 7-8 June, 10-12 September, 1 October 1865, 21-25 May 1866. See also JWH to AWM, 15 April 1866, Howe papers. Julia went on to read Fichte, whom she found very difficult. See Howe, Journal, September, 6 October, 18, 21-24 November, 10-12 December 1866, 14 January, 30 November 1867.
91. In the fall of 1865 Julia began her third series of lectures with "The Ideal State," *Christian Examiner*, August 1866. The following spring she began work on an essay variously entitled "Ideal Necessity," "The Two Necessities," and "Man *a Priori* and *a Posteriori*." This was delivered in Northampton in August of that year. Julia worked on "Representation" and "Opposition" the following winter. A copy of the Northampton lecture and fragments of "Representation" and "Opposition" are in the Howe collection, box 5, Houghton Library.
92. Howe, "Introduction to Ethical Lectures," lecture, 1867, Howe collection, Houghton Library.
93. Ibid.
94. Julia Ward Howe, "Position of Woman," [1867], Howe collection, box 5, Houghton Library.
95. Howe, *Reminiscences*, p. 372.
96. Julia Ward Howe, Untitled manuscript, n.d., Howe collection, box 8, Houghton Library.

CHAPTER ELEVEN

1. Julia Ward Howe, *From the Oak to the Olive: A Plain Record of a Pleasant Journey* (Boston: Lee and Shepard, 1868), p. 189.
2. Howe, Journal, 7, 15 February, 13 March 1867.
3. Elliott, *Three Generations*, p. 79.
4. Howe, Journal, 24 March-17 April 1867.
5. Tharp, p. 202.
6. Howe, *Oak to Olive*, pp. 49-50.
7. Ibid., p. 45.
8. Howe, Journal, 26 May 1867.
9. Howe, *Oak to Olive*, p. 66.
10. Ibid., pp. 64, 151-52, 161-62, 225-29, 232-33, 268.

11. Howe, Journal, 1 May 1867.
12. Ibid., 4 May 1867.
13. Ibid., 2-20 June 1867.
14. Howe, *Oak to Olive*, p. 202. See also Schwartz, *Samuel Gridley Howe*, pp. 282-86.
15. Julia reported that at a meeting for Crete in Boston, the audience gasped when Chev announced he had fought for the Greeks in their revolution. He was a youthful-looking man. Howe, *Reminiscences*, p. 313. See photograph, Richards and Elliott, 1: facing p. 340.
16. Howe, *Journal*, 24 June 1867. Howe, *Oak to Olive*, pp. 186-89, contains a colorful description.
17. Howe, Journal, 3-8, 9, 13, 20, July 1867.
18. Ibid., 19-22 August, 28 September 1867.
19. Ibid., 6, 25 September 1867.
20. Ibid., 29 October 1867.
21. Ibid., 30 October, 1, 14 November 1867. Chev did permit Julia to read in public if it benefited Crete. JWH to LWCT, 23 February 1868, Howe collection, Houghton Library.
22. Ibid., 17, 27 November 1867.
23. Ibid., 9, 22 November 1867. Julia first learned of this in Europe in July. See JWH to LWCT, 18 July 1867, Howe papers.
24. Howe, Journal, 31 October, 21 November, 29 December 1867, 26 January, 1 March 1868.
25. Ibid., 23 April, 8 June 1865.
26. Ibid., 13 April 1868.
27. Ibid., 30 December 1867.
28. Ibid., 5 September 1867.
29. Ibid., 12 March 1865, 7 October 1866, 5 February 1868.
30. Ibid., 9 August 1867.
31. Ibid., 23 June, 28 August 1865, 31 July 1866. See also JWH to Anna Elliot, 4 February 1869, manuscript collection, Boston Athenaeum.
32. Elliott, *Three Generations*, p. 34.
33. Howe, Journal, 29, 30 December 1867.
34. Elliott, *Three Generations*, p. 7.
35. Ibid., p. 34.
36. Richards, *Stepping Westward*, p. 20.
37. Howe, Journal, 4 May 1865.
38. Ibid.
39. Ibid., 5 September 1867.
40. Ibid., 22 December 1867. See also 26 November 1867.
41. Ibid., 24 February 1868.
42. Ibid., 16 March, 26 April 1868.
43. Ibid., 1 February 1868.
44. JWH to AWM, 4 October 1868, Howe papers.
45. Howe, Journal, 1, 23-26 March 1868. See also 2, 30 March, 1, 24 April 1868.

46. Ibid., 2 July, 15 August 1868.
47. Ibid., 11 November 1867, 2 February 1868. See also 1, 2, 29 March, 12, 13 April 1868. Also Howe, *Reminiscences*, p. 284.
48. Howe, Journal, 26 January 1868.
49. Ibid., 1 January, 1 February, 24 April 1868. See also 2 July, 17 October 1868.
50. Julia Ward Howe, "Behold I Make All Things New," sermon, 1869, Howe collection, box 1, Library of Congress.
51. Karen J. Blair, *Clubwoman as Feminist: True Womanhood Redefined, 1868-1914* (New York: Holmes & Meier, 1980), p. 33.
52. Howe, *Reminiscences*, pp. 281-303.
53. Ibid., pp. 281-83. "Alice in Wonderland's changes were not more bewildering than are the changes one seems to undergo under the pressure of other peoples' ignoring of truths which we must know in order to live." Julia Ward Howe, "Address to the Free Religious Association," [1867], Howe collection, box 3, Library of Congress. The address appears in two folders; this quotation is from the first folder.
54. Howe, Journal, 18 November 1867.
55. Howe, "Address to the F.R.A." Julia held other religions in low esteem. She found Catholicism superstitious, authoritarian, and outdated ("Address to the F.R.A."; Julia Ward Howe, "Religious Power," sermon, n.d., Howe collection, box 4, Library of Congress). She compared Mormonism to prostitution (Julia Ward Howe, "Distinctions Between Philosophy and Religion," address to the Parker Society, n.d., Howe collection, box 2, Library of Congress). She complained that the faith of the Brahmins was too abstract, too laissez-faire, and without sufficient practical application ("Address to the F.R.A."). The Islamic faith she hated because of its contemporary role of persecuting Christians in the Middle East and Eastern Europe.
56. Julia Ward Howe, "Religion considered as the essential expression of the relation between God and Man," sermon, n.d., Howe collection, box 3, Library of Congress. Although these sermons are undated, the ideas expressed in them are so close to those in her journals and essays that I have used them to portray her religious convictions in the late 1860s.
57. Howe, "Address to the F.R.A."
58. Howe, Journal, 7 August 1865.
59. Howe, "Address to the F.R.A."
60. Howe, "Religious Power."
61. Howe, "Address to the F.R.A." A few years later Julia stated the same idea simply. "The practical piety of our time looks neither up nor down, but strait before it, at the men and women to be relieved, at the worst to be done." Julia Ward Howe, "The Halfness of Nature," lecture, 1875, Howe collection, box 1, Library of Congress.
62. Howe, "Behold."
63. Howe, "Address to the F.R.A."
64. Howe, "Address to the F.R.A.," second version.

65. Julia Ward Howe, sermon delivered to the Free Religious Association, n.d., Howe collection, box 3, Library of Congress.
66. Howe, "Solitude and Religion."
67. Howe, Journal, 31 May 1865.
68. Howe, "Solitude and Religion."
69. Julia Ward Howe, "The Kingdom of Heaven is at hand," sermon, [1871], Howe collection, box 1, Library of Congress.

CHAPTER TWELVE

1. DuBois, *Feminism and Suffrage*, pp. 162-65.
2. Ibid., pp. 166-67, 169-70.
3. Ibid., p. 165.
4. "Woman's Rights Convention," *National Anti-Slavery Standard* 29 (14 November 1868) (cited hereafter as *NASS*).
5. DuBois, *Feminism and Suffrage*, pp. 165-66.
6. "Woman's Rights Convention."
7. "Boston Correspondence," *NASS* 29 (28 November 1868).
8. Ibid.
9. "Julia Ward Howe's Address."
10. Howe, *Reminiscences*, pp. 374-75. Julia may have formed this dislike during the winter of 1866-1867, when Lucy Stone was stumping the state on behalf of resolutions that would remove sex and race restrictions from the suffrage provisions of the Massachusetts State Constitution. DuBois, *Feminism and Suffrage*, pp. 65-66.
11. Howe, *Reminiscences*, p. 375.
12. Julia Ward Howe, "Debt to Pioneers."
13. The best discussin of the formation of the New England Woman's Club is available in Blair, *Clubwoman as Feminist*, pp. 31-34.
14. Julia Ward Howe, "Address to the New England Woman's Club," New England Woman's Club papers, folder 43, Schlesinger Library, as quoted in Clifford, *Mine Eyes Have Seen the Glory*, p. 174.
15. "Women Organize," *NASS* 25 (4 July 1864).
16. "Boston Correspondence," *NASS* 25 (17 December 1864).
17. Howe, *Reminiscences*, p. 311.
18. Julia Ward Howe, "Had I One of Thy Words, My Master," sermon, n.d., Howe collection, box 9, Houghton Library. Maud recalled a night in 1890 when Julia, then in her eighties, spoke of this realization. She told Maud that after reading a paper to the Parker Fraternity, which no one understood, she "determined to live from experience, from thinking about people and about life, and to think no longer about thoughts." Elliott, *Three Generations*, p. 225.
19. Five years later Julia crystallized this conviction that activity was essential. "Desk dreamers end by being mental cripples. Divorce [of study from life] is not

wholesome nor holy. Life is a perpetual marriage of real and ideal." Howe, "Halfness of Nature."

20. Howe, *Reminiscences*, pp. 375, 372.
21. Ibid., p. 376.
22. Thomas Wentworth Higginson, "Colonel Higginson on Mrs. Howe," clipping, Howe collection, vol. 4, Schlesinger Library.
23. If Stone's speech on November 18, 1868, resembled her earlier one, she maintained that just as blacks needed the vote to protect their wages and contracts, so women needed the ballot to protect themselves when they ventured into the workplace. Just as the vote would elevate the black man, increasing his self-respect and sense of responsibility, so it would uplift women and assure their self-esteem. "Lucy Stone's speech at the Brooklyn Academy of Music," *NASS* 28 (26 December 1867).
24. Julia Ward Howe, Speech to the Cleveland Convention, 1869, Howe collection, box 9, Houghton Library, pp. 2, 3-4, 10.
25. Ibid., pp. 10-11.
26. Howe, "Solitude and Religion."
27. Howe, "Behold."
28. Ibid.
29. Ibid.
30. Howe, Journal, 27 May 1871.
31. Richards and Elliott, 1: 300.
32. Clifford, *Mine Eyes Have Seen the Glory*, p. 200.
33. Howe, *Reminiscences*, pp. 380-90.

Bibliography

I. *Primary*

An obvious place to start the research of Julia Ward Howe's life is her autobiography, *Reminiscences*. Unfortunately for the biographer, an autobiography can be many things besides history. It is sometimes literature; it is sometimes self-justification. In most cases, it is an attempt to make a sensible pattern from the tangents, contradictions, and backtracking of human life. In Victorian times, moreover, an autobiography written for publication strove to uplift the reader by introducing individuals of estimable character.

Julia Ward Howe belonged to the latter school. She believed that the lives of the people she knew were lives full of instruction. As a consequence, a great deal of her autobiography describes men and women (mostly men) whom Julia admired during her lifetime. Nine pages are devoted to Frederick Henry Hedge, a Transcendentalist minister and thinker, for example. Theodore Parker earned ten pages, and James Freeman Clarke, another Transcendentalist minister, received eight pages of description. Julia devoted eight pages to the bizarre Polish Count Adam Gurowski while giving exactly the same number to her husband of thirty-two years. One frustrating feature of Julia's autobiography, then, is her constant sidetracking to take a look at other people.

Whether she intended it or not, the focus on others also helped take the focus off Julia herself. Consequently, a great deal of Julia's life simply did not get into her book. As was the case with many Victorians, Julia saw no virtue in discussing the seamy aspects of life since such discussion provided no instruction or inspiration. Therefore, she left out almost every unpleasant thing that ever happened to her or to her family. The most serious omission of this sort concerns her husband. In life, they quarreled frequently, particularly over the direction Julia's life was to take. She whitewashed their unhappy marriage and, in another cover-up, made no mention of her eldest daughter's emotional disturbances.

The autobiography has other faults as a source. One is Julia's vagueness about the timing of various events. In some cases, this may be for the sake of convenience, to tidy up her life a bit. For example, she does not say when it was that she switched to James Freeman Clarke's church. This allows her to use the switch as a link between her descriptions of Parker and Clarke; it becomes a stylistic device to link two very different halves of her life. Julia is also vague about dating her support of the abolitionist movement. She implies that she joined these reformers in 1851 when in fact her support came in 1859. Because she later looked back in admiration on the abolitionists and because she wished to cultivate her own reform credentials, Julia pushed back the actual date of her involvement.

While her autobiography is not great literature, it is full of drama, put there by Julia to bring her accomplishments into focus. Her description of her conversion to woman suffrage is a case in point. Her recollections about the writing of the "Battle Hymn of the Republic" are likewise dramatic, pitting a little mother against the echoes of a great war. In recalling her participation in the founding of the New England Woman's Club, Julia again uses the device of minimizing her initial role. The contrast between this and her later activity brings the picture of Julia Ward Howe as dedicated clubwoman into sharp relief.

The sins of this autobiography, whether of omission or commission, place limits on its usefulness. I did use the *Reminiscences*, however, in describing Julia Ward Howe's reactions to things. These reactions are not absolute truth; that she recalled her father as exceedingly strict does not necessarily mean that he was unjust and unfair. Nevertheless, they convey a section of Julia's reality. Whether or not her father was excessively strict, it is important to know that Julia thought he was. Because so many of Julia's reactions to her life as recorded in her *Reminiscences* are borne out by other sources, particularly her letters, her journal, and memoirs written for other purposes, I have tended to trust the autobiography in this regard.

I have also relied on the autobiography for descriptions of people and places. Even if not accurate to the last detail, these are colorful and explicit. They provide one more way for Julia Ward Howe's voice to sound through these pages. In some of these cases, I could not find outside testimony to corroborate Julia's descriptions. This may have permitted errors to creep in. If so, they are errors of good nature, for Julia allowed very little criticism of others to creep into her memoirs.

Confirmation or contradiction of Julia's *Reminiscences* lies in the many books and boxes of manuscript material turned over to research libraries by Julia Ward Howe's descendants.

The Julia Ward Howe collection at the Library of Congress contains manuscript versions of her lectures and sermons as well as correspondence concerning her peace work (1870-73) and the New Orleans Exposition, for which she headed a Woman's Department (1885-86). These papers are well organized.

The Julia Ward Howe collection at the Schlesinger Library contains some correspondence and a great many scrapbooks full of clippings. The correspondence is well organized, but the scrapbooks follow no thematic or chronological pattern.

At the Houghton Library repose two major Howe collections. One, the Howe papers, is enormous, containing materials relating both to Julia Ward Howe and Samuel Gridley Howe. All these papers have been cataloged, and a bound finding aid simplifies recovery of individual items. This collection contains the bulk of Julia Ward Howe's correspondence to her family and all of her journals. The second collection, the Julia Ward Howe collection, is a thoroughly disorganized but very rich source. This collection is housed under two different call numbers. The first call number identifies several folders; the second, ten boxes of manuscript sermons, lectures, and poems. Items for the first call number have no special identification in my footnotes beyond Howe collection, Houghton Library. Items under the second call number are identified by box as well as by collection. Other materials at the Houghton Library, not cataloged with either collection, include correspondence between Julia Ward Howe and her niece, Margaret Terry Chanler, and correspondence between Julia Rush Cutler Ward and Samuel Ward. Correspondence between Julia Ward Howe and various friends, such as Henry Wadsworth Longfellow and James Russell Lowell, are also available at Houghton.

Other research collections deserve mention. The Julia Ward Howe papers at the Sophia Smith Collection, Smith College, contain a great deal of correspondence from the second half of Julia's life, mostly concerning suffrage and club work. The sizable Samuel Ward papers at the New York Public Library contain the bulk of the Ward family correspondence in addition to the papers of Julia's brother, Samuel Ward, Jr. The Boston Athenaeum not only owns a copy of every one of Julia Ward Howe's published titles, but also possesses a few odd letters concerning Julia Ward Howe.

As if they, too, suspected Julia would one day leave to posterity "some great work," Julia's family and friends saved her letters. For some periods the correspondence is so profuse that Julia's mood changes can be plotted on a month-by-month time line. This is especially true for the period 1844-56. The correspondence is not so abundant for other periods, but it still includes hundreds of items. On the other hand, if Julia Ward Howe saved any letters from her family, they did not end up in these collections. Almost all her letters from her children, husband, and sisters have disappeared. Perhaps she never saved them in the first place. Perhaps these were among the letters and papers Julia threw out and burned. After Chev's death, she destroyed a great deal of their correspondence, according to his wishes. As an old woman, Julia burned a considerable number of papers; family correspondence may have ended up in the ash heap then. As a result, the vast majority of letters concerning Julia in these collections were written by her to family and friends. She lived so long and wrote so much that the record is fairly complete, with the exception of the late 1850s and the late 1860s.

Julia's absentmindedness extended to dates. She almost never dated a letter completely. When she did, she occasionally did it wrong. Her worst fault was leaving off years, a lack her sister Annie always supplied. The catalog at the Houghton Library supplies some dates for undated letters. These letters were the work of Annie or Julia's daughter, Laura. For the most part, these additions are reliable. I have not used the dates other than Julia's, however. If, through internal evidence, I was able to date the letters, then those dates are enclosed in brackets in the footnotes.

II. *Secondary*

Two biographies of Julia Ward Howe, both out of print, provide interesting overviews of her life. Laura E. Richards and Maud Howe Elliott, two of Julia's daughters, wrote a two-volume biography of their mother entitled *Julia Ward Howe, 1819-1910*. According to the title page, a third daughter, Florence Howe Hall, assisted. Forty years later, Louise Hall Tharp published *Three Saints and a Sinner: Julia Ward Howe, Louisa, Annie, and Sam Ward*.

The former biography is by far the more complete. In thirty-two chapters, accompanied by numerous illustrations, Richards and Elliott cover every major event in their mother's life. They quote extensively, though not always completely, from Julia's letters and journals. This decision to let Julia "speak for herself" is a strength of the book. Also, the authors made a great effort to put events in their proper chronological sequence, avoiding the mushiness of Julia's autobiography.

Laura Richards idolized her mother. A great-niece has observed that "Laura E. Richards was convinced her mother was a mystical saint—and you can imagine the compaction of that fun-loving, executive do-er that resulted!"

Maud Howe Elliott was not as star-struck, but she nevertheless admired her mother intensely. This love and respect inclined both daughters to adhere to the Victorian view of biography to which their mother subscribed. Both saw their biography as a source of uplift as well as of gentle amusement. They hoped to sustain their mother's legacy of belief in progress, of Christian faith, and of cheerful optimism by leaving a record of her achievements and awards. They stressed her industry, integrity, benevolence, and piety.

They also omitted things. In their effort to smooth out rough edges, they minimized her periods of depression, glided over her selfish or unfair opinions, and omitted references to her unhappy marriage. They did this not only in their connecting narrative, but also in the excerpts they chose from letters and journals. They carefully edited Julia's angry or deeply unhappy commentary from all the passages they included in their book.

Because Richards and Elliott stuck close to their chronological plan, they never stepped back to examine the texture of a span of years. They never tracked the development of any single aspect of Julia's life. Social life, family life, and study are handled as they come up but never as long threads needing to be untangled in the skein of Julia's life. Because Richards and Elliott had access to family papers that are still available to the public, I have used their quoted sources from time to time. Whenever possible I used a similar sentiment from another source to strengthen the evidence.

Since both women had vivid recollections of their relatives and of the houses and places they lived in as children, I have relied on them extensively on those topics. They are also useful as sources for Julia's early life. Particularly helpful are the daughters' own reminiscences: Laura Elizabeth Richards, *Stepping Westward* and *When I Was Your Age*, Florence Howe Hall's *Memories Grave and Gay*, and Maud Howe Elliott's *Three Generations*. (These memoirs, combined with other works they wrote about their father and uncle, meant that the Howe family kept volumes about their relatives appearing every three to eight years from 1893 until 1938.)

Despite the Pulitzer Prize given to the Richards and Elliott biography, there was room for a full and interpretive account of Julia Ward Howe's life. Louise

Hall Tharp's book did not fill the void. *Three Saints and a Sinner* is a group biography treating Samuel Ward, Jr., Julia Ward Howe, Louisa Ward Crawford Terry, and Annie Ward Mailliard in one volume. So intrigued was Tharp by their early years that the truly productive second half of Julia's life had to be squeezed, along with the activities of her brother and sisters, into the last fifth of the book.

Tharp's work suffers in ways that go beyond simple imbalance. With so many characters crowded into one volume, Tharp was unable to examine any one in depth. To fill in gaps left by skimpy research, Tharp invented dialogue or imputed motivation. Despite access to all the family papers, Tharp made use of only a section of them, focusing on letters far more than on journals. While more honest about Julia's flaws of character and unhappy marriage than her predecessors, Tharp still is guilty of the most exasperating flaw of all—consistent failure to identify her sources.

In the mid-1960s, when Deborah Clifford began her research, no scholarly biography of Julia Ward Howe had yet been produced. Clifford helped remedy the lack. Her *Mine Eyes Have Seen the Glory: A Biography of Julia Ward Howe* is a well-written scholarly study, likely to stand for a long time as the best one-volume biography of Julia Ward Howe. The major limitation of the work is one of space. Fitting a ninety-one-year life into one volume required the compression of some of Julia's activities and ideas.

PRIMARY SOURCES

A. Memoirs by Julia Ward Howe

Howe, Julia Ward. *Reminiscences*. Boston: Houghton Mifflin, 1899; reprint ed., New York: New American Library, 1969.

Julia Ward Howe collection, Houghton Library, Harvard University, Cambridge, Massachusetts.

"Childhood." n.d.
"New Yorker in Boston." 1906.
"Story of My Girlhood." n.d
"Untitled reminiscence." 1891.

B. Ward and Howe Family Memoirs

Elliott, Maud Howe. *This Was My Newport*. Cambridge, Mass.: Mythology Company, 1944.
_____. *Three Generations*. Boston: Little, Brown, 1923.
_____. *Uncle Sam Ward and His Circle*. New York: Macmillan, 1938.
Fraser, Mary Crawford. *A Diplomat's Wife in Many Lands*. 2 vols. New York: Dodd, Mead, 1910.
Hall, Florence Howe. *Memories Grave and Gay*. New York: Harper, 1918.
_____. *The Story of the Battle Hymn of the Republic*. New York: Harper, 1916.
Richards, Laura Elizabeth. *Letters and Journals of Samuel Gridley Howe*. 2 vols. Boston: Dana, Estes, 1909.
_____. *Samuel Gridley Howe*. New York: Appleton-Century, 1935.
_____. *Stepping Westward*. New York: Harper, 1918.
_____. *Two Noble Lives: Samuel Gridley Howe and Julia Ward Howe*. Boston: Dana, Estes, 1906.
_____. *When I Was Your Age*. Boston: Estes & Lauriat, 1894.
Richards, Laura Elizabeth, and Maud Howe Elliott. *Julia Ward Howe, 1819-1910*. 2 vols. Boston: Houghton Mifflin, 1916.

C. Published Works by Julia Ward Howe

Howe, Julia Ward. *From Sunset Ridge: Poems Old and New*. Boston: Houghton Mifflin, 1898.

_____. *From the Oak to the Olive: A Plain Record of a Pleasant Journey*. Boston: Lee and Shepard, 1868.

_____. "The Ideal State." *The Christian Examiner*, August 1866.

_____. "Last Letter to Sammy." Edited by Deborah P. Clifford. *Harvard Library Bulletin* 25 (January 1977): 50-62.

_____. *Later Lyrics*. Boston: J. E. Tilton, 1866.

_____. *Leonora, Or the World's Own*. Howe collection. Houghton Library, Cambridge, Massachusetts.

_____. "Newport Correspondence." New York *Tribune*, 1859.

_____. "A Note on the 'Battle Hymn of the Republic.' " *The Century* 34 (December 1877): 629-30.

_____. *Passion Flowers*. Boston: Ticknor & Fields, 1854.

_____. *A Trip to Cuba*. Boston: Ticknor & Fields, 1860.

_____. "What Life Means to Me." *Cosmopolitan*, July 1906.

_____. *Words for the Hour*. Boston: Ticknor & Fields, 1857.

Howe, Julia Ward, ed. *Boatswain's Whistle*. Boston, November 1864.

D. Other Works by Julia Ward Howe

Julia Ward Howe collection, Houghton Library, Harvard University, Cambridge, Massachusetts.

Eva and Raphael. Novel. [185?].
"The Fact Accomplished." Lecture. [1865?].
"Fichte and Spinoza." Lecture. n.d.
"Had I One of Thy Words, My Master." Sermon. n.d.
"Introduction to Ethical Lectures." Lecture. 1867.
"Ireland." Lecture. 1910.
"Limitations" ["Three Degrees of Law"]. Lecture. 1864.
Manuscript poems. 1834-1868.
"Moving Forces." Lecture. [1865?].
"Olympia's Letters." Essay. [185?].
"Opposition." Lecture. 1867.

"Position of Woman." Essay. [1867].

"Representation." Lecture. 1867.

Speech to the Cleveland Convention. 1869.

"Spinoza." Lecture. n.d.

"To write a book." Essay. [185?].

"A True History." Short story. 1867.

"Universal Truth Cures Special Sorrow." Essay. [185?].

An untitled manuscript concerning women's rights. [1867?].

"The Woman's Rights Question." Essay. n.d.

"Your head is wild with books, Sybil." Essay. [185?].

Julia Ward Howe collection, Library of Congress, Washington, D.C.

"Address to the Free Religious Association." Speech. [1867].

"After the fire, a still, small voice." Sermon. [189?].

"Behold I make all things new." Sermon. 1869.

"Brook Farm." Lecture. n.d.

"Distinctions Between Philosophy and Religion." Lecture. n.d.

"Doubt and Belief" ["Philosophy and Religion"]. Lecture. 1863.

"The Ethical Office of the Drama." Speech. 1902.

"For the fashion of the world passeth away." Sermon. n.d.

"The Halfness of Nature." Lecture. 1875.

Hippolytus. Play. 1861.

"The Kingdom of Heaven is at hand." Sermon. [1871].

"The liberty wherewith Christ has made us free." Sermon. n.d.

"Limitations." Lecture. 1864.

"Moral Trigonometry" ["Moral Triangulation"]. Lecture. 1863.

"Polarity." Lecture. [1864].

"Polarity II." Lecture. [1865].

"Proteus." Lecture. 1863.

"Religion considered as the essential expression of the relation between God and man." Sermon. n.d.

"Religious Power." Sermon. n.d.

Sermon delivered to the Free Religious Association. n.d.

"Solitude and Religion." Sermon. n.d.

"The world lost in darkness and sin." Sermon. n.d.

Julia Ward Howe collection, Schlesinger Library, Radcliffe College, Cambridge, Massachusetts.

"Debt to Pioneers." Speech. 1904.

E. Other Primary Sources

National Anti-Slavery Standard, July, December 1864, December 1867, November 1868.
Parker, Theodore. "The Public Functions of Woman." *Essays and Addresses on Woman Suffrage*. n.p., n.d.

SECONDARY SOURCES

A. Works about Julia Ward Howe and Her Family

Clifford, Deborah P. "An Invasion of Strong-Minded Women: The Newspapers and the Woman Suffrage Campaign in Vermont in 1870." *Vermont History* 43 (1975): 1-19.
_____. *Mine Eyes Have Seen the Glory: A Biography of Julia Ward Howe*. Boston: Little, Brown, 1979.
Schwartz, Harold. *Samuel Gridley Howe, Social Reformer, 1801-1876*. Cambridge: Harvard University Press, 1956.
Steele, Robert V. P. [Lately Thomas]. *Sam Ward, "King of the Lobby."* Boston: Houghton Mifflin, 1965.
Tharp, Louise Hall. *Three Saints and a Sinner: Julia Ward Howe, Louisa, Annie, and Sam Ward*. Boston: Little, Brown, 1956.

B. Works Concerning the History of American Women

Blair, Karen J. *Clubwoman as Feminist: True Womanhood Redefined, 1868-1914*. New York: Holmes & Meier, 1980.
Conrad, Susan Phinney. *Perish the Thought: Intellectual Women in Romantic America, 1830-1860*. New York: Oxford University Press, 1976.

Cott, Nancy. *The Bonds of Womanhood: "Woman's Sphere" in New England, 1780-1835*. New Haven: Yale University Press, 1977.

_____. "Young Women in the Second Great Awakening in New England." *Feminist Studies* 3 (Fall 1975): 15-29.

Davis, Rebecca Harding. *Life in the Iron Mills, or the Korl Woman*. Foreword by Tillie Olson. Old Westbury, N.Y.: Feminist Press, 1972.

DePauw, Linda Grant. *Four Traditions: Women of New York During the American Revolution*. Albany: New York State American Revolution Bicentennial Commission, 1974.

DuBois, Ellen Carol. *Feminism and Suffrage: The Emergence of an Independent Woman's Movement in America, 1848-1869*. Ithaca: Cornell University Press, 1978.

Faragher, John Mack. *Women and Men on the Overland Trail*. New Haven: Yale University Press, 1979.

James, Edward T., ed. *Notable American Women*, 3 vols. Cambridge, Mass.: Harvard University Press, 1971.

Jeffrey, Julie Ray. *Frontier Women: The Trans-Mississippi West, 1840-1880*. New York: Hill and Wang, 1979.

Kuhn, Anne L. *The Mother's Role in Childhood Education: New England Concepts, 1830-1860*. New Haven: Yale University Press, 1947.

Melder, Keith. "Ladies Bountiful: Organized Women's Benevolence in Early Nineteenth-Century America." *New York History* 47 (July 1967): 231-54.

Sklar, Kathryn Kish. *Catharine Beecher: A Study in American Domesticity*. New Haven: Yale University Press, 1973.

Smith-Rosenberg, Carroll. "The Female World of Love and Ritual: Relations Between Women in Nineteenth-Century America." *Signs* 1 (Autumn 1975): 1-29.

_____. "The Hysterical Woman: Sex Roles in Nineteenth-Century America." *Social Research* 39 (Winter 1972): 652-78.

Strouse, Jean. *Alice James: A Biography*. Boston: Houghton Mifflin, 1980.

Welter, Barbara. "The Cult of True Womanhood: 1820-1860." *American Quarterly* 18 (Summer 1966): 151-74.

C. Other Works

Ahlstrom, Sydney E. *A Religious History of the American People*. New Haven: Yale University Press, 1972.

Allmendinger, David. *Paupers and Scholars: The Transformation of Student Life in Nineteenth-Century New England*. New York: St. Martin's Press, 1975.

Benedict, Michael Les. *A Compromise of Principle: Congressional Republicans and Reconstruction, 1865-1969*. New York: Norton, 1974.

Cross, Whitney R. *The Burned-Over District: The Social and Intellectual History of Enthusiastic Religion in Western New York, 1800-1850*. Ithaca: Cornell University Press, 1950; reprint ed., New York: Harper, 1965.

Fredrickson, George. *The Inner Civil War: Northern Intellectuals and the Crisis of the Union*. New York: Harper, 1965.

Friedenthal, Richard. *Goethe: His Life and Times*. Cleveland: Ward, 1965.

Gabriel, Ralph Henry. *The Course of American Democratic Thought*. New York: Ronald Press, 1940.

Griffin, Clifford S. *Their Brothers' Keepers: Moral Stewardship in the United States, 1800-1865*. New Brunswick, N.J.: Rutgers University Press, 1960.

Hatvary, George Egon. "Horace Binney Wallace: A Study in Self-Destruction." *Princeton University Library Chronicle* 25 (Winter 1964): 137-49.

Hutchison, William R. *The Transcendentalist Ministers: Church Reform in the New England Renaissance*. New Haven: Yale University Press, 1959.

Kett, Joseph. *Rites of Passage: Adolescence in America, 1790 to the Present*. New York: Basic Books, 1977.

Mott, Frank Luther. *A History of American Magazines*, 2 vols. Cambridge: Harvard University Press, 1930.

Thomas, John L. "Romantic Reform in America, 1815-1865." *American Quarterly* 17 (Winter 1965): 656-81.

Tomkins, Sylvan. "The Psychology of Commitment: The Constructive Role of Violence and Suffering for the Individual and Society." Martin Duberman, ed., *The Anti-Slavery Vanguard: New Essays on the Abolitionists*. Princeton: Princeton University Press, 1965, pp. 270-98.

Weisberger, Bernard A. *They Gathered at the River: The Story of the Great Revivalists and Their Impact Upon Religion in America*. Boston: Little, Brown, 1958.

Wiebe, Robert H. *Search for Order, 1877-1920*. New York: Hill and Wang, 1967.

Wilson, Edmund. *Patriotic Gore: Studies in the Literature of the American Civil War*. New York: Oxford University Press, 1962.

Index

Adams, Abigail, xv
Adams, John, xv
Adolescence
  in the early republic, 29-30
  for women, 210n
Aesthetik (Hegel), 119
African-American Chatauqua Circle, xvii
Agassiz, Elizabeth
  and friendship with Julia Ward Howe, 160
Agassiz, Louis, 150
  and friendship with Julia Ward Howe, 160
Alcott, Bronson
  and Free Religious Association, 189
  and New England Woman Suffrage
    Association, 193
  and transcendentalism, 51
Alcott, Louisa May
  and New England Woman Suffrage
    Association, 193
Alger, William Rounseville, 150
American Academy of Science, 173
American Anti-Slavery Society
  and Julia Ward Howe, 197
American Notes (Charles Dickens), 57
American Woman Suffrage Association
  Julia Ward Howe's work for, 199, 203
Anagnostopoulos, Michael, 183
  and marriage to Julia Romana Howe, 202
  and Perkins Institute for the Blind, 186-
    87
  and relationship with Julia Ward Howe,
    187
Andrew, John, 134
Andrew, John Albion, 134
  death of, 184
Anthony, Susan B.
  and split with Republican Party, 193
  as aid to Elizabeth Cady Stanton, 2

and Women's Loyal League, 197
Appleton, Fanny
  and Julia Ward Howe's literary career, 47
Appleton, Tom, 105
Association for the Advancement of Women
  Julia Ward Howe's leadership of, 203
Astor, John Jacob, 40
Astor, Margaret Armstrong
  and Astor-Ward split, 62
  and Julia Ward Howe's social training, 40,
    47

Balzac, Honoré de, 40
Bancroft, George
  and Julia Ward Howe's philosophical
    studies, 119, 175
Bartlett, Elizabeth Ann, xvi
Bartol, C., 189
"The Battle Hymn of the Republic" (Julia
    Ward Howe), 2, 128, 129, 136-39,
    141, 144, 157, 159, 160, 163, 169,
    184, 200, 229n-30n, 242
Beauty and the Beast, 90
Beecher, Catharine, 67
Beecher, Lyman
  on family discipline, 22
Beethoven, Ludwig van, 165
Belknap, Jeannie
  and friendship with Julia Ward Howe, 89
Benevolent Societies
  and securing of secular order, 21
Bibliographies, xi-xii
Bigelow, Susan
  insanity of, 102
Bird, Francis
  and end of the Civil War, 162
  and New England Woman Suffrage
    Association, 193

Blackwell, Henry
and woman suffrage campaigning in
Vermont, 1
Blind People
education of, 57
Boatswain's Whistle, 161
Boatwright, Eleanor Miot, xiv-xv
Bobroff-Hajal, Anne, xv
Bonaparte, Joseph, 82
Boocock, Mr.
and piano training of Julia Ward Howe,
35
Booth, Edwin
and *Hippolytus*, 142
Booth, Mary, 149
Boston
land values in, 83
and National Sailors Fair, 160-61
and reopening of Music Hall, 150-51
upper-class society in, 77, 80, 218n-19n
Boston Sewing Circle
and aid for Greek patriots on Crete, 181
The Brain Club (Boston)
and Julia Ward Howe, 151, 168, 184, 196
Bridgman, Laura, 60
and the Perkins Institute for the Blind, 57
*The British and American Women's Trade
Union Leagues, 1890-1925: A Case
Study of Feminism and Class* (Robin
Miller Jacoby), xvii-xviii
Brown, John, 155
Harpers Ferry raid of, 133-34, 138
and the Secret Six, 229n
Browning, Elizabeth Barrett, 168
Brownson, Orestes
and "The Battle Hymn of the Republic,"
137
Bryant, William Cullen, 160, 169

Camhi, Jane Jerome, xvi
Cardini, Signor
and vocal training of Julia Ward Howe, 35
Carlisle, Lady, 60
Carlson, Ralph, xiii
Carlyle, Thomas, 60
Chambers, Clarke, xii
Channing, William
and conflicts within the Unitarian Church,
51

Channing, William Henry
and Julia Ward Howe's public lecturing,
152
and Free Religious Association, 189
Chapman, Maria Norton, 228n
Chapman, Maria Weston
and abolitionism, 133
Charles Street Charitable Eye and Ear
Infirmary, 77
Chase, Salmon P., 152
Cheney, Ednah Dow
and Free Religious Association, 189
Child, Lydia Maria
and abolitionism, 133
and the New England Woman Suffrage
Association, 193
Clarke, James Freeman
and "The Battle Hymn of the Republic,"
136
and Free Religious Association, 189
and Julia Ward Howe's public lectures,
150, 152
and New England Woman Suffrage
Association, 193
in *Reminiscences*, 241, 242
and Sanitary Commission, 135-36
Clifford, Deborah, 246
Cogswell, Joseph Greene
and courtship of Julia Ward Howe, 34
and Julia Ward Howe's flirtations, 211n
and Julia Ward Howe's literary career, 38
and tutoring of Julia Ward Howe, 119
and friendship with Samuel Ward, 21
and tutoring of Samuel Ward's daughters,
35, 38
Cole, Thomas, 21
Colonial Dames, xvii
Commonwealth
Julia Ward Howe's writings for, 104-5,
151, 163
and Samuel Gridley Howe, 104, 130
Comte, Auguste
Julia Ward Howe's study of, 119, 150,
173, 190
Conway, Moncure
and "The Battle Hymn of the Republic,"
137
and friendship with Julia Ward Howe, 160

Cornell, Albert, 116
Coster, G. W., 105
Crawford, Annie, 90
Crawford, Frank Marion
  education of, 214n
Crawford, Jennie, 90
Crawford, Louisa Ward
  See Ward, Louisa
Crawford, Thomas
  death of, 182
  European travels of, 95-96
  and friendship with Julia Ward Howe, 63
  on Julia Ward Howe's marriage, 84
  and residence with Julia Ward Howe, 90
  and marriage to Louisa Ward, 78
Critique of Pure Reason (Immanuel Kant),
  175
Curtis, George William, 105, 156
  on Words for the Hour, 127
Cushman, Charlotte
  and Julia Ward Howe's literary career,
  127, 142-43
Cutler, Benjamin Clarke, Jr.
  and religious training of Samuel Ward's
    children, 25, 26
Cutler, Benjamin Clarke, Sr.
  death of, 25
  and marriage to Sarah Mitchell Hyrne
    Cutler, 6
Cutler, Eliza, 60
  character of, 209n
  childhood of, 7
  and domestic charge of the Ward
    household, 213n
  and Julia Ward Howe's clothing requests,
    70
  as role model for Julia Ward Howe, 71
  marriage of, 42, 47
  and religious training of Samuel Ward's
    children, 24-25, 26
Cutler, Julia Rush
  See Ward, Julia Rush Cutler
Cutler, Sarah Mitchell Hyrne (grandmother)
  biographical information on, 6-7, 8
  and influence on Julia Ward Howe, 14

Daughters of the American Revolution, xvii
Davis, Rebecca Harding, 219n

Declaration of Sentiments
  and Julia Ward Howe's view of marriage,
    73
Degler, Carl, xii
Democratic Review
  Julia Ward Howe's poetry published in, 39
Dickens, Charles
  on Laura Bridgman, 57
  and Samuel Gridley Howe, 60, 61
Dictionary of American Biography, xii
Divine Love and Wisdom (Emanuel
  Swedenborg), 117
Domesticity
  and female adolescence in the early
    republic, 30
  and ideals of the wealthy urban class, 9
  Victorian ideals of, 66
"Doubt and Belief" (Julia Ward Howe), 155-
  56
Dwight, John Sullivan, 113
"The Dynamic Idea of God" (Julia Ward
  Howe), 150

Eames, Mrs. Charles
  and Julia Ward Howe's public lecturing,
    152
Eastburn, Bishop
  religious teachings of, 51
  and religious training of Julia Ward Howe,
    49
Edgeworth, Maria
  Julia Ward Howe on, 61
Education
  of blind children, 57
  and piecemeal training of girls, 38
  and theories about training for young
    women, 35-36, 37
  Samuel Ward's work for, 21
Elliott, Maud Howe
  See Howe, Maud
Emerson, Lidian
  and New England Woman Suffrage
    Association, 193
Emerson, Ralph Waldo
  and Free Religious Association, 189
  on Samuel Gridley Howe, 56
  and transcendentalism, 51, 156
Equal Rights Association, 196

Eva and Raphael (Julia Ward Howe), 121-24,
125, 126, 167
Evangelides, Christy
and courtship of Julia Ward Howe, 34
Everett, Edward
and National Sailors Fair, 160-61

Family
as analogous to society, 22
Faneuil Hall Committee
and Samuel Gridley Howe, 130
Federalists
and benevolent societies, 21
Felton, Cornelius
and friendship with Samuel Gridley Howe,
59, 80
The Female Poets of America (Rufus
Griswold)
Julia Ward Howe's poems published in,
89-90
and poetry of Julia Rush Cutler Ward, 11
Feminism
See Women's Rights Movement
Fichte, Johann
Julia Ward Howe's study of, 119, 177,
236n
Field, Mrs. David Dudley, 96
Fields, Annie, 168
and Julia Ward Howe's literary career, 47
and poetry for reopening of Boston's
Music Hall, 150-51
Fields, James
and poetry for reopening of Boston's
Music Hall, 150-51
and publication of "The Battle Hymn of
the Republic," 139
Foster, Abby Kelley
and abolitionism, 133
Foster, Stephen, 152
and New England Woman Suffrage
Association, 193
Francis, Convers
and transcendentalism, 51
Francis, Eliza Cutler
See Cutler, Eliza
Francis, John
and marriage to Eliza Cutler, 42, 47

Franklin, Benjamin
and friendship with Catherine Ray Greene,
8
Freeman, Edward, 96, 105
Free Religious Association
and Julia Ward Howe, 188, 189-92
*From the Oak to the Olive: A Plain Record of a
Pleasant Journey* (Julia Ward Howe),
183
Frothingham, Octavius B., 156
and Free Religious Association, 189
Fuller, Margaret, xvi
Julia Ward Howe's disapproval of, 168
and Julia Ward Howe's literary career, 47-
48, 50, 144
and travels to Rome, 96

Garrison, William Lloyd
and "The Battle Hymn of the Republic,"
137
and Julia Ward Howe's literary career, 141
and transcendentalism, 156
Gilmore, James Roberts
and Julia Ward Howe's literary career, 165
Glover, Russell E.
and courtship of Julia Ward Howe, 34
Goethe, Johann, 125, 227n
The Goose and Golden Eggs, 90
Gore, James, 82
Graham, Isabella
charity work of, 12
religious convictions of, 11-12
and education of Julia Rush Cutler Ward,
6, 7
Grant, Mary, xvi
Greek Revolution
Samuel Gridley Howe's participation in,
56, 59
Greeley, Horace
and disputes with Elizabeth Cady Stanton,
231n
Greene, Catherine Ray
and friendship with Benjamin Franklin, 8
and influence on Julia Ward Howe, 14
Greene, William B., 136
Grimké, Sarah, xvi
Griswold, Rufus
and *The Female Poets of America*, 11, 89-90

Gurowski, Adam, 105
  in *Reminiscences*, 241

Hale, Sarah
  and friendship with Julia Ward Howe, 89
Hale, Susan, 113
Hall, David
  and engagement to Florence Howe, 181, 185
  and marriage to Florence Howe, 202
Hall, Florence Howe
  See Howe, Florence
Hedge, Frederick Henry, 189
  in *Reminiscences*, 241
Hegel, Georg
  Julia Ward Howe's study of, 119, 150, 173, 190, 226n
Heron, Matilda, 125
Higginson, Thomas Wentworth
  and John Brown's raid on Harpers Ferry, 229n
  and Free Religious Association, 189
  on Julia Ward Howe's woman suffrage activism, 198
  and New England Woman Suffrage Association, 193
  and transcendentalism, 156
High Tea at Halekulani: Feminist Theory and American Clubwomen (Margit Misangyi Watts), xviii-xix
Hilliard, George
  and friendship with Samuel Gridley Howe, 59
Hinding, Andrea, x
Hippolytus (Julia Ward Howe), 127, 142-44
Holmes, Oliver Wendell
  and friendship with Julia Ward Howe, 160
  and National Sailors Fair, 160
The Home, Heaven and Mother Party: Female Anti-Suffragism in America, 1868-1920 (Thomas J. Jablonsky), xvi-xvii
Home Weekly
  Julia Ward Howe's writings for, 163
Howe, Florence "Flossy" (daughter)
  birth of, 64, 65
  childhood of, 76, 81, 86, 88, 92-93, 96, 111-14, 128, 129, 130, 150
  engagement of, 181, 185

and Julia Ward Howe's public lectures, 185
  marriage of, 202
  on her mother's literary career, 69
  young adulthood of, 140, 163, 171
Howe, Henry Marion "Harry" (son)
  birth of, 64, 65, 81, 86-87, 88, 90, 91, 92
  childhood of, 93, 108, 140, 111-14, 141, 160
  college education of, 163, 181, 202
  mischievous behavior of, 186
Howe, Jeanette
  and Julia Ward Howe, 66
Howe, Joseph Neals, 56
Howe, Julia Romana "Dudie" (daughter)
  and aid for Greek patriots, 183
  and Michael Anagnostopoulos, 187
  birth of, 63
  childhood of, 76, 78, 81, 86, 88, 92-93, 96, 108, 111-14
  emotional problems of, 185-86
  and Julia Ward Howe's public lectures, 185
  in *Reminiscences*, 241
  marriage of, 202
  young adulthood of, 140, 141, 163
Howe, Julia Ward
  and abolitionism, 128, 130, 132-35, 138, 154-55, 168, 169, 228n, 242
  and aid for Greek patriots, 181, 183, 187, 237n
  ancestry of, 5-6, 13-14
  articles of, 104-5, 203
  and Association for the Advancement of Women, 203
  and Astor-Ward alliance, 46
  and "The Battle Hymn of the Republic," 2, 128, 129, 136-39, 141, 144, 157, 159, 160, 163, 169, 184, 200, 229n-30n, 242
  benevolent work of, 49
  birth of, 1, 13
  and *Boatswain's Whistle*, 161
  and The Brain Club, 151, 168, 184, 196
  and Laura Bridgman, 57
  and John Brown's Harpers Ferry raid, 133-35, 138
  and charity fairs, 131

childbirth experiences of, 86-87, 216n
childhood of, 13
childhood punishment of, 16
on end of Civil War, 161-62
class status of, 70
clothing of, 70
commitment of to woman suffrage, 179
and Cuban travels, 131-33, 142
and Benjamin Clarke Cutler, Jr., 25, 26
and Eliza Cutler, 24-25, 26
death of, 203
and death of
    brother Francis Marion, 82
    brother Henry, 48, 57-58, 102, 124
    father, 48, 57, 164
    Sammy Howe, 147-50, 157
    mother, 15, 16, 24-25, 63, 124, 125,
      164
    Henry Ward, 164
    Sammy Ward, 164, 184, 187
and Declaration of Sentiments, 73
depressions of, 3, 48-50, 52, 64-65, 74,
      79, 80, 81-82, 83-84, 88, 90-92, 93,
      99, 100-102, 103, 107-8, 110-11,
      114, 123-24, 128, 149, 173, 184-
      85, 187-89, 196, 202
desires of to be a boy, 37-38
disapproves of Margaret Fuller, 168
on distribution of wealth, 153
and domestic feminism, 201
and domesticity, 10, 17, 33, 39, 42, 66-
      68, 71, 74, 77-78, 79, 81, 91-92,
      93, 100, 109-10, 115-16, 202,
      213n, 216n, 217n
education of, 1, 22, 35-38, 40, 53, 91-92
and education of her children, 91, 113,
      140
entertaining of, 89, 91-92, 101, 112, 140,
      159-60, 169, 183
essays of, 120-21, 150-58, 159, 169, 173-
      75, 177-79, 184, 236n
European travels of, 60-63, 92-93, 95-96,
      181-84
and Eva and Raphael, 121-24, 125, 126,
      167
father as role model for, 46
and female friendship networks, 168, 196,
      202-3

financial difficulties of, 163-64, 165
and financial difficulties of Sam Ward, 83
first publications of, 38-39
flirtations of, 80-81, 211n
and freedmen's rights, 170, 191, 194,
      196-98
and Free Religious Association, 188, 189-
      92
frequent moves of, 109-10
and friendship with
    Henry Wadsworth Longfellow, 104,
      105
    Theodore Parker, 87, 103-4, 172, 191
    Mary Ward, 43-45, 50, 51, 52, 77, 89,
      103
health of, 76, 80, 81, 84, 107, 110, 173,
      184, 187
height of, 27
and Hippolytus, 127, 142-44
and Howe family servants, 67-68, 76
and Jeanette Howe, 66
on Samuel Gridley Howe, 221n
and husband's
    angry moods, 84
    benevolent work, 72-73
    character, 100
    courtship of, 57-60
    friends, 60, 89
    headaches, 71
    ideal of a perfect wife, 56, 59, 63-64,
      65, 70-71, 101
    marital infidelity of, 110, 116, 123,
      171, 225n
    request for a divorce, 108, 140-41
and hydropathy, 100
on individual moral autonomy, 3, 191-92
and lack of role models, 73-74
and The Ladies Social, 151
leadership qualities of, 46
and liberal Protestantism, 50-53
literary aspirations of, 64, 65, 81
literary career of, 36-37, 93-94, 95
literary earnings of, 69, 141
literary role models of, 47-48, 50
on maiden name retention, 60
and male church authority, 117, 118
on marriage, 154-55, 172
marital difficulties of, 2, 3, 17

marital expectations of, 10, 17, 46-48, 63-64, 65, 71-72, 73, 78, 88-89, 100
and motherhood, 74, 76, 85, 92, 93, 114, 166, 169, 218n
and Mother's Day, 203
and mother's influence on, 36-37
musical activities of, 30
on music's power, 208n
musical training of, 35
and National Sailors Fair, 160-61
and New England Woman's Club, 196, 202, 203, 242
and New England Woman Suffrage Association, 2-3, 193-96, 198-99
and *Northern Lights*, 165
and nursing, 87-88, 91, 101, 134
philosophical studies of, 3, 119-20, 144, 162-63, 173-74, 175-77, 178, 179, 190
physical appearance of, 33
and physical intimacy with her husband, 84, 86, 91, 101, 108, 122, 123
plays of, 125-27, 142, 142-44, 143, 200, 227n, 228n
and poetry for the reopening of Boston's Music Hall, 150-51
poetry of, 19-20, 25, 34, 37, 39, 40, 45, 48, 50, 53, 61-62, 66, 78, 82, 89-90, 91, 93, 95, 97-99, 100, 101, 104, 105-7, 111, 127-28, 136-39, 141, 144, 148-49, 157, 159, 160, 163, 167, 172, 184, 188, 200, 224n
on power, 154
pregnancies of, 63, 64-65, 76, 81, 82, 84-86, 90-91, 92, 108, 110, 122, 123, 124, 134, 225n
prenuptial contract of, 58, 102
and production of *Leonora, Or The World's Own*, 125-27, 142, 143
and publication of
  Later Lyrics, 163, 184
  Passion Flowers, 104, 105-7, 115
  Words for the Hour, 127-28
public lectures of, 144-45, 150, 151-52, 157-58, 159, 160, 162-63, 169, 170-71, 173, 174, 183-84, 185, 188, 189, 197, 200-201, 236n, 237n

racism of, 132
real estate holdings of, 58
and reform, 116
on reform and the Christian Ideal, 191
on reformers, 177-78
and rejection of traditional women's roles, 89, 99
and relationships with
  Michael Anagnostopoulos, 187
  brothers, 18-19, 39-42
  children, 111-14
  daughters, 185-86
  father, 30-33, 34-35, 40
  Margaret Fuller, 96
  Henry Wadsworth Longfellow, 41
  sisters, 19, 39, 42-43, 49, 93, 104, 111, 115, 220n
  Charles Sumner, 79, 87
  Horace Binney Wallace, 1, 97-99, 101, 102, 103
  Anne Eliza Ward, 82
  Henry Marion Ward, 186
  her Ward uncles, 26-27
  Louisa Ward, 78
and religion
  anxieties over, 30
  beliefs on, 176, 188-89
  criticism of, 238n
  and revivals, 49-50
  studies of, 3, 116-19
  and training of, 16, 18, 19-20, 22, 23, 124
and residence at
  Beacon Hill, 140, 163
  Boylston Place, 163, 171, 182, 184
  Green Peace, 79-80, 81, 110, 112
  Lawton's Valley, 109, 116, 140
  Perkins Institute for the Blind, 63, 65-66, 77, 79, 108-9, 171
  Rome, 96-98, 182
  Winthrop House, 80
and Sanitary Commission, 135-36
and Sanitary Fairs, 151
on separate spheres, 168-70, 174-75, 178-79, 201
sexuality in the writings of, 121-27, 143-44, 169

social aspirations of, 76-78, 79-80, 103, 153
and socializing in Newport, 105, 111, 112
social training of, 16-17, 32, 40-41, 47
and studies of
  Auguste Comte, 119, 150, 173, 190
  Fichte, 119, 177, 236n
  Hegel, 119, 150, 173, 190, 226n
  Immanuel Kant, 175-77, 184, 188, 190
  Spinoza, 119, 150, 173-74, 175, 190
  Emanuel Swedenborg, 89, 91, 117-19, 121, 124, 134, 176, 190, 191
and Lucy Stone, 195, 198-99, 239n
on her sweet tooth, 211n
suitors of, 33-34, 41-42, 45, 46-47
on toilet training, 88
and transcendentalism, 51-52, 117, 119, 156, 176
travel narratives of, 131-33, 183, 200
trust money of, 68-70, 83, 102-3, 114, 164, 166
and tutoring in Greek, 187
and Unitarianism, 51-52, 77
unpublished writings of, 222n
on upper class society in Boston, 218n-19n
and Horace Binney Wallace's suicide, 223n
and John Ward's estate, 164, 165-66
on Julia Rush Cutler Ward, 11
Sam Ward as role model for, 45-46
wedding of, 60
western travels of, 128, 129, 130
on women's
  character, 123, 125
  education, 123, 125, 167
  higher education, 113
  right to work outside marriage, 179
  suffrage, 178, 194, 195, 198
and women's rights movement, 166-70, 172, 178, 192
and woman suffrage campaigning in Vermont, 1, 2
woman suffrage speeches of, 199-200, 201, 202
Howe, Laura (daughter)
and aid for Greek patriots, 183
birth of, 64, 65, 85, 87, 92

childhood of, 93, 101, 111-14, 116, 140, 186
marriage of, 202
on marriage of Julia Ward Howe and Samuel Gridley Howe, 172
and writing her mother's biography, 245
Howe, Maud (daughter)
birth of, 65, 111
childhood of, 113-14, 140, 171, 181, 186, 202
on her father's temperament, 109
and writing her mother's biography, 245
Howe, Patty Gridley
and Samuel Gridley Howe's idealization of women, 59
Howe, Sammy (son)
birth of, 134, 142
childhood of, 139-40, 141
death of, 147-50, 157, 184, 187
Howe, Samuel Gridley "Chev" (husband)
and abolitionism, 91, 104, 129-30, 133-34, 172
and affection for his children, 111-12
and allocation of domestic tasks, 66, 67-68
angry moods of, 84
appearance and character of, 53, 55
benevolent work of, 72-73, 99
and births of his children, 87
and John Brown's raid on Harpers Ferry, 133-35, 229n
and conflicts with Sam Ward, 83
and courtship of Julia Ward Howe, 57-60
death of, 166, 202, 221n, 244
depressions of, 71
and domestic operations in his household, 115-16, 141
education of, 56, 57, 59
and education of his children, 91, 113, 140
European travels of, 60-63, 92-93, 95-96, 181-84
on fears of childbirth, 86
financial difficulties of, 163
and freedmen's rights, 196
friends of, 59-60, 89, 215n
and aid for Greek patriots, 181, 183, 237n
and Greek Revolution, 56, 59
headaches of, 71

health of, 140, 141, 230n
and Howe family servants, 67-68
Julia Ward Howe on, 221n
and Julia Ward Howe's
    childbirth experiences, 216n
    depressions, 64-65, 90-92, 99, 100-
        102, 103, 107-8, 173
    domesticity, 81
    entertaining, 80, 101, 159-60
    literary career, 91, 104, 105-7, 114,
        127, 141-42, 150, 170-71
    prenuptial contract, 58, 102
    public lectures, 151-52, 170-71, 173,
        184, 237n
    relationship with Horace Binney
        Wallace, 97-99, 101
    religious studies, 118, 121
    trust money, 68-69, 83, 102-3, 164,
        166
    woman suffrage activism, 198, 199
and death of Sammy Howe, 147
and ideal of perfect wife, 56, 59, 63-64,
    65, 70-71, 101
imprisoned in Prussia, 56-57
and interest in his wife's pursuits, 81
Kansas inspection tour of, 128, 129, 130
marital difficulties of, 2
marital infidelity of, 110, 116, 123, 171,
    225n
and phrenology, 67
and physical intimacy with his wife, 84,
    86, 91, 101, 108, 122, 123
purchases Green Peace, 79
real estate speculations of, 69, 83, 109,
    110, 130, 166
and Reconstruction, 162
reform career of, 2, 218n
relationships of with daughters, 185, 186
on religion and social activism, 117
in Reminiscences, 241
requests divorce from Julia Ward Howe,
    108, 140-41
and Sanitary Commission, 135-36
and theories on educating blind children,
    57
travels to Cuba, 131-33
and work with the blind, 174
and estate of John Ward, 165-66

Hugo, Victor
    on John Brown, 134
Hutchinson, Anne, 118
Hyatt, Thaddeus
    Kansas inspection tour of, 130
Hyrne, Thomas
    and marriage to Sarah Mitchell Hyrne
        Cutler, 6

An Improved Woman: The Wisconsin
    Federation of Women's Clubs, 1895-
    1920 (Janice Steinschneider), xviii
The Iroquois Bride, 18, 90

Jablonsky, Thomas J., xvi-xvii
Jackson, Andrew, 48
Jacoby, Robin Miller, xvii-xviii
James, Henry, Sr., 118
    and "The Battle Hymn of the Republic,"
        137
    and friendship with Julia Ward Howe, 160
James, Janet, xii
Janin, Jules
    and Sam Ward, 37
Jarvis, Edward
    and care of Samuel Gridley Howe's
        children, 92-93, 96
Jarvis, Fanny, 68
Jocelyn (Larmartine)
    Julia Ward Howe's critique of, 38
Julia Ward Howe, 1819-1910 (Laura E.
    Richards and Maud Howe Elliott),
    244-45

Kant, Immanuel, 119
    Julia Ward Howe's study of, 175-77, 184,
        188, 190
Keller, Rosemary, xv
Kemble, Fanny, 108
Kett, Joseph
    on semi-independence of adolescents in
        the early republic, 29
King, Charles
    and Julia Ward Howe's literary career, 39
King, Gracie, 82
King, Rufus
    and partnership with Samuel Ward and
        Nathaniel Prime, 8, 20

Kirke, Minister
and engagement to Julia Ward Howe, 41, 45

The Ladies Social (Boston), 151
Lansdowne, Lord, 60
Later Lyrics (Julia Ward Howe), 163, 184
Lays of the Western World
Julia Ward Howe's poems published in, 89
Leonora, Or The World's Own (Julia Ward Howe), 125-27, 142, 143, 167
Liberator, 130
Liberty, Equality and Sorority: The Origins and Integrity of Feminist Thought: Frances Wright, Sarah Grimké and Margaret Fuller (Elizabeth Ann Bartlett), xvi
Lieber, Francis
and friendship with Julia Ward Howe, 72, 218n
Lincoln, Abraham
election of, 134
inauguration of, 141
William Lloyd Garrison on, 137
Livermore, Mary
and Free Religious Association, 189
and woman suffrage campaigning in Vermont, 1
Locke, John, 40
Logik (Hegel), 119
Longfellow, Fanny Appleton, 105, 168
Longfellow, Henry Wadsworth, 72
and Free Religious Association, 189
and friendship with Julia Ward Howe, 104, 105
and friendship with Samuel Gridley Howe, 59
and relationship with Julia Ward Howe, 41
and relationship with Samuel Gridley Howe, 80
and Julia Ward Howe's education, 38
and Julia Ward Howe's flirtations, 211n
and Julia Ward Howe's poetry, 91
on Samuel Gridley Howe, 56
and Samuel Gridley Howe's courtship of Julia Ward Howe, 58
Lowell, James Russell
and Julia Ward Howe's literary career, 141
and National Sailors Fair, 161

McAllister, Louisa Cutler, 24
McAllister, Ward, 209n
Mailliard, Adolphe
and Samuel Gridley Howe's real estate speculations, 166
and marriage to Anne Eliza Ward, 82
and purchase of the Ranch, 184
Mailliard, Anne Eliza Ward
See Ward, Anne Eliza
Mann, Horace, 129
banquets for, 89
and friendship with Samuel Gridley Howe, 59-60, 87
Mann, Mary, 129
and New England Woman Suffrage Association, 193
Marion, Francis, 6
Julia Ward Howe on, 5
Marriage
upper-class expectations of, 47
and working partnerships between husband and wife, 72-73
Massachusetts Emigrant Aid Company
and Samuel Gridley Howe, 130
Massey, Elizabeth, xv
Matronage: Patterns in Women's Organizations, Atlanta, Georgia, 1890-1940 (Darlene Roth), xvii
Matthias Claudius (Goethe), 50
May, Abby W.
and Boston Sewing Circle, 181
May, Samuel
and New England Woman Suffrage Association, 193
Memories Grave and Gay (Florence Howe Hall), 245
Michelet, Jules, 119
Mills, James K.
and Julia Ward Howe's trust money, 68-69, 102
Milnes, Menckton, 60
Mine Eyes Have Seen the Glory: A Biography of Julia Ward Howe (Deborah Clifford), 246
Minturn, Jonas, 22
Montpelier, Vermont
woman suffrage campaigning in, 1, 2

"Moral Trigonometry" (Julia Ward Howe), 154-55, 162
Mother's Day
    Julia Ward Howe's invention of, 203
Moulton, Louise Chandler
    and Free Religious Association, 189

National Anti-Slavery Standard
    on Julia Ward Howe and the New England Woman Suffrage Association, 194, 195
National Sailors Fair
    Julia Ward Howe's work for, 160-61
New England Asylum for the Blind
    and Samuel Gridley Howe, 56
New England Woman's Club
    founding of, 196
    and Julia Ward Howe, 202, 203, 242
New England Woman Suffrage Association
    and Julia Ward Howe, 2-3
New England Women's League for Diminishing the Use of Luxuries During the War
    and Julia Ward Howe, 197
The New York American
    Julia Ward Howe's essays published in, 39
New York University
    founding of, 21
New York City
    and the Bond Street neighborhood, 23
    class structure of, 46
    religious revivals in, 49
    upper-class society in, 71
Nightingale, Florence
    Julia Ward Howe's poems to, 167
    and Samuel Gridley Howe, 59
Northern Lights
    Julia Ward Howe's writing for, 165
Norton, Charles Eliot
    and "The Battle Hymn of the Republic," 137
Notable American Women: 1607-1950: A Biographical Dictionary, xii
Nursing
    and preventing conception, 86

Orphan Asylum (New York City)
    Julia Ward Howe's work for, 49
Outdoor Circle, xviii

Paddock, Mrs., 150
Paradise Lost (Milton), 50
Parker, Theodore
    and abolitionism, 133
    and John Brown's raid on Harpers Ferry, 229n
    and friendship with Julia Ward Howe, 87, 103-4, 172, 191
    and religious studies of Julia Ward Howe, 117, 118, 121, 134
    in *Reminiscences*, 241, 242
    and travels to Cuba, 131-32
    women's rights position of, 169-70
Parkman, Frances
    and "The Battle Hymn of the Republic," 137
Passion Flowers (Julia Ward Howe), 104, 105-7, 115
Patriotism and the Female Sex: Abigail Adams and the American Revolution (Rosemary Keller), xv
Peabody, Andrew Preston
    and National Sailors Fair, 161
Peabody, Elizabeth Palmer, 113
    and Julia Ward Howe's literary career, 47, 144
    and New England Woman Suffrage Association, 193
Peabody, Lucia, 113
Peirce, Benjamin, 189
Perkins, Thomas
    and education of blind children, 57
Perkins Institute for the Blind
    and Michael Anagnostopoulos, 186-87
    Julia Ward Howe's residence at, 63, 65-66, 77, 79, 108-9, 171
    and Samuel Gridley Howe, 53, 55, 57
Phillips, Wendell
    on end of the Civil War, 161-62
A Pilgrim's Progress, 19
"Polarity" (Julia Ward Howe), 174-75, 177, 178
Pope, Micijah
    and Samuel Gridley Howe's real estate deals, 69
Positive Philosophy (Auguste Comte), 119
Powell, Aaron
    and New England Woman Suffrage Association, 194

Pregnancy
  nursing and prevention of, 86
  Victorian conventions concerning, 85
Prime, Nathaniel
  and partnership with Samuel Ward and
    Rufus King, 8, 20, 82
Prison Discipline Society, 72
*Private Woman, Public Person: An Account of
  the Life of Julia Ward Howe from 1819
  to 1868* (Mary Grant), xvi
"Proteus: or Success in Life" (Julia Ward
  Howe), 150, 153, 155
"Public Function of Woman" (Theodore
  Parker), 170

Radical Club
  See Free Religious Association
Religion
  and liberal Protestantism, 50
  and male church authority, 49, 117
  and revivals, 49
  and Second Great Awakening, 11-12
  and securing of secular order, 21
  and Emanuel Swedenborg's writings, 117-
    18
  and transcendentalism, 156
  women's conversions to, 207n
  and women's identity, 214n
Reminiscences (Julia Ward Howe), 241-43
  on Civil War, 138-39
  on death of her mother, 15, 16
  and readings before Free Religious
    Association, 189
  and chapter on "My Father," 30
  on Horace Binney Wallace, 97
Republican Party
  and end of the Civil War, 161-62
  and post-Civil War reforms, 193
  and woman suffrage, 197
Richards, Henry
  and marriage to Laura Howe, 202
Richards, Laura Elizabeth
  See Howe, Laura
Ripley, George
  and transcendentalism, 51
Rome, Italy
  conservative politics in, 96
Roth, Darlene, xv

Round Hill School, 19
  Joseph Greene Cogswell's departure from,
    35
  educational innovation at, 21
  Sam Ward's education at, 37

Sanborn, Franklin, 156
  and John Brown's raid on Harpers Ferry,
    229n
Sand, George, 40, 165
Sanitary Commission
  and Julia Ward Howe, 196
  and Samuel Gridley Howe, 135-36
  and Sanitary Fairs, 151
Sargent, John T.
  and Free Religious Association, 189, 190
Schleiermacher, Friedrich, 119
Scott, Anne Firor, xii, xiv
Separate Spheres
  and sex role prescriptions for women, 16-
    17
  and women's friendship networks, 44
  women's role in, 71
Severance, Caroline
  and New England Woman's Club, 196
  and New England Woman Suffrage
    Association, 193
Sewall, Samuel
  and New England Woman Suffrage
    Association, 193
Shaw, Anna, 84
Shurtz, Carl, 189
Sigourney, Lydia, 39
Sklar, Kathryn Kish, xi
Slavery, xiv-xv
Smith, Gerrit
  and John Brown's raid on Harpers Ferry,
    229n
Smith, Sydney
  Julia Ward Howe on, 60
Social Darwinism
  Julia Ward Howe on, 153
Society for Promotion of Industry among the
  Poor (New York City)
  Julia Rush Cutler Ward's work for, 12
Society for the Promotion of Temperance
  and Samuel Ward, 31

Society for the Relief of Poor Widows with
    Small Children (New York City), 12
Sothern, Edward Askew, 125
Sources for Women's History, xi-xiii
Spinoza, Benedict de
    Julia Ward Howe's study of, 119, 150,
        173-74, 175, 190
Spruill, Julia, xv
Stanton, Elizabeth Cady
    family duties of, 2
    and Horace Greeley, 231n
    and split with Republican Party, 193
    and Women's Loyal League, 197
Status of Women in Georgia, 1783-1860
    (Eleanor Miot Boatwright), xiv-xv
Stearns, George
    and John Brown's raid on Harpers Ferry,
        229n
Stein, Charlotte von, 227n
Steinschneider, Janice, xviii
Stepping Westward (Laura Elizabeth
        Richards), 245
Stone, Lucy
    and Julia Ward Howe, 195, 198-99, 239n
    and woman suffrage campaigning in
        Vermont, 1
    woman suffrage speeches of, 240n
Sumner, Albert, 105
Sumner, Charles, 105
    and Laura Bridgman, 57
    and friendship with Samuel Gridley Howe,
        59-60
    and relationship with Julia Ward Howe,
        79, 87
    and Julia Ward Howe's poetry, 128
    and Julia Ward Howe's public lectures,
        152, 162
    and Julia Ward Howe's trust money, 68
    and Samuel Gridley Howe's courtship of
        Julia Ward Howe, 58
    and Sanitary Commission, 134
Swedenborg, Emanuel
    Julia Ward Howe's study of, 89, 91, 117-
        19, 121, 124, 134, 176, 190, 191

Tarbell, Ida, xvi
Tasso (Goethe), 125
Telma (Julia Ward Howe), 90

Terry, Arthur Noel
    birth of, 182
Terry, Louisa Margaret (Daisy)
    birth of, 182
Terry, Louisa Ward Crawford
    See Ward, Louisa
Terry, Luther
    and friendship with Julia Ward Howe, 63
    and marriage to Louisa Ward, 182
Tharp, Louise Hall, 244, 245-46
Theological Review
    Julia Ward Howe's essays published in, 38
Three Generations (Maud Howe Elliott), 245
Three Saints and a Sinner: Julia Ward Howe,
        Louisa, Annie, and Sam Ward (Louise
        Hall Tharp), 244, 245-46
Ticknor, W. T.
    and Julia Ward Howe's literary career, 53
Torlonia, Prince
    and friendship with Julia Ward Howe, 63
Transcendentalism
    and Free Religious Association, 189
    and Julia Ward Howe, 117, 119, 156, 176
    and conflicts within Unitarian Church, 51
A Trip to Cuba (Julia Ward Howe), 131-33,
        167
    earnings from, 141
Twisleton, Edward, 98, 102, 104, 107, 119
Twisleton, Ellen, 98

Unitarian Church
    conflicts within, 51
"Universal Truth Cures Special Sorrow"
        (Julia Ward Howe), 120-21

Vermont
    woman suffrage campaigning in, 1, 2

Wallace, Horace Binney
    and Julia Ward Howe's plays, 227n
    and relationship with Julia Ward Howe, 1,
        97-99, 101, 104, 119
    suicide of, 99, 102, 103, 223n
Ward, Anne Eliza "Annie" (sister), 26, 40
    birth of, 13, 15-16
    childhood of, 19, 25
    on Eliza Cutler, 47
    European travels of, 60-62, 95-96

and relationships with sisters, 220n
and relationship with Julia Ward Howe,
    42-43, 93, 104
and Julia Ward Howe's clothing requests,
    70
and Julia Ward Howe's servant problems,
    68
and Julia Ward Howe's wedding, 60
and male church authority, 117
and marriage to Adolphe Mailliard, 82, 84
physical appearance of, 33
pregnancies of, 81, 88
and purchase of the Ranch, 184
and death of Julia Rush Cutler Ward, 16
Ward, Charles
and Julia Ward Howe's finances, 103
and Julia Ward Howe's trust money, 114
Ward, Eliza
and social training of Julia Ward Howe, 17
Ward, Emily Astor
and Astor-Ward alliance, 46
death of, 41, 63
and Julia Ward Howe's literary career, 47
and marriage to Sam Ward, 40
and social training of Julia Ward Howe,
    40-41
Ward, Francis Marion
birth of, 13
childhood of, 19
death of, 82
estate of, 164
and relationship with Julia Ward Howe,
    40, 41
on Julia Ward Howe's flirtations, 211n
on Julia Ward Howe's relationship with
    her father, 31
and ill health of Julia Rush Cutler Ward, 10
Ward, Governor Samuel
and friendship with George Washington, 7
Ward, Henry
birth of, 13
Bond street residences of, 27
business career of, 26
death of, 48, 57, 102, 124, 164
engagement of, 41-42
and relationship with Julia Ward Howe,
    18-19, 40, 41
on Julia Ward Howe's suitors, 34

and relations with father, 32
Ward, John
Bond street residence of, 27
education of, 37
estate of, 164, 165
and Julia Ward Howe's prenuptial
    contract, 58
and Julia Ward Howe's trust money, 68
on Julia Ward Howe's budding literary
    career, 39
and Prime, Ward, & Company, 83
and relationship with Samuel Ward's
    children, 26
Ward, Julia Rush Cutler (mother)
ancestry of, 5
as possible role model for Julia Ward
    Howe, 73
charity work of, 12, 21, 49
childhood of, 6-7
death of, 13, 15-16, 164
education of, 206n
ill health of, 10-11
and influence on Julia Ward Howe, 36-37
literary aspirations of, 36
literary career of, 11
and marriage to Samuel Ward, 8-11, 12-
    13, 17
and punishment of her children, 16
religious conversion of, 207n
religious convictions of, 11-12, 36
sensibility of, 30
Ward, Louisa (sister)
and Astor-Ward split, 62-63
birth of, 13
childhood of, 19, 25
criticisms of Unitarianism, 52
and domestic affairs of the Ward house-
    hold, 42
European travels of, 95-96
fatherly advice for, 30-31
health of, 208n
and relationship with Julia Ward Howe,
    42-43, 93, 104
and relationships with sisters, 220n
and Julia Ward Howe's domestic tasks, 67
and Julia Ward Howe's European travels,
    60-61, 62
and Julia Ward Howe's literary career, 76

and Julia Ward Howe's marital unhappiness, 73
and Julia Ward Howe's religious views, 214n
and residence with Julia Ward Howe, 90
and Julia Ward Howe's wedding, 60
and Samuel Gridley Howe's prescriptions for wifehood, 70
and Samuel Gridley Howe's theories on childbirth, 86
marriage of, 78, 82, 84, 181-2
physical appearance of, 33
Ward, Maddie, 88
and Astor-Ward split, 62
Ward, Maria Hall, 26
Ward, Mary
and engagement to Henry Ward, 41
and friendship with Julia Ward Howe, 43-45, 50, 51, 52, 77, 89, 103
and Julia Ward Howe's literary career, 47
and Julia Ward Howe's marriage, 213n
on marriage, 44-45
Ward, Medora
and Sam Ward, 88
Ward, Phoebe Greene, 7-8, 26
Ward, Richard
business career of, 26
Ward, Sam (brother)
and Astor-Ward split, 46, 62
birth of, 11, 13
childhood of, 19
and clashes with father, 31, 32
education of, 21-22, 37
and Julia Ward Howe's education, 38, 40
and Julia Ward Howe's literary career, 37, 40, 41, 47
and Julia Ward Howe's marriage, 63-64
and Julia Ward Howe's prenuptial contract, 58
on Julia Ward Howe's relationship with her father, 32-33
and Julia Ward Howe's relationship with Samuel Gridley Howe, 141
as Julia Ward Howe's role model, 45-46
and social training of Julia Ward Howe, 41
and Julia Ward Howe's trust money, 68-69, 83

and Samuel Gridley Howe's courtship of Julia Ward Howe, 58-59
marriage of, 40
and Prime, Ward, & Company, 82-83
on reactions to *Leonora, Or The World's Own*, 125, 126
religious training of, 24
and estate of John Ward, 164
and Medora Ward, 88
Ward, Sammy
death of, 164, 231n
Ward, Samuel (father)
ancestry of, 5, 7-8
and Astor-Ward alliance, 46
banking career of, 8, 20, 48
benevolent work of, 21, 46, 49
death of, 26, 41, 48, 57, 164
educational philosophy of, 21-22
and Julia Ward Howe's education, 22, 35-37
and Julia Ward Howe's literary career, 37, 40
as Julia Ward Howe's role model, 46
and Julia Ward Howe's role as oldest sister, 43
and Julia Ward Howe's social life, 41
and Julia Ward Howe's social training, 16
and Julia Ward Howe's suitors, 34
and influence over Julia Ward Howe's adolescence, 30-33, 34-35, 40
and marriage to Julia Rush Cutler Ward, 8-11, 12-13, 17
and Newport farm, 43-44
parenting philosophy of, 30-33, 34-35, 40
religious conversion of, 12, 20
strict morals of, 31-32
and death of Julia Rush Cutler Ward, 2, 15-16, 18, 20, 21-22
and religious upbringing of his children, 18, 20, 22, 23, 26, 46
Ward, Colonel Samuel (grandfather)
biographical information on, 7-8
death of, 20
height of, 27
Ward, Samuel Grey
and Julia Ward Howe's finances, 103
Ward, Thomas, 43

Ward, William
  business career of, 26
  estate of, 69
Washington, George, 6
  and friendship with Governor Ward, 7
Wasson, David, 189
Watts, Margit Misangyi, xviii-xix
Weiss, John
  and Free Religious Association, 189, 190
Weld, Angelina Grimké
  and New England Woman Suffrage
    Association, 193
Welles, Gideon, 152
When I Was Your Age (Laura Elizabeth
    Richards), 245
Whipple, Edwin Percy, 150
  and National Sailors Fair, 161
Whittier, John Greenleaf, 104
  and "The Battle Hymn of the Republic,"
    137
  and National Sailors Fair, 161
Willay, Caroline, 113
Williams, Henry, 113
Wilson, Edmund
  on "The Battle Hymn of the Republic,"
    137
Wilson, Henry
  and New England Woman Suffrage
    Association, 193
Wingspread Conference, xiii
Winthrop, Robert
  and Boston charity fairs, 131
Winthrop House
  Julia Ward Howe's residence at, 80
The Woman's Journal
  Julia Ward Howe's writings for, 203
"The Woman's Rights Question" (Julia Ward
    Howe), 168
Woman Suffrage
  and freedmen's rights, 196-98, 240n
  Julia Ward Howe on, 178, 194, 195, 198
  Julia Ward Howe's commitment to, 179
  and Republican Party, 193
  Vermont campaigns for, 1, 2
Women Against Women: American Anti-
    Suffragism, 1880-1920 (Jane Jerome
    Camhi), xvi

Women's Central Association of Relief for
    the Sick and Wounded of the Army,
    134
Women's History Sources: A Guide to Archives
    and Manuscript Collections in the
    United States, xii
Women's Loyal League
  Julia Ward Howe refuses to join, 196-97
Women's Rights Movement
  and Julia Ward Howe, 192
  Julia Ward Howe's leadership in, 3
  and married women's property rights, 166,
    234n
  and split with Republican Party, 193
  and Declaration of Sentiments, 73
Women's Trade Union League (WTUL), xiv,
    xvii-xviii
Woods, Leonard
  and Julia Ward Howe's literary career, 38
Words for the Hour (Julia Ward Howe), 127-
    28
Working Women in Russia Under the Hunger
    Tsar: Political Activism and Daily Life
    (Anne Bobroff-Hajal), xv
Wright, Fanny, 167
Wright, Frances, xvi

Scholarship in Women's History: Rediscovered and New

GERDA LERNER, Editor

1. Bartlett, Elizabeth Ann. *Liberty, Equality, Sorority: The Origins and Interpretation of American Feminist Thought: Frances Wright, Sarah Grimké, and Margaret Fuller*
2. Boatwright, Eleanor Miot. *Status of Women in Georgia 1783-1860*
3. Bobroff-Hajal, Anne. *Working Women in Russia Under the Hunger Tsar: Political Activism and Daily Life*
4. Camhi, Jane Jerome. *Women Against Women: American Anti-Suffragism, 1880-1920*
5. Grant, Mary H. *Private Woman, Public Person: An Account of the Life of Julia Ward Howe From 1819-1868*
6. Jablonsky, Thomas J. *The Home, Heaven, and Mother Party: Female Anti-Suffragists in the United States, 1868-1920*
7. Jacoby, Robin Miller. *The British and American Women's Trade Union Leagues, 1890-1925: A Case Study of Feminism and Class*
8. Keller, Rosemary. *Patriotism and the Female Sex: Abigail Adams and the American Revolution*
9. Roth, Darlene Rebecca. *Matronage: Patterns in Women's Organizations, Atlanta, Georgia, 1890-1940*
10. Steinschneider, Janice C. *An Improved Woman: The Wisconsin Federation of Women's Clubs, 1895-1920*
11. Watts, Margit Misangyi. *High Tea at Halekulani: Feminist Theory and American Clubwomen*